GROWING UP
EXISTENTIALLY

Ronald J. Manheimer

GROWING UP
EXISTENTIALLY

A Journey from Absurdity to Consciousness

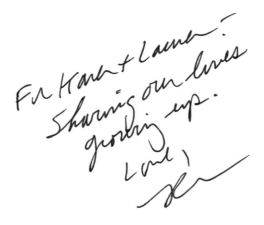

JORVIK
P R E S S

ISBN-10: 0-9863770-5-8

ISBN-13: 978-0-9863770-5-1

Library of Congress
Catalog No: 2017948420

Cover design: Keith Carlson

First edition

JORVIK PRESS

5331 SW Macadam Ave., Ste. 258-424,
Portland OR 97239

JorvikPress.com

About the Author

Ronald J. Manheimer holds a PhD from the History of Consciousness interdisciplinary graduate program of the University of California at Santa Cruz. His dissertation, *Kierkegaard and the Education of Historical Consciousness*, led to his first book, *Kierkegaard As Educator* (University of California Press, 1977). In 2003, an award-winning Korean translation of this book appeared with a new introduction by the author.

Manheimer has taught at UC Santa Cruz, San Diego State University, The Evergreen State College (Olympia, Washington), Wayne State University (Detroit), the Smithsonian, and the University of North Carolina at Asheville, where until his retirement in 2009 he held a joint appointment as Research Associate Professor of Philosophy and executive director of the NC Center for Creative Retirement (now OLLI, the Osher Lifelong Learning Institute).

In his *A Map to the End of Time: Wayfarings with Friends and Philosophers* (Norton, 1999), Manheimer demonstrates the fruitfulness of combining dual interests in philosophy and narrative studies. This work has been translated into Chinese and Korean. His newest book, *Mirrors of the Mind: Reflecting on Philosophers' Autobiographies* (Jorvik Press, 2015) extends this pursuit by capturing transformative moments in the first-person narratives of renowned thinkers.

Currently, Manheimer teaches philosophy courses at OLLI, conducts enrichment programs for elementary schoolchildren, chairs UNCA's Center for Jewish Studies steering committee, is Chair Elect of the BJH Foundation of the Carolinas, serves on the editorial board of two academic journals, and provides consulting for non-profit organizations.

Acknowledgments

My students in two separate courses on existentialism have been an inspiration for this book. Imagine the benefits of having such participants as an existential psychoanalyst, a philosophy Ph.D. with a dissertation on Nietzsche, and a man who told us the following story shared by his 90-year-old father, a retired dentist in Chicago.

In a phone conversation about his son's studying the French philosophers, the father recounted a conversation he'd had with a writer at a party years ago. The writer was bemoaning his French lover's refusal to marry him because of her longstanding commitment to a man back in Paris. The Chicago writer turned out to be the novelist Nelson Algren, the lover, Simone de Beauvoir, and the boyfriend back home, Jean-Paul Sartre. Adding to this, another classmate dug out the yellowing pages of her undergraduate essay for a college French literature class in which she had, in French, tried to come to terms with the love triangle in de Beauvoir's *L'Invitée* (*She Came to Stay*).

I am also grateful to readers of earlier drafts of this work: Rob Neufeld, Harry Moody, Denise Snodgrass, Elyn Selu, Steven Wall, Peggy Noel, Robert Warner and my wife, Gail Manheimer. My editor, Peter Stansill, remains my intrepid guide in matters of persistence and perseverance.

By way of disclosure, personal anecdotes sprinkled throughout this book are sometimes fictionalized to honor the confidentiality of friends and acquaintances, or in instances in which I could not acquire permission to use the subjects' names or details about their lives. Names in first-use quotation marks will indicate modification.

Ronald J. Manheimer, Ph.D.
Asheville NC

To our grandchildren:

Levi, Grayson, Asa,

Benjamin and Noah

CONTENTS

1. Absurdity

My attraction to philosophy began the way attractions to new ideas have for so many others – I was handed an assignment. Our high school English teacher, "Mr. O'Brien," had high expectations. We were to choose from a list of themes for the term paper. "Compare Shaw's Superman with Nietzsche's *Übermensch*?" My eyes glazed over. "Compare Gide's *The Immoralist* with Camus' *The Stranger*?" Something stirred within.

That seemingly random choice is how the philosophical orientation known as existentialism first entered my world. Existential themes and concepts would surface repeatedly, each time announcing or precipitating a new challenge or moment of decision.

In this I was not unique. Earlier generations had responded to the voices of existential philosophers, novelists, playwrights and filmmakers. That calling took many names, such as rebellion, liberation, authenticity, solidarity and emancipation. The season of my assignment was winter, 1960; the place, Detroit. Not yet seventeen, I was departing on a journey of a lifetime.

Library Epiphany

For several weekends I would be seated at a massive oak table at the marble-lined main branch of the Detroit Public Library, thumbing through volumes of the *Reader's Guide to Periodical Literature* in search of articles about the two French authors. Albert Camus' *The Stranger* is about Meursault, a diffident young French Algerian who, seemingly without any clear motive, kills an Arab man on a beach near Algiers and is sentenced to death. Andre Gide's *The Immoralist*, published in 1902, forty years before Camus' novel, concerns a young Frenchman, Michel, whose diary tells us about his search to find his authentic self, a quest that takes him to Arab villages in French colonized North Africa where he discovers an attraction to young boys.

Both novels, I noticed, in their final pages present their protagonists looking up into the North African night sky. For Meursault it's the dark sky "spangled with its signs and stars," their brilliance opening his heart "to the benign indifference of the universe." The stars, says Meursault, mirror his own existence like a "brotherly" embrace (Camus, 75). For Michel, the brightness of the moon is "almost terrifying," as it floods into the room where his wife Marceline lay dying of tuberculosis (Gide, 195). He cannot hide from its rays. He's like a fugitive caught in the beams of a searchlight. Signs, stars, the moon – were these important? Mr. O'Brien liked his students to craft phrases like "vivid parallelism" or "uncanny coincidence." Would he know the message Meursault and Michel had found in the darkness?

I was aware that Camus was friendly with a philosopher named Jean-Paul Sartre and that he, in turn, was frequently associated with the novelist Simone de Beauvoir. The threesome was linked to a philosophical movement popularly dubbed existentialism, and all three characters admired the more senior Monsieur Gide. There must have been something existentialist in his writings, too. But what was it?

The protagonists of both novels seemed to have come to the end of their respective ropes. Almost literally for Meursault, though it is not the noose but the guillotine he must face, and, metaphorically, for Michel whose journey has brought him to the point of immobility and despair. Michel has summoned three of his closest friends to comfort him, as he lies prone on a mat in the interior courtyard of his North African desert village abode.

Death, or at least facing death, seemed to be important to the existentialists, many of whom had a few years earlier emerged from five years of the German occupation of Paris where they had seen a great many deaths, especially violent ones, firsthand. Camus and Sartre had taken part in the French Resistance. The war must have influenced de Beauvoir, too. In one of the sources I hoped to use in a footnote for my paper, she wrote that human beings, of all other animals, suffered from a "tragic ambiguity" because, despite their freedom to make what they will of their lives, humans are also consciously aware that they are mortal and will, at some unpredictable moment, perish. Given this feature of the "human condition," we cannot escape the question: what is the point of doing anything (de Beauvoir, *Ethics of Ambiguity*, 8)?

People were tiptoeing around the library, pulling heavy volumes from shelves in the cathedral-like reference room and totting them over to a spot staked out at one of the tables. They seemed so focused, so determined. I felt adrift, as if looking down from the room's vaulted ceiling and seeing myself, a small figure in an enormous space filled with an eternity's worth of knowledge and ideas.

Starry nights, murder under a hot Mediterranean sun, dying in a North African oasis town with its twisting, stone-paved streets and palm trees, what did this mean to me, a mere high school student who had never seen death face to face, never stood in desert moonlight and did not speak French. I was just trying to get a decent grade on a paper for Mr. O'Brien in order to graduate and go to college where, as a pre-med student, I would probably have little time to delve further into existentialism.

Before I finished my day's task, filling out index cards with quotes and sources, the head of a man seated across from me behind a pile of books loomed up as he pushed the stacks apart. A round face with puffy cheeks, hair parted down the middle, he pointed to my copy of *The Stranger* and shook his head in apparent disapproval of my reading choice. He should have known I hadn't chosen these books; they were part of a school assignment.

But then he leaned forward, grinned from ear to ear, and in the appropriate library voice whispered, "He's dead, you know?" Was he referring to the condemned character Meursault? Yes, by now, the character probably would be dead.

The man stood up. He was wearing a corduroy sport jacket with a dress shirt, open at the neck. He removed a pair of gold-rimmed glasses.

"An accident. Automobile. Ironic, wouldn't you say?"

Ah, he must have been talking about Camus, the author, not the character in his novel. The man glanced around, perhaps to see if anyone else was listening. I, too, looked around but the other patrons seemed completely focused on their research as if, even as grownups, they had term papers to write.

"He was supposed to have taken the train," the man continued, nodding and then shaking his head as if Camus had been one of his best friends. "Instead, he accepted a ride in a sports car with his publisher. Reckless.

The man drove too fast. A terrible smash up. What an absurd way to die for such a great writer."

Was the man going to start to cry, right there in the public library? He didn't. He put his glasses back on and pointed at my reference books and my index cards. "Put that in your paper. Camus' was an absurd death." With that he sat down and bowed his head as if in prayer.

That was the first time it occurred to me that authors were mortal flesh-and-blood individuals like the people walking around in the public library. Camus had been no more real to me than Meursault; both were fictional characters, the one on the cover, the other inside the book. But Meursault hadn't died by the time I turned the last page of *The Stranger* and now, oddly, Camus had. Perhaps if that's what the man in the corduroy jacket meant by calling it absurd, it's true that a car accident did seem an unglamorous and sadly ironic way to die for a famous writer who had won a Nobel Prize in literature and was a survivor of four years of serving in the French Resistance.

The moon-faced man at my table had taken it personally, as if Camus had been a relative or acquaintance. Still, Camus' automobile death wouldn't fit into my term paper. What did absurdity have to do with the stars in the desert sky?

ALIGNING THE STARS

Mr. O'Brien was impressed with my disquisition on the topic of Death and Stargazing in the novels of Camus and Gide. "What better place to project one's destiny than the night sky," I enthused. The "existential challenge," I noted and footnoted in my paper, is an aspect of (another footnote) the "literature of extremes," life and death encounters that serve to "shatter the shell of indifference" that "embalms the protagonist" who has yet to discover "his unique existence on the stage of life." Unfortunately, for the likes of Meursault and Michel, this awakening comes "a bit too late." But not for us readers who, if we are up to the challenge, may likewise be shaken from our "plodding conformism, settled mediocrity, and fear of the freedom and responsibility to make our lives our own."

These phrases I remember in kind because during stints as a college philosophy teacher I would come across similar bits of rhetoric in my students' papers. How is it that at such a young age we can acquire such profound insights merely by searching through the *Reader's Guide* (and today Google Scholar) to find our way into the volumes of arcane journals where the meanings of life are so beautifully and intelligently illuminated?

At the end of the class, the term papers having been returned with grades and comments, we seniors said our farewells to our esteemed teacher. Watching us shuffling out of the classroom, Mr. O'Brien motioned me aside.

"Well, Manheimer," he began. "What are your plans? College, I presume." I nodded in the affirmative. "Yes, good. And to what will you devote your studies? Do you know?"

I murmured that I was pre-med. "Oh," said Mr. O'Brien, frowning. "Too bad." And with that, he shook my hand, patted me on the shoulder and dismissed me.

Mr. O'Brien's parting comment lingered in the stale air of the high school hallway. What had he meant? That I had not yet had my brush with death and therefore was not initiated into the ranks of those who were truly alive; the nonconformists, sensualists, outsider types; people who refuse to fulfill other people's dreams but who have the courage to risk forging their own destiny? Should I then pursue a cure for a life-threatening disease, commit myself to a capricious murder, or seek out strangers whom I might embrace in the shadows of some lane or alleyway? The answer to these questions remained hidden.

COLLEGE KNOWLEDGE

Seven months later, on an unusually warm autumn afternoon, I stepped through the doorway into my first college discussion group, part of the Monteith College social science curriculum. A new, small liberal arts college on the sprawling urban campus of Detroit's Wayne State University, Monteith was one of a new breed of undergraduate schools designed to encourage students to think independently while learning in the context of an interdisciplinary and integrated four-year curriculum.

Newly matriculating students received a letter inviting them to sign up for Monteith, explaining the school was launched with funds from the Ford Foundation in response to a perceived lack of creative initiative on the part of newly minted graduates such as engineers and chemists.

Monteith, with its small student body, its own student center and low student-faculty ratio would be a kind of "Oxford at Wayne State."

But Oxford was in faraway England. Its students paraded around in capes. Nevertheless, invited to enroll in a special college, I accepted.

I found a seat at the large seminar table. As the teacher read off the registration list of the students, I realized from the ending of the last names that many of my classmates had probably grown up in one of Detroit's many ethnic neighborhoods.

Our teacher introduced himself as Dr. Otto Feinstein. Balding, soft-spoken, with a faintly European accent, he reminded me of my high school physics teacher who, as a youth, was supposed to have fled the Nazis in the 1930s. Dr. Feinstein's sport coat looked a bit rumpled and his necktie slightly askew. He asked us to introduce ourselves and to say a few words about how we viewed the world that seemed to be changing so dramatically.

This was surprising. Did we, his students, have views about "the world?" Turned out, some did. A boy who worked part-time as a newspaper carrier talked about how he had gone to union meetings but the chairman would never call on him to answer his questions. A girl took out a handful of flyers that she distributed inviting us to come see a free movie, *Ivan the Terrible*, at a place called Debs Hall. Another talked about life in Poland under the Communists. It seems his father, who ran a restaurant in the ethnic Hamtramck neighborhood, was also editor of a left-wing Polish newspaper. Awed at the worldliness of my fellow students, I sat there in silence.

A few weeks later, consuming plates of spaghetti at a campus eatery with a few classmates and "Otto," our teacher, we were expressing our anxieties about what we wanted to do in life compared with what our parents expected would come out of our college educations. Nodding thoughtfully, Otto asked whether we'd heard of a new book about American youth and the future of society. It was called *Growing Up Absurd*. Maybe we would find it helpful.

There was that word again. Absurd. The faces of the other spaghetti eaters mirrored the anxiety and uncertainty I was feeling. Were we living in a condition of absurdity or were our lives themselves absurd? The world of received values that we had grown up with seemed suddenly antiquated and oddly unhelpful to the challenges of the social changes that had followed in the aftermath of World War II. The contest of the nuclear superpowers, the U.S. and the Soviet Union, racism and school desegregation, the newly documented poverty in Appalachia, revolutionary ferment in colonized countries of South America and Asia. Twirling the strands of pasta, I decided my next stop would be the bookstore.

GROWING UP ABSURD

Growing Up Absurd was not quite what I expected. The author, Paul Goodman, wrote about a newly labeled problem of social deviance: juvenile delinquency. I couldn't see how learning about kids engaged in gang fights or incarcerated for stealing cars was going to provide me with a guide to a life that I hoped to make my own.

Still, there was something about the way Goodman described America's wayward youth that made them sound vaguely heroic, if not revolutionary. With their petty thefts and loose morals, their beer drinking and foulmouthed backtalk, Goodman's "kids" were, he argued, the product of a society that had little or nothing to offer them. It was the "system of society" with its gray-flannel suited businessmen and repressive governmental bureaucracies that had led young people into unfocused revolt and flailing antisocial behavior that fomented juvenile delinquency. To "grow up absurd," proclaimed Goodman, was to come of age in a society of mindless, repetitive jobs, fear-driven social conformity, and the impersonal bureaucracies of industry and government.

Juvenile delinquents, Goodman conjectured, were not so different from another type of deviant group, the socially self-marginalizing Beatniks. Both were repelled by what Goodman called "the Organized System and its dominant values." That System operated "against human nature," and the consequence, said Goodman, was that when a society failed to provide young people with the tools and resources to thrive, "they'll fill the gaps with eccentric substitutes."

Though these appeared to be meant as cautionary words, it seemed like Goodman was actually inviting us, American youth plagued by the malaise of meaninglessness, to mull over the possibilities of eccentric substitutes. In short, *Growing Up Absurd* was less a treatise on misbehaved youth than a critique of American society, less a piece of social science research than a call to rebellion.

Probably there was not a direct causal relationship between reading *Growing Up Absurd* and my involvement in the civil rights and the early stages of the anti-Vietnam War movements while a student at Monteith. The book was just one among many influences that shaped my outlook. Yet I continue to wonder, of the hundreds of books and people that vied for attention, why was I predisposed to some and not to others?

GOODMAN IN DENMARK

Five years after pondering over his portrayal of American youth, I watched the curly haired, bespectacled Paul Goodman take a pinch of stringy tobacco from a pouch and mash it into the bowl of his pipe before striking a wooden match and igniting the aromatic tinder. We were seated across from one another in a circle of people about my age dressed in jeans or shorts, sandals or hiking boots. A few were barefoot. New Experimental College was holding its annual summer retreat in a creaky seaside hotel in the village of Humlebæk, 40 kilometers north of Copenhagen, Denmark. Paul, as everyone called the social critic and novelist, was one of the resident faculty members that semester.

I had taken the overnight boat from the island of Bornholm where, in my year of hitchhiking through Europe after graduating from college, I had found a job working for room and board as a farm laborer. Arriving at the hotel in the early afternoon, I took a short nap to make up for my loss of sleep on the ship. When I awoke, there was Goodman sitting in a chair across from my bed. He introduced himself and we started to talk.

Walking down the hotel hallway headed to the gathering downstairs, Paul took my hand. This, I considered, was something of a European gesture as I had seen men in Italy and Greece walking arm in arm. Later, I would discover, that Goodman, a bisexual, was a notorious flirt with younger men.

Goodman knew about Monteith College. He liked the idea that the college was run as an experiment to see how a broad range of freshmen, rather than exclusively honors students, fared in a college that featured small discussion groups, an integrated curriculum, lots of personal contact between students and faculty, and opportunities for students to innovate. Indeed, Monteith had turned out to be the hotbed of student activism on the Wayne State campus. This ranged from launching film and folk festivals to organizing demonstrations against discrimination in student housing.

Moreover, as I explained to Paul, a few of us seniors had taken it into our heads that we were ready to function as teachers and course innovators. We had championed an initiative in which students would educate one another. We called it "Cooperative Self-education." These were accredited courses vetted by the faculty and monitored by a willing teacher since grades would be given and credits awarded. I had taught two such courses, "Writing as Self-Expression" and later, with a fellow student majoring in filmmaking, "Art and the City." The city in this latter case was Detroit and the class met in various locations ranging from the offices of the City Planning Commission to one of the new twin high rises, Lafayette Towers, designed by Mies van der Rohe, which gave residents a view of the Detroit River. Paul thought I should share my story about Monteith and I agreed to do so.

Maybe it was because of living and working on a dairy and poultry farm and beginning to dream in a new language that, as soon as I started talking, my former life in Detroit and at Monteith felt like ancient history. I tried to be informative but, as Goodman later commented, "For someone involved in an exciting educational venture, you sounded kind of bored with the idea and, frankly, your talk was boring."

This was embarrassing. I had let the group down and wondered what had happened to me. As the first in my family to go to college, Monteith had marked a huge change in my life. I had discovered, as one of my teachers called it, "the life of the mind." My time at Monteith had also helped me to see that becoming a medical doctor was not my calling.

A rich and complex world had opened up and I was eager to explore the possibilities. But diverging from the known or predictable path, while exciting and mind-expanding, had left me feeling more than a little lost. Maybe that's why I fell in with the New Experimental College group. I needed to be in a place and among a group of people that would provide a setting to continue my search for the values and meanings that would replace the ones I had discarded.

The rector of New Experimental College was a maverick Danish educator named Aage Rosendal Nielsen. A charismatic figure, Augie, as everyone called him, was well known in Denmark for launching an organization called the Scandinavian Seminar for Cultural Studies, a program that brought American undergraduates to Scandinavia's culture- and craft-oriented *folkehøjskoler* or "people's colleges," for a yearlong program.

Augie had a slight stutter, which I soon noticed his students picked up, so that conversations were marked by hesitant Rs, Ss, and Ts. There was an inch-long scar above his right lip that had attained legendary status. "Th-th, that's from where Augie fell from a hayloft on his parents' farm." Or, "It was when he was r-running after sabotaging the g-g-Germans during the Occupation." After I told the group in Humlebæk about Paul Goodman's influence on my efforts to escape absurdity and the dreariness of Detroit, Augie said I should read something of the Danish philosopher Kierkegaard. I asked him why and he responded with his laryngeal: "R-r, Ron. It's j-j, just a hunch."

READING KIERKEGAARD

The Humlebæk hotel's sun porch was lined with built-in bookshelves. Many of the books were in Danish. As my reading ability in that language was still at a ten-year-old's level, I passed over them. But there were some paperbacks in English, including a translation of Kierkegaard's best-known work, the two-volume *Either/Or.* I began reading random chapters of the first volume, what I dubbed the *Either* half, since the volume seemed to hold independent essays rather than a logically progressive sequence.

The book baffled me. It began with a collection of irony-laced aphorisms including one that asks: "What is a poet?" And answers that he is an unhappy man who hides a deep anguish and so suffers like the legendary men "who were slowly roasted by a gentle fire in the tyrant Phalaris' bull – their shrieks could not reach his ear to terrify him, to him they sounded like sweet music" (Vol. 1, 19). After the aphorisms came a series of essays on drama and literature and a long excerpt from "The Diary of a Seducer."

The writing in the first volume was supposed to come from the hand of a young man whom we only know as A. The whole book was purport-edly composed from a bundle of documents that the book's editor, with the obviously made-up name of Victor Eremita, found in an antique desk he bought at an auction and in which he discovered the papers hidden in a secret compartment.

Most of what I found in the writing of Mr. A., or in Danish, Herr A., seemed to be about how to demonstrate great wit, erudition and an impressive vocabulary without getting caught up in anything too serious. In other words, A. possessed a dreamy, melancholy poetic sensibility. And while he demonstrated literary brilliance he used it to dance away from binding commitments.

How, I wondered, was this book going to help?

Turning to the second volume, the one I had named the *Or*, I found two very long essays that were presented as letters written by a middle-aged man whose profession was a lower court judge. He's called B. but somewhere was reference to a first name, Wilhelm or, in English, William. The letters are addressed to the first volume's Herr A. Basically, B. was telling A. to grow up and get a life and not think that he could keep on living like some dashing romantic poet who feels superior to others because he refuses to play the game of joining into the conventional life of middle class existence.

B.'s tedious exhortations made me want to go back and read more of what A. had to say. After all, I too was an aspiring poet and would-be romancer; perhaps his outlook might be more appealing. Still, I plugged on with the weighty words of Mr. B. And there was the section in which B. tells A. that he has to "give birth to yourself" through some kind of self-impregnation (Vol. 2, 206). That phrase and another – "Choose yourself" – brought me to a halt.

I looked up through the small windowpanes of the sunroom at the leaves of nearby birch trees. The movement of the branches made the light flicker across my face. Had I chosen myself? What an odd question. How could a person not have chosen himself or herself? That's when it hit me. By moving away from the place and life in which I had grown up and by deferring the education and career path that had somehow seemed my destiny, I had unchosen myself.

Maybe this is what Augie had in mind when he recommended Kierkegaard. That I would find my life situation reflected somewhere in the pages of one of his books.

The truth was, from the time I read Camus and Gide and looked with their ill-fated characters up into the night sky, and then read Paul

Goodman's account of juvenile delinquents as rebels, I had found my affinity with absurdity.

To many people absurdity means that something is ridiculous, pointless, or meaningless. But to me, my unchoosing adventure signified life without preset limitations, it meant that one could leap boldly out of the past and the place and family in which you had grown up into an unknown yet welcoming future.

In short, absurd meant liberation, finding oneself on a fresh map of life with paths that had yet to be trod or even surveyed. Herr A. was to me the absurdist hero of *Either/Or* while the judge Herr B. was the comic straight man.

HISTORY OF CONSCIOUSNESS

After three years serving on the staff of New Experimental College, I returned to the U.S. to start graduate school at UC Santa Cruz. I enrolled in a brand new doctoral program with the unabashed title, History of Consciousness. There, at Santa Cruz, I came under the intellectual tutelage of two professors, Albert Hofstadter and Maurice Natanson, the former a specialist in aesthetics and Continental philosophy (he was a translator of the German philosopher Heidegger) and the latter an internationally well-known scholar in the phenomenology of the social sciences.

On reaching Santa Cruz I had lost interest in Kierkegaard but not before making the discovery that I had been caught in one of his literary-philosophical traps. *Either/Or*, I learned, was designed to entice readers to see themselves in the mindset of either A. or B. with A. representing the "aesthetic" stage of life (live for the moment, avoid commitments, maintain an ironic standpoint towards all others) and B. representing the "ethical" (become part of the universal human community, embrace your destiny, find enduring values through career, marriage and friendship). The reader was meant to vacillate back and forth between identifying with now the free-spirited (though occasionally melancholy) A. and then the well-adjusted good burgher, Judge Wilhelm, Herr B.

So it came as another ironic twist that for a dissertation topic I would wind up writing on "Kierkegaard and the Education of Historical Consciousness." This came about after I had formulated an idea that I wanted to investigate how philosophers viewed human development as compared to the then-current views of developmental psychologists.

The latter focused on what was normal or deviant from normal while the former dealt with what was ideal or possible but also with the obstacles that stood in the way. The idea that fascinated me was that we move through stages of life that can be understood not only psychologically but also philosophically as meaning-constructing positions.

At the time I vaguely suspected I was looking for this theory of philosophical life stages to serve as a map for understanding my own life. The framework of life stages also seemed useful for carrying out what I thought would be my career as a college teacher since it would be invaluable to understanding what evaluative life outlook my students might possess and how, then, I would communicate with them.

When I described the study I wanted to undertake in order to write my dissertation, my advisor, Professor Hofstadter, immediately said, "What about Kierkegaard?" He probably saw the frown on my face. "You know, Ron, Kierkegaard's book, *The Stages on Life's Way*? Wouldn't that be a good starting point?" I wanted to say that I had already started and finished with the Dane but out of deference to my advisor I agreed to take a fresh look. Because I had now formulated my quest, my reentry into the Kierkegaardian realm proved propitious.

Kierkegaard was to teach me yet one more variation on the meaning of absurdity. He quotes the Second Century (C.E.) Christian author Tertullian's *credo quia absurdum*, "I believe by virtue of the absurd." Here the absurd is something incomprehensible, a being who is at once mortal and immortal, the paradoxical man-god Jesus. Here was a theological challenge to the mind that clings to the criteria of rationality.

Thanks to a Danforth Foundation Fellowship, I completed my dissertation in Denmark, writing it in a farmhouse overlooking the Limfjord that cuts through the northern peninsula of Jutland. Coincidentally, this was an area not too far from the windswept heath on which Kierkegaard's father had grown up as a poor shepherd boy before being plucked up by an uncle and set down in Copenhagen where he eventually became a wealthy wool merchant. By the time of my return to Denmark, I had made a decisive leap into the "court" of Judge Wilhelm. I was married, working on a career-oriented dissertation, and was soon to be a father.

EXISTENTIALISM ECLIPSED?

Existentialism has long been eclipsed by philosophical movements in France and beyond, such as structuralism, post-structuralism and deconstructionism. Research in the neurosciences has come to overshadow existentialists' theories of human consciousness. But these have only led to fresh debates about how far we determine our own destinies.

Nevertheless, the lives and ideas of Camus, Sartre, de Beauvoir, and their predecessors, Kierkegaard and Nietzsche, have remained both visible and relevant. Anthologies of new scholarship like the *Bloomsbury Companion to Existentialism* (2011) have been reassessing existentialism in light of these subsequent emergent schools of thought. They aim to show how the work of Sartre and de Beauvoir anticipated and contributed to them.

A novel, *The Meursault Investigation* (2015), has come out presenting an Arab point of view on Camus' *The Stranger*. New editions of Kierkegaard's voluminous works continue to be reprinted. Sarah Bakewell's *At the Existentialist Cafe* (2016) was a bestseller – she conveys the ideas of the existentialists through their life stories and the historical context in which they lived.

As for my own small part, I have been offering courses on the existentialists in a lifelong learning program. My courses quickly fill with 35 enrollees, often with a waiting list of 50. At the younger end of the spectrum, students at Brown University favored a course on existentialism as their top choice in a recent summer warm-up series for incoming freshmen. No doubt, existentialism is still alive and relevant. Its cluster of ideas and assertions about what it means to be human continue to resonate with the most profound challenges to our lives.

Each of the chapters in this book deals with a single, though closely related, idea prominent in the existentialist universe. These are the stars in the night sky into which I first gazed many years ago. As Kierkegaard put it, the existential thinker's task is that of a "personal appropriation process." Accordingly, I share some of my appropriations to convey what existentialism has meant to me at different moments and to others with whom I believe I have shared these meanings. I am mindful of Simone de Beauvoir's assertion in the second of her memoirs, *The Prime of Life*, that shedding light on one's own life might lead to "illuminating the lives of others" (8).

Not everyone leads their life as a series of infatuations with ideas nor finds the concept of the absurd a guiding star in the dark night of the soul. This book is intended for those who do.

REFERENCES

Bakewell, Sarah (2016). *At the Existentialist Cafe*. New York: Other Press.

Beauvoir, Simone de (1948). *The Ethics of Ambiguity*. Tr. Bernard Frechtman. New York: Citadel Press.

_____ (1973). *The Prime of Life*. Second edition. Tr. Peter Green. New York: Lancer Books.

Camus, Albert (1946). *The Stranger*. Tr. Stuart Gilbert. New York: Knopf.

Daud, Kamel (2015). *The Meursault Investigation, a novel*. New York: Other Press.

Gide, Andre (1961). *The Immoralist*. Tr. Dorothy Bussy. New York: Knopf.

Goodman, Paul (1960). *Growing Up Absurd: Problems of Youth in the Organized System*. New York: Random House.

Joseph, Felicity, Jack Reynolds, and Ashley Woodward (2011). *The Bloomsbury Companion to Existentialism*. London: Bloomsbury.

Kierkegaard, Søren (1959*). Either/Or*. Tr. Harold Lowrie. New York: Doubleday.

_____ (1988). *Stages on Life's Way*. Tr. Howard Hong. Princeton: Princeton University Press.

2. NOTHINGNESS

If the existentialists' use of the absurd is to shake us from the slumber of deadening rituals and repressive social conventions, then our second star, nothingness, is the source from which the absurd draws its power. But how can a concept of non-being or negation prove fruitful to the discovery of new meanings?

Much fun, if not consternation, from philosophers of a non-existentialist disposition has been directed at this ephemeral idea, yet the experience of nothingness is so familiar that it usually goes unidentified. Its formative moments are many. The child's building a tower of blocks only to knock it down to build anew. The adolescent's dawning awareness that he or she is not a replica of a parent but can pursue a different life course or, conversely, choose to embrace and extend a family's heritage. A young college student, away from home for the first time, plunged suddenly into a world of diverse beliefs and opinions, discovering that meanings are not fixed but fluid and multiform.

Anyone engaged in creative enterprises will recall moments in which something – an image, idea or mathematical equation – bursts forth precisely at the point of impasse and mental immobility. Yes, something can come not exactly from nothing but from the suspension or negation of the previously known, believed, or imagined. The void of nothingness rarely occurs without a certain degree of tension, conflict or turmoil. Nothingness has always been an unruly if not dangerous idea, as a young clergyman who discovered its connection to social change understood.

HEGEL AND DR. KING

In the spring of 1953, a student pursuing a doctoral degree in systematic theology at Boston University submitted the last of six required essays. It bore the ponderous title, "An Exposition of the First Triad of Categories of the Hegelian Logic – Being, Non-Being, Becoming."

The 24-year-old grad student, Martin Luther King Jr., was finishing up a two-semester seminar devoted to the study of the 19th century German idealist philosopher Hegel, whose works had a profound influence on both religious and secular existentialist thinkers, especially the Dane, Kierkegaard (who both imitated and mocked Hegel) and the French, Sartre and de Beauvoir (who adapted Hegelian ideas to their purposes).

The BU student, also fascinated with the sources of existentialism, struggled to grasp Hegel's assertion that reality (that which is, or Being) is shaped through and through by thought, not in a subjective sense as a projection of the human mind, but as an identity of the mind and its object, the world. An ordained minister with a part-time pulpit in Atlanta, he was deeply immersed in heady academic subjects while simultaneously caught up in the race-relations turmoil back home. How would Hegel's logic be of any help?

King had chosen Boston University as a multicultural setting where he could study ethics and philosophy. In his final essay he sought to decipher what is called the "first triad" of Hegel's logic. "Being," King writes in his essay, is "the highest abstraction, that which is common to every conceivable object in the universe." This bare abstraction, devoid of determinants or features, is "completely empty and vacant." This vacancy, however, "turns out to be not anything."

In Hegel's special way of tracing the fundamentals of thought, which he called "dialectical reasoning," the category of Being generates its opposite, that of Non-Being or Nothing. While they form an inseparable polarity, Being and Nothing are not rigid opposites. They pass back and forth into one another as things and thoughts come into being and disappear from being. The dynamic they set up brings animation and transformation into an otherwise non-temporal logic. "Becoming," the third term of the triad, King notes, doesn't eradicate Being and Nothing, rather they are, as Hegel puts it, *aufhaben*, a term usually translated as "sublated." This is the key to Hegel's logic: Becoming preserves Being and Nothing in a dynamic unity.

King learned from Hegel that Being-Nothing-Becoming were not only the foundational building blocks of human consciousness but also the conceptual mechanism that drove historical change. That any seemingly fated or fixed moment of history – a reigning school of painting or architecture, an entrenched monarchy or oligarchy, a system of class hierarchy – could and would eventually be overturned.

While King rejected Hegel's account because it seemed to turn individuals into pawns rather than agents of social change, he lauded Hegel's assertion that "growth comes through struggle." In June of 1955, now the pastor of Dexter Avenue Baptist Church in Montgomery, Alabama, Martin Luther King, Jr. received his degree and became Dr. King. Six months later, he emerged as one of the key leaders of the Montgomery boycott of the city's segregated bus system.

The lesson Dr. King gleaned from Hegel's logic is that socially entrenched, fixed states of affairs such as conditions of racial and economic injustice are not inevitable and are certainly not ordained by a transcendent power. They can be overcome, sublated, through what Hegel called "the power of the negative." To accomplish this there would have to be a process of consciousness-raising and mobilization.

King, recently acquainted with Gandhi's Indian emancipation model of *ahimsa*, non-violent resistance, merged this form of civil disobedience with Hegel's logic of historical change to yield the strategy and philosophy that reenergized the black civil rights movement. Dr. King sought to overturn the laws of American apartheid and to seek the same goal as Hegel's charter course of history: Freedom.

In his 1958 book, the *Stride Towards Freedom: The Montgomery Story*, King cites Hegel as an inspiration for nonviolence. He called Hegel's logic of historical consciousness, "the third way open to oppressed people in their quest for freedom." And he inserted into the dialectic of change his own set of opposites, "acquiescence and violence," bending to the oppressive status quo versus manifestly overthrowing the system. King sought to avoid "the extremes and immoralities of both" (213). He believed the path of becoming was forged through the power of the negative.

NOTHING AS SELF-OVERCOMING

My encounter with Dr. King occurred in June of 1963, two months before the famous March on Washington and King's "I have a dream" speech. As a new participant in social change, I was one of an estimated 250,000 people marching along Detroit's Woodward Avenue towards the site of Dr. King's speech at the city's downtown convention arena. Active in the civil right movement, I was thrilled to be a tiny speck in this sea of people, black and white, many of them with arms linked, some singing, some dancing, talking, laughing, and all in apparent agreement that the time for change had come.

I, too, was linked with someone of color, "Gwendolyn," a young woman who had recently come into my life in a way that had suddenly made racial equality more than a slogan on a picket sign. While I had some black friends, mainly from among the students in my college, I had never had a close relationship with a black person. I chastised myself for feeling apprehensive about drawing closer to Gwen; nevertheless I was hesitant about stepping across a line – no, a chasm – over which Gwen was inviting me to leap.

I had met Gwen a few months earlier at a civil rights training retreat at a camp about two hour's drive from campus. We were to learn about the techniques and meaning of non-violent resistance. One evening, someone had brought out a guitar and a semi-circle had formed in the dining hall around the stone fireplace. People either started a song for the others to join in or called out a song title to see if the singing would spring up. Seated on cushions or sprawled across the wooden floor, the singers seemed to grow closer together as night came on. I became aware of Gwen when someone dropped a fresh log on the fire and it flamed up illuminating her shimmering brown face as it tilted towards me. I had the feeling that she was sizing me up. How committed was I? Was this just another white liberal who, in a moment of crisis, would walk away from the conflict? It was then that I committed an incredible *faux pas*.

In a lull in the singing, I shouted out "Summertime," the popular tune from *Porgy and Bess*. What followed was an awkward silence, broken by the sound of hisses and moans, and a few outright "No, Man!" exclamations. Fortunately, in the dim light, no one could see my reddening face. It hit me. The song and the story reflected a white person's view of impoverished blacks living in the slums of Charleston, SC. Hardly the right choice of song for our interracial group. My suggestion, I realized, showed my lack of sensitivity and my hopelessly middle-class white upbringing. Was there some way I could slink out of the room?

"Okay, people," the voice beside me called out. "You know, Ella sings this song. We know what it means. It's a beautiful song. Very black, you know. Very, very black."

A hand touched my shoulder. I raised my shamed face and watched her pursed lips humming the beginning of "Summertime." Slowly, the group joined in. After that, Gwen became my mentor in black-white relations. She shared some of the lore of her family background and drew insightful portraits of various black leaders in our group that helped me understand both their anger at white society and dedication to the cause of black civil rights. If our relationship had stayed on that level I wouldn't have come to stand at the edge of the chasm.

So there we were marching down Woodward, arms around each other's waists. By then we both knew what this meant or might mean. If we were to become further romantically involved, I would be making the leap into uncharted territory. The prospect of involvement with a black woman who seemed comfortable with the expression of her affections and, I sensed, more experienced as a lover, further increased my anxiety. If I leapt, I would be radically redefining my identity.

My involvement in the civil rights movement had already opened my eyes, not only to the history of racism in America, but my inadvertent participation in that racism by virtue of the family and social class into which I had been born. I had, in Hegelian (and, later, Sartrean, terms) become an Other to myself. Regarding myself from a different standpoint, I realized my strangeness as a historical entity, as a white body and mindset, as other-than a person of color. The tension of self-division, of becoming other to my Self, had already set in. Gwen was calling me to go further, to overcome the boundaries of my white identity to deliver myself from the restraints of prejudice, not just in a theoretical and intellectual way, but a fully embodied one. Her smiling face was asking me: Are you ready for an interracial relationship? Are you ready to let go of who you think you are, ready to move from what you have been into the realm of what you are not-yet?

Mental paralysis set in. Our furtive moves towards one another were made further complicated. A former boyfriend who had been serving in the Navy reappeared on the scene and their attraction flared up. I didn't want us to go our separate ways and yet I lacked the courage to persist.

How tangled were the issues of love, race and the cause of social justice. In this situation I sought someone else's perspective. I turned to my new friend, Bob, a fellow Monteith student who, while majoring in chemistry, was interested in just about every new idea and emerging movement. Thick bodied, bespectacled with slicked back hair, Bob had been a high school football player as well as an honor student.

It was morning. We were in the student cafeteria, me sitting before a cup of coffee, Bob wolfing down a waffle smothered in syrup. Bob chewed and nodded as I told my story. But when I concluded with "So, Bob, what do you think I should do?" He looked down at his empty plate and then looked up and smiled.

"You know," he said, gesturing with his fork, "Sartre talks about this." I'm sure I looked puzzled. What had Sartre written about race relations and love conflicts?

"Moral ambiguity, the key to existentialism. In this situation, there's no simple right or wrong answer," said Bob. "Besides, Sartre says when we ask someone for advice, we already know what they're going to say." He paused letting this sink in. "That's why we pick this certain person." I waited for him to fill in the missing blanks.

After a long silence, Bob took a packet of sugar from a plastic holder on the table and set it down in front of me. He slid beside it a plate dotted with puddles of syrup.

"Let me offer you this analogy," he said. And pointing at the sugar packet, "This is you," he said. "The result of refinement. Crystalline. Before that, you were syrup." He swiped his finger across the plate and licked off the syrup. "Actually, you've shifted back and forth between syrup and crystals a number of times. That's how we develop. Liquid, solid, liquid and so forth. But now you're more or less grown up. Crystallized. So the challenge is whether you're willing to go back into a state of syrup. That could be exciting. But it's fluid, uncertain, you feel the ambiguity. Or you can stay the way you are, crystalline. Safe." Bob rocked back in his seat.

How was this syrup and sugar analogy going to tell me what to do? Observing my continued confusion, Bob pulled himself back to the table.

"Look, Ron, you're not a blueprint for being Ron Manheimer, you're a work in progress. And you've reached a crystalline state. If you take up with Gwen, you will be making a public statement. And that's important because maybe you want to make a public statement about dating a black girl and how race doesn't matter, only our humanity matters. And she'll be making that statement, too. So you will both be redefining yourselves. And to do that, you will have to turn into syrup, at least for a while. And eventually, I guess, you'll recrystallize."

Now I began to understand Bob's analogy. If I pursued my relationship with Gwen, I would be undefining and redefining myself to myself and to others. I would be in a kind of suspended state. Syrupy, fluid; not crystalline, solid.

Bob leaned over sideways and dragged a book bag up from the floor. He rummaged around in it. "Ah, yes," he said. "Here is Sartre's lecture on defining yourself and embracing the syrup of nothingness. See if this helps."

NOTHINGNESS AND FREEDOM

The little book was titled *Existentialism is a Humanism*. It was transcribed from a lecture Sartre gave in 1945 shortly after the liberation of Paris. By this time Sartre was already well known for his pre-war novel *Nausea* and wartime plays *No Exit* and *The Flies*. Far fewer people had tried to read his major philosophical tome, *Being and Nothingness*, written while Sartre was a prisoner of war in 1940 and published in 1943. Most were too busy either scrounging for food or blowing up rail lines and bridges to halt the flow of German soldiers from reaching the front.

But now people flocked to the lecture hall of the *Club Maintenant* (Club Now) on October 29, 1945 to hear him defend the philosophy then known among the intellectually curious as *L'Existentialisme*. Had Sartre spoken about syrupy and crystal states of being as analogies to nothingness and being?

I did enjoy reading this little book. Bob had told me it was an oversimplification of a difficult topic but it would get me properly oriented. Right from the start, the book drew me in like I'd been part of the crowd seated in the smoke-filled room.

Sartre knew a large portion of his audience would be hostile. I think he was probably counting on it. The Communists, in whose ranks he could name many friends including former Resistance fighters, contended that since existentialism was based on pure subjectivity, its hypothetical individual would remain indifferent to the cause of freeing the under-classes from economic and social oppression.

From their side, the Christians accused the existentialists of rendering all values and actions gratuitous since in denying the existence of God, the very basis of morality as grounded in the eternal truths of the com-mandments, everyone could do exactly as he or she pleased.

Existentialism was thus shut off from the plight of the working classes and the oppressed peoples rising up in countries colonized by European powers while the atheistic version of the philosophy flung open the door to chaos and immorality.

A skilled debater, Sartre began by stating the claims of the opposi-tion. It was true, he said, that existentialism embraced Descartes' start-ing point, the doubt-produced discovery of the Cogito. And giving that discovery a slightly existentially emotional spin, Sartre qualified it, "as the very moment in which man comprehends his isolation" (18). And it was also true that the version of existentialism he shared with his fellow exis-tentialists, Simone de Beauvoir and Maurice Merleau-Ponty, rendered the concept of God irrelevant and, with that, they had dismissed all values and moral imperatives that depended on the authoritative utterances of a supreme being and that being's representatives on earth.

I could picture many of the audience members shaking their heads, their arms folded against their chests. Meanwhile, the short, bespecta-cled Sartre paused to take a puff on his iconic pipe. Then he threw several analogies at the audience for which they were completely unprepared. First, came a paper knife, then a cauliflower, and finally, a chocolate éclair.

Sartre explained. A desktop accessory, a paper knife is used to slit open envelopes or cut the edges of untrimmed book pages. When a craftsman designs a paper knife, said Sartre to his bewildered audience, he does so from a concept he has in mind. He already knows what the purpose of the knife is and how it should look. As a concept, the craftsman's knife already exists in his mind. Therefore, the conceptual model is its essence and the manufactured result is its existence, in that order.

Many people believe human beings are like paper knives. They origi-nate in the "divine intelligence" of a "superlative artisan" who installs them on the earth with latent qualities and inherent purposes. These human beings owe their very existence to the will of a kind and perfect mind. As such they are equipped not just to open envelopes but also to open their minds to the inherent power of reason that discloses that their essence preceded their existence.

However, said Sartre, human beings are not at all like paper knives. Since the superlative artisan is a fiction but human subjectivity in the form of the Cogito is, as Descartes demonstrated, an indubitable fact, the first principle of Existentialism is that first human beings exist and then, as they encounter themselves through the power of consciousness, they determine their own values and purposes and, in doing so, manifest their essence.

Driving the paper knife deeper into the minds of his listeners, Sartre then asserted that human existence is not born from the mind of a divine intelligence but actually comes out of "nothing" (22). Picking up on the term *geworfenheit*, coined by Heidegger whose works he had studied, Sartre says that human beings are "thrown into existence" (22). They are thrust into the future-impelled motion as a being whose condition is to become. Always bent toward the future, human beings set themselves to the task of having projects, ones that they can and must freely claim as their own. That's all an individual is, proclaimed Sartre, nothing more than the sum of his or her actions, nothing more than their lives. Actually, he didn't say "his or her," he said "man."

No doubt Simone de Beauvoir took note of this unselfconscious and yet clearly sexist convention of speech. Why was it that "man" was to stand for "everyone," she pondered? Not wanting to sidetrack fellow existentialists, she pocketed this thought and decided she would write a book about the presumptions of male superiority.

The kind of nothing out of which something arises is what we might call sheer possibility, the as yet unrealized actions that give shape and direction to our lives. It's not as dire or dramatic as nothing at first sounds. And it's not quite Descartes' nothing, which is more the nothing of cancellation or suspension of beliefs and perceptions under the powerful scrutiny of doubt. Sartre's nothing is more radical than Descartes' because he also gets rid of the idea of a perfect being to whom we are accountable, which also helps him to dispose of a whole mélange of middle class presumptions, pretensions and pretexts since they are imposed, not selected, projects of conscious choice.

Sartre has a good sense of humor. Having shown the irrelevance of the paper knife he next presents some other items that human beings are unlike – "a patch of moss, a spreading fungus, or a cauliflower" (23). Did anyone laugh or were they still puzzling over how Sartre had managed to pull human existence out of nothingness? Sartre was no naturalist. He preferred urban environments with their boulevards, cafes, tobacco shops and *boulangeries*. Mosses, fungi and cauliflowers, as part of the material world, have no consciousness and so they claim no projects. We cannot find out by asking them whether a supreme intelligence planted them.

The Communists probably were still chuckling over Sartre's theological irreverence when he turned to address their criticisms. Here, once again, he proved himself as deft a conjuror as Descartes, while attempting a trick his predecessor could never have imagined. Like Descartes, Sartre had discovered something else in the Cogito besides the consciousness of the existing subject. It was not the concept of a perfect being like the one that had insinuated itself into Descartes' mind, instead it was "the presence of the other."

The man who becomes aware of himself "directly in the cogito," announced Sartre with a flourish, "also perceives all others, and does so as the condition of his existence." In other words, the starting point of all philosophy, subjectivity, human consciousness, the outpouring from nothing, also directly implicates the real presence of other consciousnesses, without whose presence it would be impossible to establish oneself as an "I think." Moreover, this Other is not derived through a series of observations or speculations. The Other arises in a preconscious immediacy as intimately part of the Cogito as its own existence.

We are immediately thrust into a social world, says Sartre that is characterized by "intersubjectivity." And while "man," unlike mosses, fungi and cauliflowers, does not have a fixed nature, man does participate in the "universal human condition" which is to exist within the consciousness of other subjectivities and to suffer or enjoy their gaze, caress, praise or condemnation.

Not satisfied to have restored the world of other consciousness to the domain of pure subjectivity, putting the capitalized Other where, centuries earlier, Descartes had found the capitalized God, Sartre makes his boldest leap, one designed to appease his comrades on the Left and the one to which my friend Bob must have been referring. When we make a choice, argued Sartre, especially a choice that implies certain moral values, we not only choose for ourselves, we choose on behalf of all mankind. How should we understand this audacious claim?

The decision to marry or to have children or to join a certain political party is not only an individual act, it is a public affirmation of a value for which we serve as a champion. The decision to marry someone is also a vote in favor of the institution of marriage. Opting to have children is an affirmation of the value of parenthood. Political affiliation is a state-ment affirming the social ideals we consider best for our society or nation. Therefore, social solidarity is not only an imperative of a freely choosing being; it is also an inescapable reality.

Even a negative decision – not to marry, not to have children, not to collaborate with the Nazis – is a choice and a commitment to others. So, Comrades, says Sartre, you see, existentialism is not indifferent to the plight of the downtrodden. In fact, it is quite the opposite. The only way we can act indifferently is by deceiving ourselves that our freedom is not in some important way bound up with others. Moreover, says Sartre, those who justify their indifference to the plight of others because they claim to be powerless to act, or believe what happens in the world is a matter of the will of a higher intelligence, or that social change is controlled by forces of historical inevitability, these individuals are, he proclaims, "cowards."

Did a cheer go up from Sartre's previously dubious Comrades? It's doubtful. Sartre ended his talk by explaining that existentialism was a type of humanistic philosophy. Given its unique understanding of con-sciousness and intersubjectivity, replacement of God with human Others, its notion of "thrownness" as the human condition of moving beyond oneself by losing oneself on the verge of each moment of choice and regaining oneself in the moment of arrival of becoming oneself, existen-tialism stood for liberation from everything that would deny or suppress human freedom.

After a round of mixed applause, a question and answer period was announced. A man, who remains unidentified to this day, stood up and asked Sartre why he used terms like "abandonment," "despair," and "anguish," when he wrote in *Being and Nothingness* about making choices. After all, said the man, "anguish and despair are hardly common emotions." It's not recorded in the transcript of the lecture and Q and A period whether there was a glint in Sartre's eye or an ironic smile on his lips when he said to the man: "Obviously, I do not mean that when I choose between a pastry and a chocolate éclair, I am choosing in anguish" (54). Having given the audience cauliflowers, he now offered dessert.

While he does not at this moment give the historical background to his use of these seemingly emotive terms, those already in the know would understand that abandonment, anguish and despair were ontological dispositions or conditions of Being, terms serving as the coin of the realm for Sartre's formulation of the existential tradition he was defending.

He had not invented these terms; he had inherited them. From the man whose works he studied for a year at the Institut Français in Berlin, Martin Heidegger, he absorbed the idea that human beings experience an undercurrent of unspecified fear or dread that has no tangible explanation as due to a real threat to a person's safety. These emotional tones or moods sometimes erupt into conscious awareness when we are making critical choices that heighten our sense of responsibility, uncertainty and risk. Many decisions are irreversible, involve others and have important, sometimes life-and-death, consequences. Not surprisingly, we experience anxiety about our acts and choices, anxiety that we even have the freedom and responsibility to exercise our choices. Sometimes we'd rather not have to act or choose.

Delving into this later, I learned that Heidegger meant something more when he talked about "angst." There are times, said Heidegger, when we get this odd feeling that everything around us is a phantasm, especially when we acknowledge that everything in our environment is the product of our own consciousness. At such moments, says Heidegger, we sense that everything is "slipping away" or "drawing away" and that the whole world feels strange, alien (*Being and Time*, 227). That feeling, really it's more than an emotion, it's a state of all-encompassing consciousness, brings with it the sensation of anxiety. Heidegger, who wrote about this in his native German, used the word "*unheimlich*," which means something like our English word, "uncanny," and is made up of the literal sense of "un-homeness," or that we are "not-at-home" in the world at this moment. Heidegger says of this angst-provoking epiphany: "The only thing that remains and comes over us--in this drawing away of everything--is this 'nothingness.'"

Pastries and chocolate éclairs aside, given these serious choices that reveal to us our human condition, that we are radically free in every moment to determine ourselves and, at the same time, proclaim our commitments and values to others, we might have some feelings of trepidation. But, Sartre would say, echoing Heidegger, that's not a bad thing because when we have these insights, then our condition of freedom is enhanced as we step out of the daze of ordinary and mechanical behavior to step into the circle of a spotlight that illuminates our full presence of being-in-the-world. In this sense, what was lost or slipped into nothingness comes back to us even more powerfully as the miraculous condition of being alive.

For Sartre, the nothingness of human consciousness mirrors the moral neutrality of the universe, unguided as it is by any deity and the mute indifference of nature. While Sartre's notion of what he called facticity (situatedness) may sound like primeval raw material waiting to be formed, and acts of choice sound like bringing order out of chaos, Sartre's nothingness reveals itself as the opposite. It is the power of the negative that turns the received condition of order into chaos so that the creative act of self-definition may occur.

APPLIED NOTHINGNESS

So what had I learned from reading this book? It did not discuss syrup or sugar crystals, though there were cauliflowers and éclairs. I did recognize the point that Bob had been trying to make with his tabletop analogy. We do become crystals out of the syrup of finding our way to an independent identity from the fluid state of childhood and adolescence. But we never truly become set or fixed beings. That's an illusion but sometimes a comforting one. Faced with difficult choices for which there are no clear cut rules or where social conventions no longer have a hold on us, we may enter, once again, a fluid-like state of uncertainty triggered by the possibility of finding a new position in a new situation. Dissolving back into syrup and entering the state of suspension or stepping into the unknown because now surpassed condition of the givens of our crystallized life, we experience the nothing that is the beckoning of the not-yet that only we can determine by making choices. And when we do this, we "choose for all mankind" in that we cannot help but to assert a value position.

The crossroads I faced with Gwen made me aware that what seemed a narrowly personal choice was, at the same time, a politically tinged one.

Must important personal choices always carry moral and political implications? These, I was learning, were inescapable.

When we delve into its multiple meanings, we quickly become aware
that along with its duality of fullness and emptiness, nothingness marks
a disruption in the taken-for-granted flow of everyday consciousness.
Martin Luther King, Jr.'s use of the boycott, the march, and the sit-in
were all both assertions (of human rights) and negations (of economic
and racial inequality). King was making history by disrupting history
as the condition of the status quo. Like Gandhi, he knew that freedom
requires both the outward transformation of the social order and an
inward transformation in how the individual regards his and her moral
situation. In other words, nothingness triggers the realization that time
is both quantitative and qualitative, both outward and inward. The
latter is what philosophers call "temporality," a concept I will further
explore in Chapter 4.

REFERENCES

Descartes, Rene (1968). *Discourse on Method and the Meditations.* Translated by F. E.
   Sutcliffe. London: Penguin Books.

Heidegger, Martin (1962). *Being and Time,* translated by John Macquarrie and Edward
   Robinson. New York: Harper & Row.

King, Martin Luther, Jr. (1953). "An Exposition of the First Triad of Categories of the
   Hegelian Logic – Being, Non-Being, Becoming." https://kinginstitute.stanford.edu/
   king-papers/documents/exposition-first-triad-categories-hegelian-logic-being-non-
   being-becoming

_____ (1958). *Stride Towards Freedom: The Montgomery Story.* New
   York: Harper and Row.

Sartre, Jean-Paul (2007). *Existentialism Is A Humanism.* Translated by Carol Macomber.
   New Haven: Yale University Press.

_____ (2013). *Nausea.* Trans. Richard Howard. New York: New Directions.

3. Becoming

Given their emphasis on critical choices that can often mean breaking away from the forces that have shaped one's life, it is not surprising that existential writers and thinkers would find great significance in the word "becoming." In the previous chapter, we touched lightly upon the concept in understanding Hegel's triad, being-nothing-becoming. Now it ascends as the third star in the existentialists' sky.

For the French existentialists, becoming means becoming a person through the process of self-emancipation and self-actualization. For Kierkegaard, "giving birth to yourself," and especially coming to terms with the both finite (or bounded) and infinite (or unbounded) dimensions of your existence as central to the process of "becoming a Christian," gives a religious meaning to the concept of becoming. It is mainly Kierkegaard's stages of life conceptualization that preoccupied me in 1968, as I was becoming a candidate for a Ph.D. in the History of Consciousness at UC Santa Cruz. A certain window framed my outlook.

My Professor

High Street winds its way up the hillside from downtown Santa Cruz. The road crosses what was then the new entrance to the university where, if you turned in and drove half a mile, you would come upon clusters of rectangular white stucco-clad dorms and classroom buildings, jutting up out of the pasture lands and wooded slopes of what a few years earlier had been the Cowell Ranch.

But had you turned off High Street before the university entrance, you would find yourself in a quiet residential neighborhood lined with modest, brick ranch-style houses, each with its requisite picture window. If the curtains were open, you could make out the silhouette of a couch, a horizontal mirror or landscape painting mounted above a fireplace mantel. And if you came closer and peeked in, you'd see a hearth containing pristine white birch logs. As for the inhabitants, looking out they could admire a patch of lawn, a strip of sidewalk, parked cars, and beyond, the arched eyelet windows of metal garage doors.

I had on several occasions looked both from within and without a certain picture window in a house off High Street when meeting with my thesis advisor, Professor Albert Hofstadter.

My Professor, as I addressed him in my mind, and his wife, Mrs. Hofstadter ("Manya," he'd call out to her), had a few years earlier migrated from Manhattan, where they had lived and worked most of their lives. I knew from our conversations that, for them, the ranch house was a novel dwelling place that contrasted to the high-rise apartment building where they once lived near Columbia University on the upper West Side.

I pictured them on a wintry day braving the harsh winds that wound through the skyscraper canyons of Manhattan as, luggage in hand, they bundled into a cab on Riverside Drive and a few hours later emerged into the balmy air of a seaside California town. Santa Cruz was then most notable for a pier that extended a quarter mile out into the Monterey Bay, on which, if you drove to the very end, you could sit in a restaurant eating a fresh Crab Louie while watching the surfers ride the waves on Steamer's Lane, or venturing back to the beachside amusement park you could feel the rumble and hear the screams emanating from a wood lattice-built roller coaster.

Upon entering the Hofstadters' living room of Scandinavian modern sofas and teak chairs, first-time visitors would be surprised to see two grand pianos, the curves of their cabinets nested together. The curly grayed-haired and bespectacled Mrs. Hofstadter had been a concert pianist earlier in life and My Professor was also musically accomplished in his own way. The juxtaposition of the pianos in the long living room allowed the couple to exchange nods to synchronize the playing of duets. The piano was not her only keyboard, as Mrs. Hofstadter would attend many of her husband's lectures where she took notes and later typed them up in aid of My Professor's latest writing project.

In May of 1968 I was sitting across from the good doctor (he invited me to call him Albert but I felt more comfortable with Professor) in his home office, a converted bedroom at one end of the house. We were discussing details about researching and writing the essay required by second-year students in the History of Consciousness program. Once a student's advisor had approved the essay, a group of three or four faculty members, the orals committee, would read it and then grill the student on its contents. If they were satisfied, the student would then be "advanced to candidacy" to go on to write the dissertation. But what if they weren't satisfied? I understood that there was an exit door Master's degree that would gracefully mark your departure from the Cowell Ranch.

THE ESSAY

It was a strange time to be doing something as conventional as writing a dissertation, since so much of normal life had been disrupted by student strikes, sit-ins, marches and demonstrations that turned violent, and a general atmosphere of protest that raised serious questions about what life might hold for us graduate students in the future. It wasn't just the big events that were taking place in nearby Berkeley with the helicopter tear-gassing of the whole campus and surrounding neighborhoods or the National Guard, in battle gear, marching down Telegraph Avenue. These kinds of confrontations were taking place across the country, mainly in reaction to the United States' involvement in Vietnam and, as we were soon to learn, its secret war in Cambodia. Newscasts of Black civil right demonstrations and urban riots added more fuel to the fires of impending doom.

Just then we were also hearing about a major uprising of students and workers in France. Though perhaps long simmering, it surprised everyone since it hadn't been organized by a political party, trade union or official student organization but had erupted seemingly out of nowhere. What was provoking the youth of Paris to turn out into the streets and join with workers to shut down the entire country? After all, France had lost its former colony, Vietnam, after the disastrous 1954 battle of Dien Bien Phu.

Sitting in his swivel leather office chair turned away from his desk and electric typewriter, My Professor had been reminding me of the first time we met face to face. Freshly arrived at Santa Cruz, I had barged into his campus office and began telling him, without so much as a "how do you do," that I wanted to pursue my own semi-independent course of study in order to explore a certain idea that had captivated me in the years between my undergraduate education and return to formal academic study.

So preoccupied was I in sharing my ideas that I barely took in the nodding and smiling man in a plaid shirt, his thinning brown hair combed back, his belly gently expanding his khaki pants and sporting a professorially incongruous pair of red sneakers. But before I could take another breath and continue my monologue, he lifted a sheet of paper that he waved in the air.

"Uh, Ronald," he began. "According to this list, I'm supposed to be your advisor." He extended his other hand, which I looked at uncomprehendingly. Then, the blood rushing to my face, I extended mine. We shook. "Good to meet one of you new History of Consciousness students," he said, motioning for me to sit down in one of the two chairs positioned against the opposite wall.

Lowering myself into the chair, I reviewed the situation. Before me sat Professor Hofstadter, a distinguished philosopher from the East Coast. His brother, Robert, was a Nobel Prize-winning physicist at Stanford. The whole Hofstadter clan was famous for intellectual and scientific accomplishment. Shouldn't he be wearing a jacket and tie and be hunched over some German manuscript? And who was I to be issuing demands to this famous Heidegger translator and editor of a widely used anthology in courses on aesthetics? True, I had certain ideas about what I wanted to study and I had applied to Santa Cruz because it looked like the kind of place where an independently minded individual like myself would be free to make his or her own way. Now, a year after this first meeting, I had come to realize my naïveté.

My Professor turned and picked up a glass of water that stood on his desk and called out his wife's name. No answer. Taking a sip, he continued, "Do you remember how you came into my office and sat yourself down and told me you wanted to do an independent study of the relationship between theories of human development and theories of history? Oh, and weren't you going to mix in a little Jungian psychology and maybe just a touch of Hegelian dialectics?"

"Yes," I said. "I guess I was a little presumptuous."

"That's one way to put it," he laughed. "Where did you cook all that up? It wasn't while you were an undergraduate. You told me something about working on a farm on some Danish island in the Baltic and then living in some hippie commune. I don't suppose they studied Hegel there." My Professor chuckled.

I squirmed a little in my chair. Though we were on cordial terms, I was not accustomed to sharing much about my personal life with him, nor did he share with me much about his personal life except for some cautionary tales drawn from his own academic career and a few asides about his son, also enrolled in a graduate program at Santa Cruz, whose lifestyle experiments worried him.

I had once told My Professor about taking time off to hitchhike around in Europe after college. I mentioned working on a dairy farm on Bornholm but not the part about following my girlfriend Susan out to the island. He knew I borrowed books by mail from the U.S. Embassy library in Copenhagen, novels like Dreiser's *An American Tragedy*, and Henry James's *The Ambassadors*, then more contemporary works like Saul Bellow's *Adventures of Augie March*. Inspired by my own disorienting experience as an American city boy now living on a Danish farm that had been in the same family for 13 generations, I started borrowing immigrant-themed novels such as Henry Roth's *Call It Sleep* and *The Rise of David Levinsky*.

"Oh, I read that years ago," he said of the latter. "Abraham Cahan, right?"

"That's right," I said. "And from there I gravitated toward American intellectual history. For instance, I read your cousin's book, *Anti-Intellectualism in American Life*."

"A good book. You know, Richard won a Pulitzer for it?"

"Yes," I replied, "but I wasn't aware at the time." I explained that I had been somewhat isolated, occupying a small bedroom under the roof of a farmhouse that must have been two hundred years old. I didn't see an English-language newspaper and I was already starting to have dreams in Danish. This was my inner life, the bookworm, the dreamer, while my outer was eating breakfasts of dark rye bread layered with strong cheese and tromping around pig pens, cow stalls, and chicken coops.

I was learning to operate a tractor and later was loaned out to an apple juice producer whose factory was housed in the metal barn of his nearby farm. In my outward life, except on weekends when I'd bicycle to see my girlfriend and stay over at the Folk High School, I spoke a toddler's level of Danish, enough to answer how I'd slept, ask for the cheese, and take instructions about udders and snouts.

"You were having your own immigrant experience," My Professor had commented. "It's when you leave your country and culture behind that you really first start to see what it was all about. Every college student should have this experience. For many people, it's the first time they realize that a big part of who they are is where they come from."

"Yes, I guess that's right," I said. "You get to see yourself more objectively as an actor in history." I had made my island vigil sound like a great adventure. What I hadn't said is that I had felt very adrift in those months of living mainly in my head while my body changed from the flabbiness of my physically inactive undergraduate years, to growing strong and sturdy as I adapted to farm labor, and increasingly attuned to the life of the senses.

I had come to enjoy the pungent smells of animal manure mixed with hay, feel the sharp bite of persistent winds coming off the Baltic Sea, and alert to the shifting gray veil of the Danish winter with its early night falls and chalk-line morning horizons. I'd be riding home on my bicycle, the cone of its headlight searching for the country road's edge, feeling my body drained after a day of maneuvering wheelbarrows of pressed crushed apples across a cobbled courtyard and up onto a set of narrow wooden planks ascending a huge pile of composting apple pulp. One misstep and over went the wheelbarrow, your rubber boots sinking down in the apple mash up to your tucked-in pants.

I had desperately wanted to have adventures and to see the world outside beyond the grit and grime of Detroit. Well, now I was doing both. But Bornholm was not Paris or London, the farm was not the Louvre or the British Museum, my Danish "parents" were not famous writers or artists, and working in an apple juice factory alongside a pair of Danish laborers who yelled commands to keep the machines from breaking down was not like a job in a bookstore on the Left Bank.

"Albert?" Mrs. Hofstadter stood in the doorway. "Don't forget, you have a department meeting on campus at three."

"Thank you, darling." He turned and picked up a folder from his desk and opened it. "Let's see. You've given me this rough outline. And, uh,

I've made some notes. Yes, and this title." He looked at me wrinkling his brow. "Kierkegaard and the Education of Historical Consciousness." My Professor rubbed his clean-shaved chin. "Quite a mouthful. Do you think it may be a bit too ambitious? I want to make sure you can find your way so that I can put that doctoral hood over your shoulders one of these days."

I appreciated my Professor's concern. Unlike some thesis advisors I'd heard about, he was not throwing up one new obstacle after another for the would-be doctoral candidate to jump over. Certainly, there were requirements. For example, I would have to pass a language exam in Danish. In a way, my "ambitious" project was due in no small part to the influence of My Professor himself.

THE HEGEL SEMINAR

During that first conversation in his campus office when I became his advisee, Hofstadter had gently dissuaded me from pursuing the independent study that I wanted him to supervise. He suggested that it would be a good idea, "just, you know, to get your bearings," that besides a required "proseminar" for all first-year History of Consciousness students, I might want to sign up for his Hegel seminar.

During my self-guided studies that took me from American intellectual history to the Jungian-influenced history of consciousness that aimed to synthesize mythology, history and psychology along with the study of primitive art and anthropology, I also read a little Greek mythology, developmental psychology, and books on theories of history (known as historiography). I frequently came across references to Hegel, the philosophical system builder of mid-nineteenth century German philosophy. I was intrigued and took the plunge into several of Hegel's major tomes. But I soon found I was over my head in arcane terminology that required considerable familiarity with his predecessor, Kant, as well as a grasp of British empiricists like Locke and Hume and ideally some understanding of Aristotle's logic, and so on.

Clearly, there was something important in Hegel's philosophy. It had been highly influential among European philosophers and social thinkers ranging from Kierkegaard to Marx. But the density of the work had stymied me. Besides, I couldn't exactly refuse Hofstadter's almost fatherly advice. So I agreed to sign up for the seminar, figuring once I had bowed to his suggestion I would later be in a better position to renegotiate my plan.

The class, conducted in a seminar room in the campus library, met weekly for three hours with a short break in the middle. It came as nothing less than a revelation. All of my self-concocted ideas about how theories of individual human development could be merged with theories of historical evolution were to be found in the Hegelian vision of the world's evolving consciousness. After just two class meetings, everything that I had previously (as My Professor had put it) "conjured up" turned out to have occurred to – clearly a genius, Hegel. Yes, and so much more! I was dumbstruck, awestruck, humbled. It was imperative. I must concentrate my studies in philosophy.

With My Professor as our pathfinder, the small group of graduate students worked through the Wallace and Miller English translation of Hegel's *Philosophy of Mind*. Since the book had gone out of print, Hofstadter had gotten permission from the publisher to have photocopies made for the dozen or so students enrolled in the class. The reason for the tome's unavailability was that Hegel's mid-nineteenth century prominence had long been eclipsed by Anglo-American analytic philosophy. This school of thought had completely dismissed the kind of grand system building (Hegel dealt with every imaginable topic, from psychology to the history of art, religions east and west, even the natural sciences) that so fascinated the nineteenth century German philosophers.

Coming to prominence if not dominance in academic philosophy in the years after World War II, the analytic philosophers believed that Hegel and his various misguided followers who believed history was marching along toward an apotheosis, had contributed to bringing about the kind of world-dominating totalitarianism of Nazi Germany and Stalinist Russia, ideologies that justified the murder and subjugation of millions of people for the goal of bringing the history of the world to a magnificent culmination in one unified and purified system of government, culture and peoplehood. For members of the analytic school, the historical evidence clearly indicated where a philosophy of "Absolute Spirit" would lead – to catastrophe.

Only empirically testable, linguistically logical, scientifically verifiable propositions were worth consideration, as these procedures would free the mind from prejudice, superstition, muddle-headedness, and in general the whole history of metaphysics which had been shown to be based on misuses of language, faulty logic and outmoded scientific theories about nature, cosmology, biology, psychology, sociology and history itself.

Historical thinking of the Hegelian type was dismissed as folly. History contained no messages about progress or about the inevitable achievement of complete human emancipation. There was no Spirit or, in Hegel's German, *Geist*, that drove human events through the pendulum swings of opposed pairs of trends. Hegel asserted that these trends would then culminate in a fresh synthesis that preserved elements (now regarded as partial truths) of the two previous movements in its more comprehensive conceptualization. This fused conceptualization, in turn, would fragment again into disunity and a repetition of the same pattern – what Hegel called the Dialectic, an underlying logic that unlike Aristotle's static set of rules and categories, embraced time, development and historical change as an evolutionary process. The analytic philosophers threw Hegel's pendulum out the window.

History, argued the analytic school, was no crystal ball in which those equipped with knowledge of the Dialectic could grasp "world historical becoming." Certainly, there were small lessons to be learned about futile wars, failed political and economic ideas, and the hunger for power of the tyrants whose people fed their delusions and, when the leaders failed, self-righteously hanged or decapitated them in the public square.

If there was something like divine providence, as Hegel inferred, it wasn't operating in history. Such a belief might be useful for individuals suffering from lack of direction or guilt over some indiscretion. Moreover, the idea of an invisible hand of destiny guiding the actions of generals, monarchs, presidents, prime ministers and Führers, who were unaware they were pawns of what Hegel called "the cunning of reason," was a complete fabrication. There was no empirical evidence to support this farfetched point of view.

And so the intellectual market value of Hegelianism plummeted to almost complete worthlessness. At best, it was something for the historians of philosophy to recount in their tales of past-misguided thinking. And, thus, the demise of Hegelianism. But, as has often happened in the history of philosophy, a discredited, seemingly irrelevant philosophy suddenly appears in a new light and its premises get reevaluated. And so we get such philosophical movements as the neo-Aristotelian, neo-Thomists and neo-Kantian.

There had already been the post-Hegelians, among them Karl Marx who identified what he regarded as a hidden truth in Hegel's theory of history. For Marx, Hegel's Dialectic was more accurately about real-world economics ("dialectical materialism") than the ephemeral *Geist*. It pointed toward the inevitable liberation of the working classes and the culmination of history in a totally egalitarian society in which workers controlled the means of production through the apparatus of the state. They were no longer alienated from the products they produced (but previously could not afford) or from the means by which they were produced (formerly controlled by capitalist bosses).

Also grouped by scholars into the category of post-Hegelian was Kierkegaard, who fought a battle with the Hegelians he encountered among the intellectuals and clerical authorities in his hometown of Copenhagen. In truth, you could not really appreciate Kierkegaard or the school of thought that eventually turned into what he helped to launch, existentialism, without understanding Kierkegaard's battle with the influence of Hegel. For it is often the case that one philosophy is so engaged in repudiating another by demonstrating its inadequacies and contradictions that it becomes entangled with that philosophy forever.

And so it is for many students and scholars who enlist themselves in the contest of opposing philosophies, enamored with the claims of one over the other, only to discover they cannot do without their enemy because without that opposition, taken on its own merits, their favored philosophy seems to lose its vitality, if not its raison d'être.

Ironically, Hegel seemed to have anticipated his detractors as inevitable players in the dialectic of historical consciousness. I wondered, had he made me one of them?

THE INDEX

"Now, Ron," My Professor said, turning in his chair as he flipped through the proposal. "I think it would be helpful for you to make an index of key terms in Kierkegaard's *Concluding Unscientific Postscript*. Have I ever shown you my method for indexing a book?"

I shook my head. All of his students were familiar with Hofstadter's huge, tab-separated three-ring binders of typed notes that he opened on a desk or podium in front of him when conducting a seminar. But what exactly he was looking at we did not know.

My Professor pulled one of the blue cloth-covered binders off a shelf beside his desk. He laid it across his knees and opened it. "Look here, Ron." I dragged my chair over and looked down upon the typed sheets of paper that, at first, appeared to be a maze of irregularly indented short paragraphs.

"This is one I did on Heidegger's *Being and Time*," he said, pointing. "You see, first I made a list of the key words in the book and then I reread it in German and English for, well, maybe the fourth or fifth time. See now how I noted the way Heidegger defined or made special reference to certain key terms in each place of the book and I noted the page number as well. That way, I came to understand all the different formulations of the term, how Heidegger associated it with other terms, the slight variations in the German usage and how they were translated, and so on. It was as if I were entering into Heidegger's mind when he was planning out his own book." He looked up at me. "I know it's a lot of labor and it can be tedious, but once you've done this spadework, you save yourself a lot of time down the road. And, besides, you'll always be able to use the index in doing future research or teaching."

"Yes," I murmured, "I see." I didn't really see. And it did seem like an incredibly tedious task. However, Kierkegaard's weighty tome, what scholars called *The Postscript* for short, was probably the Dane's lengthiest and most comprehensive philosophical treatise. It was easy to get lost in its numerous arguments, anecdotes, parable-like stories and frequent, sometimes sardonic, uses of Hegelian terminology. And I constantly had to flip back and forth in the book (which contained a meager index) to trace a reference or an idea or to find a passage I meant to flag in the margin for later citation in my essay. Besides if My Professor had made a suggestion to help improve my understanding of the material, I should do it. Though he would never ask to see the index, I wanted to be able to voluntarily show it to him. So, the next day I started on the task.

I made a list of important terms that Kierkegaard used repeatedly: Aesthetic, Anxiety, Authority, Authorship, Autonomy, Becoming,

Choice, Christianity, Communication, Consciousness, Despair, Dialectic, Discourse, Doubt and so on through to Universal-human, Wholeness, Will, and Xenophon (a student of Socrates). As I looked at the list, I saw ahead of me hour upon hour of rereading the 600+ page book that Kierkegaard teasingly designated as a "postscript" to a previous book, the rather slender *Philosophical Fragments*, a work in which he compares Socrates and Christ as teachers.

Despite the tedium, as I plunged into this daunting task something unexpected happened.

I was plucking out uses of the term "Becoming" and having to create multiple context such as "Becoming a self," "Becoming, Hegel's triad," "Becoming and subjectivity," "Becoming as coming-into-being of self-consciousness." Growing fatigued by this contextual enumeration, I put down my book and notepad. Leaning back, I closed my eyes. My mind drifted to My Professor's comment about adapting to life in a foreign country where you have to learn to use its language and decipher the behavior of its inhabitants. To fit into the new environment you also needed to let go of the one you left behind.

Who I used to be when I lived in Detroit was a sort of given, reinforced by everyone and everything around me. But now with all of these mirrors removed I had to establish new relationships to people and places, though I had minimal equipment to accomplish these tasks. Before, despite whatever turmoil and change was part of my life, it was circumscribed by the faces of family, friends and teachers, the customs of dress, the rules of the road, and so on. People frequented my memories, anticipated my habits; they knew what I liked to eat, to read, to talk about. I had substantiality. I might have doubts about myself but other people came along who didn't because they recognized me, in their own way, as I recognized them in my way. I existed, I owned myself; I had being (crystallization).

Lacking the language skills, I couldn't tell my Danish "family" how I liked to kid around and that I had an ironic sense of humor. I was a city boy but now I had awakened to the significance of the Baltic wind, the icy rain, the coming and going of light, the danger of an angry sow, the artificial insemination of cows and the birth of calves, the taste of strong coffee poured into small ceramic cups, the staccato chatter of visiting farmer neighbors coming over for an evening coffee party.

A family album was taken out revealing pictures of jeeps filled with German soldiers and then one of a hammer and sickle-flagged tank with a boy (my Danish father?) riding along on top, grinning and waving. (I later learned that Russian troops occupied Bornholm for about a year at the end of the Second World War.) All of this and a thousand things more cut me off from the past and threw me into a present in which my past life was submerged if not negated.

I wrote letters to my parents and friends trying to describe this new life but I soon realized that, to them, it would sound like make-believe. It was as if I were acting in a play somewhere, and when the play was over I would walk out through the wings and come home, where I would reappear unchanged; the familiar son, brother, cousin and friend. Only this Danish island farmstead was my real life now because I had chosen to meet it each dark wintry morning: throwing myself into cleaning out stalls, breaking up bales of hay for the cows, garnering elementary use of the language to figure out what was true of the Danish culture in general, what was unique to the island culture of Bornholm, where spoken Danish was inflected with a Swedish lilt, what was idiosyncratic in my new family, what made the people around me laugh or cry, and what I intended to do with my new life. In short, I was in the process of Becoming.

In retrospect, I realized I had reenacted Hegel's logical triad of being, nothing and becoming. The substantiality of the past dissolved into the nothingness of a present that was yet overly abundant with the new and unfamiliar. Here was the pulse, the driving engine, the dialectical force that animated all of life – world history and, lo and behold, my history. And it delivered to me a beautiful though at times anguished feeling of disorientation, bewilderment and dislocation.

My new situation caused me to reflect on the life I had once lived, to see it as if for the first time in all its parameters with all the unself-conscious assumptions. Then, in the next moment, I would be spearing football-sized sugar beets and flinging them up beside the chipper that would turn them into fodder for cows, or I'd be cranking up a tractor on a cold morning by adjusting the choke and the throttle just so. Here was the Hegelian dialectic of self-determination in which I had to become alien to myself in order to discover myself. I had to put my world into suspension in order to begin to understand that world through the movements of history that generated it.

And so I sat in a chair beside my bed under the steep sloping orange tile farmhouse roof and read about one of my almost ancestors, the Russian Jewish emigrant boy, David Levinsky. I learned from him what it takes to survive among the tenements and pushcarts of the Lower East Side, which was the life of my parents' parents. But I had not fled a homeland out of fear for my family's life. I had the luxury to voluntarily take up residency in a new one.

Still, I knew that Kierkegaard's "becoming" was not identical to that of Hegel's. Kierkegaard's becoming was passionately religious, not rationally reflective. Kierkegaard kept you in a state of becoming because that was the truth of the human condition – uncertainty, risk, inner contradiction, despair over ever resolving all the conflicts of one's inner and outer life, a passionate seeking after wholeness while maintaining awareness of the constant shadow of death. But what if you had no interest in becoming a Christian or, for that matter, "becoming" a Jew as an inward confrontation with the Biblical prophets? Would Kierkegaard's theory of life stages still have merit?

KIERKEGAARD'S VOICE

My Professor had advised me, "Write about what truly interests you. Don't think about writing a dissertation as just a series of hurdles you have to jump over." He told me about his own experience, about how his thesis advisor had suggested a technically difficult topic having to do with seventeenth-century English philosopher John Locke's causal theory of perception. It was an interesting philosophical problem about which Hofstadter's then young contemporaries were publishing journal articles. It wasn't important that the student, Albert Hofstadter, have a personal interest in the subject. "Later, when you're a professor," his advisor told him, "you can find subjects to write about that interest you." My Professor shook his head. "He was disingenuous. Oh, I guess he meant well."

It was great to hear that I had free rein regarding what to write about and how to go about doing it. That created additional problems because the more I knew of Kierkegaard – both the man and his philosophical and theological works – the more he loomed up from the grave in a Copenhagen cemetery to chide me:

'Your task in life is not to become another Kierkegaard. I never wanted followers. I wanted my readers to seek to become themselves and to discover that if they took that risk, they would walk in the ways of our Savior.

'Why do you think I insisted that Socrates' irony was his way of life and not just a method for conducting an argument? Why do you think I repeated, over and over, that you couldn't be a Christian in Christendom just by going to church and taking communion? No, you had to strive and struggle with yourself, with what is finite in you and what is infinite. Christianity is the experience of Christ's way, and only secondarily a doctrine and a set of rituals. Besides, you're a Jew, and Christ is the historical stumbling block to your people. How can you write about me without being a hypocrite or becoming a convert? You're trying to be something that you are not.'

Yes, it was true. A conundrum. How had I ended up in this situation caught between the maker of metaphysical castles, Hegel, and their would-be destroyer, Kierkegaard? I had no idea that becoming an individual could be so difficult. After all, I was just working on a dissertation, not actually putting my life on the line.

The Hegel Revival in France

Thinking back to the seminar of 1967, I came to realize that My Professor was ahead of his time in teaching American students about Hegel. Widespread renewed interest and new English translations of Hegel works would come soon. In part, this new interest arrived as a ripple effect from a rediscovery of Hegel on the Continent.

Credit for the Hegel revival in France is generally accorded to two men: Alexandre Kojève, a Russian émigré, multilingual scholar and, later, an important figure in planning for the Common Market, and Jean Hyppolite, a philosopher and university professor who in 1939 translated Hegel's groundbreaking work, *Phenomenology of the Spirit* from German into French.

Kojève's prewar lectures at the Ecole Pratique des Hautes Etudes attracted a wide spectrum of people, including liberals, Catholics, novelists, communists, surrealists, structuralists and figures from the emerging group that would be dubbed the existentialists, and who would become luminaries of French intellectual life.

Hyppolite's translation of and commentary on the *Phenomenology* went through numerous editions while he lectured at the Sorbonne to students who became major figures in post-war French intellectual life, especially those affiliated with post-modernism such as Foucault, Deleuze, Althusser and Derrida. (Readers unfamiliar with these figures might enjoy Elizabeth Roundinesco's *Philosophy in Turbulent Times*, translated from French by William McCuaig and published by Columbia University Press in 2010.)

Hegel's writings are voluminous and his works, not unlike that of most philosophers, reveal that over time he produced various revisions to his approach and theoretical formulations. Scholars refer to the "early" Hegel in contrast to his middle, late and, even later, the posthumously published works. Consequently, different thinkers grant special relevance to certain phases in the development of Hegel's ideas in light of the social, political and cultural conditions of their present moment. In the case of Kojève, it was Hegel's formulation of what is loosely translated as the "master-slave" relationship, and for Hyppolite it was the "unhappy conscious-ness." Despite the terminological density of Hegel's writing, these colorful phrases indicate Hegel's capacity for coming up with imaginative titles.

The master-slave relationship is, for Hegel, a stage in the development of consciousness. Like the British empiricist philosophers, Hegel acknowledges that consciousness emerges as sensate, that is, as awareness of the world as presented to the body through the five senses – simple awareness of objects. So far, there is no self-aware receiver of these sensations and perceptions and the subject, the individual, remains in a state of passivity.

But then, says Hegel, there arises in the subject a feeling that something is lacking and from that the motive of desire is born. This desire is not for material objects but for the individual's coming into possession of his or her own confirmed reality. This sense of reality can only come from recognition bestowed by another human consciousness as a meeting of beings who experience both lack and desire. And with that elementary interaction, says Hegel, human beings are hurtled into the drama of history and society. If this sounds a little like the story of the Garden of Eden and the loneliness of Adam, the murderous contest between brothers, and the exile from paradise, that Biblical story only goes to show

how a philosophical idea may first reveal itself in the narrative form of an ancient myth.

Unlike the Adam and Eve narrative, which initially presents humans as in a state of blissful contentment, the Hegelian account is immediately fraught with conflict since each recognition-seeking consciousness competes for attention with the other. Hence, says Kojève quoting from Hegel's *Phenomenology*, a "struggle to the death between men" ensues. This struggle is not over property or self-preservation, claims Hegel, but for "prestige" (Kojève, 40).

Hegel asserts that the first interactions among men were wars of prestige. For evidence of that, we might think of the Nordic and Celtic sagas that depict the battles of warrior kingdoms not merely for control of land but as demonstrations of heroic superiority, which could only be proven through the willingness, indeed, enthusiasm, to wield a sword or spear and fight to the death. As it turned out, not everyone among the defeated died, rather they were subjugated by the victors to slavery and consequently assigned the tasks to build monuments, till the soil, and mine and smelt ores for making tools." Meanwhile, the victors functioned as free men, nobles who would as masters supervise the enslaved and enjoy the spoils of their labors.

Eventually, in the history of the evolution of consciousness, there arose the order of the aristocrats and the peasant serfs, of ruler and ruled. But the story doesn't end there since the movements from within the history of consciousness are unstoppable. What happened is that the masters became dependent on the slaves who had gained considerable knowledge of taming nature through planting, sowing and reaping and through building edifices and making tools. Moreover, the status of the masters, their very recognition, depended on the lower status of the slaves who would bow down to them. In this sense, the two groups were co-dependent.

However, servile recognition could not satisfy the master, only that rendered voluntarily by another freeborn person could do the job. Meanwhile, the slaves became increasingly aware of the power they had acquired through knowledge and skill and of the dependency of the masters on their existence. The masters could only try to hold onto power through maintaining the status quo – which they did by insisting that the order of things is necessitated by the laws of nature and by divine decree (think: "divine right of kings"), while the slaves, who had been in subjugation through fear of pain and death at the hands of their masters, longed for freedom from oppression.

Kojève's interpretation and fresh focus on the master-slave relationship spoke to the prewar unrest in the increasing conflicts between the wealthier classes (and then, especially, the bourgeoisie) and those who labored in factories, mines and shops or who struggled to survive by renting and tilling land owned by the large estate holders.

The Russian Revolution had already occurred, demonstrating Marx's Hegelian-inspired historical theory that the slave class, now the proletariat, would eventually rise up to take control of their own destiny and of the means of production. Kojève was not, however, a proponent of Russian-style revolution. He was more interested in emphasizing how, in Hegel's account, the role of work could become ennobling and affirming, rather than oppressive, when it functioned as a part of the individual's sense of dignity and of the community's pride in its accomplishment.

So while Kojève exerted considerable influence on individuals of a Marxist persuasion, he also influenced those attracted to a new "philosophical anthropology" which illustrated that the process of the becoming of humanity was animated by the dialectical movement from the finite of the given (subjugation) to the infinite of possibility (freedom of self-determination) and back from the infinite to a new finitude embodied in the formation of the state.

There are numerous examples, especially that of the relationship of the colonizer to the colonized in many parts of the world, that mirror this depiction of the master-slave relationship, lending credibility to the Hegelian account of the interrelationship of history, consciousness and social change. But decolonization would come later in the post-war years. Before the wars of liberation, Kojève's influence would reveal itself in the formulations and vocabulary of Sartre and de Beauvoir as well as that of their friend Merleau-Ponty (more about him in Chapter 5). In part, this would resonate with their Marxist orientation to the forces of social change but also to their beliefs in the dynamic and evolving structure of consciousness that, driven by the motives of lack, desire, and recognition, announced that freedom was the ultimate purpose of human existence.

Jean Hyppolite exerted equal influence through his interpretation of Hegel's philosophy, particularly in the Hegelian account of the "unhappy consciousness." For Hyppolite, Hegel's *Phenomenology* was not the story of how consciousness evolves outwardly through historical stages but rather the story of Hegel's own evolving thought process, which in turn reflected the developing consciousness of humanity. This would mean that an attempt to understand one's own consciousness would be inseparable from delving into how the present historical era might reveal itself as an intrinsic part of one's individuality.

In this sense, Newton's famous comment, "If I have seen far, it is because I have stood on the shoulders of giants," would be true for all of us. We are each a product of our time and are therefore given the advantages of a vast accumulation of knowledge, should we choose to appropriate it. Hegel, for Hyppolite, was one of those extraordinary people who, by means of his erudite knowledge and brilliant mind, could comprehend within the compass of his own mind the entire history of thought that for him led to the present moment.

Hyppolite did not assume that everyone could be a Hegel but he did surmise that anyone willing to make the "voyage of discovery" that is self-conscious reflection, could enter upon a similar exploration. That voyage, according to Hegel, required a process by means of which the individual would have to make of him- or herself an object to be considered reflectively and therefore to be separated from the immediacy of consciousness. Human beings thus experienced a state of incompleteness as they anticipated a unity of self-knowledge that remained elusive.

Hegel's depiction of "unhappy consciousness," as the finite individual seeking after that which is infinite, could be seen as a search for the absolute, for God. And some interpreters have read Hegel in this way. But Hyppolite did not want to turn Hegel over to the theologians. For him, Hegel was a humanist. Man needed to separate himself from himself in order to become himself, said Hyppolite, following his interpretation of Hegel.

Crucial in Hyppolite's revival of Hegel in the context of the emerging post-war philosophies of existentialism and post-modernism, was the rendering of consciousness and its history as fundamentally and inextricably social. Unlike the major figures of the French philosophical tradition, such as Descartes, who located the center of the self in autonomous reflection, outside society, outside history and even outside everyday experience, the Hegelian account denied that an indubitable *cogito* was the bedrock of a theory of knowledge or of an ontology.

The consequences of World War II, the quick defeat of the French forces, the total failure of the liberal-bourgeois order of society and government, the ensuing leadership vacuum, and the direct experience of the master-slave relationship that was the French population's occupation under the Nazis, made the Hegelian philosophy of history and human consciousness tantamount to a divine revelation.

THE MAY 1968 UPRISING

While I was once again sitting in My Professor's home office, students were occupying buildings, first on the campus of Paris University at Nanterre and then at the ancient French university, the Sorbonne. They then summoned Jean-Paul Sartre to come speak to them. He and Simone de Beauvoir had already signed a declaration in support of the student uprising that appeared in the French newspaper, *Le Monde*, on May 8th. Two days later, their names, along with that of other leftwing French intellectuals, appeared below a manifesto in *Le Monde* that characterized the movement as an effort to escape an "alienated order" of society, not just a protest demanding university reform.

Then on May 12th, Radio Luxembourg carried an interview with Sartre in which he came out in favor of the students' tactics of confrontation and street fighting. And on the 20th, the news weekly *Le Nouvel Observateur* printed an interview between Sartre and the charismatic figure of the twenty-year-old Daniel Cohn-Bendit, known in the press as "Dany the Red," whose comic provocateur antics served as a catalyst to a completely unprecedented, unanticipated festival-like month-long protest movement that was so chaotic and spontaneous as to remain loosely titled the "May Festival" or the "Student Revolt" or just "May 68." In retrospect, one might compare the series of mass street demonstration, sit-ins, teach-ins, and working committees generating manifestos as akin to the Occupy Wall Street protest that occurred on September 17, 2011 in Zuccotti Park in New York's financial district. This in turn spawned the Occupy movement against social and economic inequality that swept the U.S. and later spread to other countries.

While Sartre and de Beauvoir were trying to figure out whether the student protest that soon drew in working people from a wide swath of industries and offices was the long dreamed-of amalgam of socialism and democracy, I was working away at my index, only dimly aware of what was going on in France.

The newspapers and mainstream magazines were struggling to make sense of this wild youth party that seemed to have new spokespersons and leaders every other day. They noted that the protesters had rebuffed the French communist party as well as the trade unions that had not been a part of the uprising and were themselves scrambling to try to play a role, only to then be rejected by the protestors as part of the problem, not the solution. The staunch Marxists, for their part, were dumbfounded. The workers were not the long-championed proletariat because here were technicians whose work with their hands was only to press buttons and keys, and here were office workers and even their supervisors. Besides, factory workers in France were reasonably well paid, received adequate vacation time, and enjoyed many of the benefits of so-called "late capitalism." If this was a revolution, it was not one that Marx would have recognized.

The French street party, which included a complete national shutdown of all businesses, brought people together from across a wide spectrum of ages and social classes to talk about their feelings of living in a commodity-driven culture that clung to business and school hierarchies that seemed outmoded, uncreative, and resistant to change. The long-standing governmental bureaucracy had turned into a technocracy that dehumanized both its employees and the citizens whom it was supposed to serve.

Everyone seemed to want a say in how things were done. Workers wanted increased self-management of the means of production and the quality of the products they made. Students wanted more relevance in their curricular studies, they wanted to help select new faculty members, and they wanted less formal and more personal interaction with their teachers and amongst themselves. In all of this, Sartre realized he had a new role to play. Not as the prophet of a Marxist-Existentialism who would tell the students what to do and say, but as a supporter and facilitator who would be learning alongside them about this new generation that saw him as an old man who had written some dense and mostly out-of-fashion books of philosophy and a few plays that still seemed relevant.

As it had done with Sartre and de Beauvoir in their heyday, the American press made fun of the quirky French uprising and labeled some of its youth leaders as communist agitators. But the uprising grew dangerously viral and looked as though it was heading to a full-scale revolution that would bring down the government and lead to anarchy. We would later learn that the French president, De Gaulle, had secretly fled France with his family for several days. But then he came back and offered concessions. University officials agreed to reopen the universities and engage in discussion with students. Workers declared the party was over and went back to their assembly lines. No sweeping legislative changes initially took effect. And yet, so shocking had been the events of May that the repercussions continued to travel through all levels of French society for years to come, in many cases leading to major social changes.

Meanwhile, I plodded away at finding the various meanings and uses of "Becoming" in *The Postscript*. I could see that becoming was closely linked to the saga of personal development which Kierkegaard understood as a calling forward into one's future, a sense of personal destiny that was not driven by antecedent experiences or unconscious motives. Kierkegaard announced the challenge: not by means of intellectual rationality through which to achieve understanding of one's place in history but passionate yearning to overcome the separation of what one was and what one could become as an individual in an increasingly mass society. He offered numerous critiques of Hegel's concept of becoming that in his assessment submerged the individual's development into the development of the national culture and, more globally, into "world historical becoming."

Periodically, coming up for air out of the ocean of the Kierkegaardian text clinging to my little plastic raft, a yellow highlighter, I would catch glimpses on television and in the *New York Times* of Sartre and de Beauvoir marching with a throng of banner-waving students in the streets of Paris. But what did that protest have to do with me, an American graduate student in the History of Consciousness program? After all, I didn't feel alienated from my teachers or fellow students. We weren't competing but, rather, were engaged in mutually supportive dialogue because we received only individualized, not comparative, evaluations. I wasn't regimented into a meaningless set of technical exercises demonstrating my facility with philosophical language, though I would soon have to take my Danish language exam but that was just to translate a few pages of *Philosophical Fragments*.

And yet, closer to home, there were bigger and bigger demonstrations taking place in Berkeley against the war in Vietnam, a war the U.S. had taken over from the French who had abandoned their former colony and their imperial role in Indochina. Thereafter, following the Geneva Accords, Vietnam had been divided into its north (communist) and south (pseudo-democratic, emperor-controlled) halves. Though I was a bit older than the targeted population of young men, it was still possible that I might be drafted and sent to Vietnam. The Civil Rights Act had just been signed in April so who knew what that might mean in terms of the Black Power movement. And Robert Kennedy was running for president. This dynamic, youthful figure could easily have been among the protestors in the streets of Paris. Surely, he would usher in a new age as his brother had begun to do before his becoming had been cut short by an assassin's bullet.

THE MARCHING MURAL

The morning fog was just burning off as I sat in the Hofstadter's living room balancing a cup of coffee on my knee as I waited for My Professor to finish a telephone conversation with his publisher. I gazed out of the picture window spotting a squirrel flitting from branch to branch in what Mrs. Hofstadter had told me was a service berry tree. Just then, I had not only Kierkegaard's but also my own becoming on my mind. I was think-ing about becoming a married man. My girlfriend and I had been living together for almost a year. She was finishing her undergraduate degree while working in a bookstore. When I finished my essay and passed my oral exam, I could apply for a one-year fellowship to write my thesis. These funds would allow me to travel back to Denmark where I would be in closer communion with Kierkegaard, the master of becoming.

My girlfriend and I were in our mid-20s and so, for her at least, the biological clock was ticking. Though perhaps not biological, there was something ticking in me too. As Kierkegaard had predicted, I was losing my enthusiasm for the aesthetic stage of life and feeling the tug of the ethical. Until that time, in my extended post-adolescent years, I was enamored by the process of becoming my own person. I had charted a course, by happenstance, opportunity, or just bumbling along. I told myself that following my heart betokened heeding the call of my destiny. But now it wasn't just my own heart that I needed to heed.

I enjoyed graduate school for all that it opened up to me of the world of ideas and of my fellow students whose quirky theories and scholarly obsessions of delving into the esoteric (e.g. dolphin linguistics) and the beautiful (e.g. Kant's theory of the sublime) fascinated me. I was working hard, yet having fun. What better place to think about the historical becoming of the world than the hippie-commune-pocketed mountains of mind-expanding Santa Cruz, a place of infinite possibilities? But then, looming on the horizon was finitude. My two-year required residency period was coming to an end. I could write my dissertation from anywhere in the world but it had to be done within a limited period of time. Besides, I would have to earn a living after my fellowship ran out.

Living for the journey, not the destination, was great but now it was time to arrive somewhere, and have something to show for my effort. I started to realize I wanted products – a book coming out of my doctoral thesis, a title, Dr. Manheimer, a partner for life, and living progeny, too. I was in a state of shock. While Kierkegaard was never able to fulfill the marital ideals of the ethical, about which he wrote so enthusiastically under the guise of Judge Wilhelm of *Either/Or*, I could enter into matrimony as an enduring and committed love relationship, pursue work in the form of an engaging and fulfilling career, and embrace friendships as mutually enhancing relationships. I wanted these aspects of what I deemed the good life.

The phrase I picked up somewhere, "becoming a part of the world, not just its observer," reverberated in my mind. And so a new term entered my Hegelian-Kierkegaardian vocabulary. For in addition to the triad of being, nothing and becoming, there surfaced in me something new and different: "belonging."

My Professor and his wife were my Judge Wilhelm and the Judge's unnamed wife. I admired the way the Hofstadters belonged to one another. They held hands while walking across campus, they shared musical scores at the piano, they had a son, and even a little fox terrier named Kimmy. They had a history together. Moreover, My Professor had a string of publications to memorialize his own process of scholarly becoming. At the same time, the Hofstadters were showing signs of age – graying or thinning hair, a little unsteadiness when standing up from a chair, My Professor's greater reliance on his written lecture notes and three-ring binders. Belonging meant risking the loss of attachments, the failure of commitments. Belonging meant foregoing the open-ended horizon that was forever in process, meant making irreversible choices, and meant accepting death as the finality of belonging to the earth.

What I saw through the Hofstadters' picture window were the scenes of my possible futures. Would I one day, books and note papers scattered around, be sitting in my ranch house, my wife rattling silverware in the kitchen or sitting at the piano playing a Chopin étude while I ruminated about the success of my career, my books and articles, academic battles, promotions and disappointments, the unexpected directions our children had taken, my aching knees? Maybe I would rather be as serene as the serviceberry tree balancing a squirrel on one of its limbs. Then I heard a voice calling me from the other end of the house. "Manheimer, where are you?"

In his retrospective study, architectural historian Sandy Isenstadt cites a 1934 article in *House and Garden* magazine that heralds the coming popularity of the picture window, described in the magazine as "a single piece of polished plate glass set into one wall of a room" that would give the householder visual access to a "changing vista" that "paints what is, in effect, a marching mural on your wall."

It was hard for me to imagine the Hofstadters' picture window framing a pastoral view instead of the cream-colored station wagon, students walking by in spring, and the rain gutter lined roofs of ranch houses across the street. I surmised that for the Hofstadters their marching mural was more likely the lines of a musical score for two pianos. Perhaps from their recent trip to Italy, memories of strolling along in front of Raphael's fresco in the Apostolic Palace of the Vatican, The School of Athens, out of whose vanishing point perspective come strolling Plato and Aristotle. As for me, my marching mural was a string of words in black print – Aesthetic, Anxiety, Authority...

REFERENCES

Hyppolite, Jean (1974). *Genesis and Structure of Hegel's Phenomenology of Spirit.* Translated by Samuel Cherniak and John Heckman. Evanston: Northwestern University Press.

Isenstadt, Sandy (2006). "The Rise and Fall of the Picture Window." In *Housing and Dwelling: Perspectives on Modern Domestic Architecture,* edited by Barbara Miller Lane. London: Routledge. Pp 208-309.

Kojève, Alexandre (1969). *Introduction to the Reading of Hegel.* New York: Basic Books.

Poster, Mark (1975). *Existential Marxism in Post-war France: From Sartre to Althusser.* Princeton: Princeton University Press.

4. Temporality

If absurdity, nothingness and becoming are a cluster of stars in the existentialists' night sky, then the following star exerts the gravitational force that shapes their movements. The existentialists, be they thinkers, writers or visual artists, endeavored to explore and express not the linearity of time that is associated with motion and distance, but the spatiality of inner-time consciousness or "temporality." They aimed to capture what an influential but not existential French contemporary, Henri Bergson, called the qualitative multiplicity of consciousness or the "durational" moment (Bergson, 93). Becoming archeologists of temporality, they dug down into layers of memory and brought forth images they assembled into a collage of the present moment.

In just such a simultaneity of past and present, a picture and an ink well brought me back to the hour when my high school teacher, Mr. O'Brien, handed out the list of essay topics. Now, through the Internet grapevine, I'd heard from classmates that he was planning to attend our 50th high school reunion. A great deal had happened in those five decades. After a long marriage I went through a divorce. Now I was recently remarried. I wasn't sure whether my new wife, Gail, would be keen on accompanying me on this journey into the past. But, to her credit, she was game.

Class Picture

Meandering with Gail along a hallway lined with banks of low, dark green lockers, my eye was drawn to the open wall spaces hung with bulletin boards on which were affixed photos of kids, crayon drawing of houses and buildings, and watercolor depictions of rainbows and clouds. A group of our classmates had organized a visit to our neighborhood elementary school on the Friday afternoon preceding the big 50th anniversary high school reunion.

Walking down the brown linoleum hallway, I didn't think about the idea of temporality, I experienced it. "I'm walking through my past," I said to Gail, who nodded. "No," I corrected myself, "I'm walking alongside a whole new generation of black kids who now live in my old neighborhood." I pointed at the faces of the children on the bulletin boards.

"You're doing both," said Gail.

"Yes, both in the same moment. It's like our timelines are braided together."

"Yours and mine?"

"Uh-huh, and these kids, and my classmates who you're about to meet."

"Can't wait. Did you bring the picture?"

I showed her the folder.

A message had gone out via email asking us to bring photographs from the period if we had them. Where was that cardboard box of photographs I had carted around from one attic or basement to another? Digging through the pictures – me in my peddle-driven fire truck smiling under a plastic fireman's helmet, my, I now realized, sister looking sexy in short shorts and a well filled-out stripped blouse standing on our front porch, her hand resting on the shoulder of a boy in a plaid shirt – and then, finally, what I had been seeking: a class photo.

This was the first time I had looked carefully at the picture, studied it as an artifact. The boys are in short sleeves and the girls in flowery blouses so it must have been taken close to the end of the school year. I counted 49 of us standing in rows organized by height with a few seated on the floor in front of the group. Cutouts of starfish and mollusks tacked to a bulletin board protruding behind us indicate the setting was in one of the two science classrooms. The hands on a clock on the wall above our heads stand at 3:25.

In anticipation of this moment, I had the 5 x 7 black and white photo enlarged and slipped it into a manila folder. It was from this protective cover that I drew it out and held it forth in a circle of classmates who had gathered in the hallway in advance of a tour of the building. My fellow time travelers were graying and bald-headed men, some like myself sporting beards and mustaches, and well-preserved blond, brunette and redheaded women.

Those who had remained in the city or its suburbs still socialized with one another. So they laughed as they vied to put names to the faces, their own among them. It amazed me when two or three pointed and looked over at me. "There you are, Ronnie." It had actually taken several seconds for me to identify myself and now, these many years later, not having seen each other for decades, and wearing a beard and glasses and many of the signs of age, how could they know the pictured face and body and this current one belonged to the same person?

Meanwhile, selfies were taken. Of those absent, some deaths – by suicide, drug overdose, a landmine in Vietnam, or from a car or a boating accident – were reported. A few, it was told, were living abroad in places like Israel, Canada, and Scandinavia. Then two young African-American teachers took us on a tour of the building, which now seemed a miniature version of the one we walked through in our memories. The teachers were very proud of the school, its innovations and accomplishments. And they clearly loved the children. At the end of the tour, one of our troop, "Mitch," a madcap, fast-talking, smart-ass kid who always wore wild-colored shirts, very diplomatically asked our guides if we could see the boiler room. They exchanged puzzled looks. Noting their discomfort, Mitch crossed his arms over his head and explained, "Air raid drills."

One of the teachers agreed to lead those of us who were interested down the stairway to the basement. Gail stayed with a group of her new-found women friends while a few of us made the descent down the concrete stairs to the places still bearing the red and green outlines that designated where each class would sit near the throbbing boilers, hoping the all-clear signal would soon be sounded.

THE INKWELL

Not all of our homeroom classes had been in the two-story orange brick building. What had become of my third and fourth grade classrooms known as "the portables"? While some of us were born just ahead of the post-war baby boom, the elementary school soon became overwhelmed with new enrollees amongst whom there were some with foreign accents.

The principal, "Mr. Campbell" – he'd been a World War I ambulance driver and was known to everyone, including us children, as Sarge – would hire additional teachers, but there was nowhere to put them or their charges. I only learned this at the reunion from my fifth grade girl friend, Anita, whose mother was then president of the PTA.

Sections of the portables were trucked in and assembled upon a grassy strip beside the gravel playground. Children and teachers would climb a short flight of wooden stairs to a landing positioned in the middle of each one. A door opened into a mudroom where, in inclement weather, I would drape my coat onto a row of hooks below which, in winter, I set my snowy galoshes to drip onto the wooden floor. A black potbellied coal fired stove sat towards the rear middle of the mudroom surrounded by a makeshift iron railing on which a small metal sign warned, "Hot."

From the mudroom, depending on our grade level, our classroom was either to the left or the right. We children were arranged alphabetically, sitting in rows of solid wooden desks supported by curved wrought iron legs that connected the tops to attached seats. Each desk had a small, round corner hole that, from the blue and black stains that rimmed them, showed that previous users had dipped pens in inkwells. Our main writing implements were yellow pencils that sat nicely in slots carved along the top edge of the surface. When it came time for cursive writing exercises, we took fountain pens equipped with ink reservoirs out of our pencil cases.

There was something enticing about these inkwell holes that led me to peer down into the void that opened into the lower shelf of the hinged tops. Occasionally, I tipped crumpled notes, worn erasers, and sometimes an errant button into the inkwell hole. The vestige of another time, the empty circle made me wonder, who were the children that had used these desks and where had they gone? The inkwells spoke of the past yet everything about our school directed us to the future and what lay beyond the classroom at the other end of the portable.

GENERATIONAL TIME

After we had punch and cookies provided by the current school PTA for our reunion group and said our farewells until the next evening, I led Gail out a side door and along an outside pathway to the cyclone fenced playground. The portables were gone. Only an imprint of unkempt grass marked the site. We wandered diagonally across the playground while I shared memories of playing games of tag and Red Rover before the morning school bell sounded.

I explained to Gail that I found it comforting to encounter my gray-haired male and generally well-preserved female classmates, especially since I had so long ago moved away from the city and had not, on family visits during the intervening decades, bumped into them in a restaurant or shopping center in the suburbs. Comforting because we were witnesses for one another to a wholly other time in our lives that marked the beginning of a remarkably new era, one that would transform us. We were contemporaries, yes, and members of a birth cohort – the leading edge of what would, decades later, be labeled the Baby Boom Generation.

What seems especially strange now is how many ideas and revelations, in far off places under vastly different conditions from ours, were already set into motion during our elementary school years. Words emerging out of the ruins of European cities would not reach us until ten, twenty or thirty years later. It's not that we were such literary intellectuals. Many of my classmates would probably not have voluntarily read the words of these European novelists and philosophers. But their impact, the scratchings of the pen, the pounding of the typewriter, would reverberate into our cultural milieu through movies, TV dramas, even articles in popular magazines such *Time* or *Life*.

As I scuffed around on the graveled playground of my youth the question lingered. Just as we were drawn back to the important places and faces of our formative years, was there some compelling reason to hold a reunion with voices of those who had influenced us, directly or indirectly, in our adolescence and young adulthood? Or would rereading the novels, essays and works of philosophy of the existentialists be like traipsing around the halls of our elementary school and descending into the basement boiler room? Nostalgic, yes; but hadn't the all-clear been sounded long ago?

"Ron," Gail summoned my attention. "I enjoyed meeting your schoolmates. Especially the women. What a talented bunch. And funny, too. Isn't it amazing how our lives have changed with the times?"

"It is amazing. They've had interesting lives and careers."

"Which reminds me," said Gail, pulling her cell phone out of her pocketbook. "I've got to make a couple of calls to clients and, besides, I'm hungry. Can you take me somewhere for a bite to eat?"

As we got back on the freeway heading out to the suburbs where we were staying, Gail's observation about the women among my peers welled up. It was true that their lives had undergone an even more dramatic transformation from what, in the sixth grade, anyone might have expected. A book that contributed to this transformation and had a profound influence on feminists such as Betty Freidan came from the pen of a key figure in the existentialist movement.

WOMEN'S HISTORY

While I was conjuring up my future by gazing into the empty inkwells of the portables, readers in the United States, especially women, were peering into the English translation of Simone de Beauvoir's 1949, two-volume *Le deuxième sexe*, consolidated into a one volume work, *The Second Sex*. While I would not discover the book for more than a decade, in 1952 American readers, especially women were learning that they shared a history as an oppressed group. The book's American reception mirrored what had happened a few years earlier on the Continent.

When it first appeared in France, de Beauvoir's scathing critique of women's second-class citizenship came as a great shock to readers in France, women and men alike. The lengthy, well-researched work provided a systematic treatment of the oppression of women both historically and in the modern age. French readers were unprepared for her candid account of taboo topics such as women's sexual initiation, lesbianism, menstruation, pregnancy, and menopause. While the book sold well in France, criticism abounded, much of it negative. One incensed reviewer accused de Beauvoir of being "a poor neurotic girl, repressed, frustrated, and cheated by life." Another, that she was "humiliated by being a woman." The Vatican added the title to its Index of Prohibited Books.

De Beauvoir's affront was that she applied to women's lives the credo she shared with her compatriot philosopher, intermittent lover, and life-long friend, Jean-Paul Sartre, that "existence precedes essence." In short, a child "is not *born* a woman, but *becomes* one" (249). Only a small part of women's lives and roles are predetermined by the dictates of biology (the purported "essence"), the rest, her analysis showed, is the product of cultural mores, social stereotypes and ingrained attitudes (the situation in which she experiences her "existence").

The idea of "Woman" (she often used the singular to signify the general) is a socially and historically constructed one. And since women's roles are the result of legal and economic status, are deeply influenced by social class and suppressed by covert or overt misogyny, they can be changed. By extending the women's suffrage movement into the whole range of gender identity issues and sounding the clarion call to awareness and self-determination, de Beauvoir provided the research and analytical framework that would help kindle the fires of the 1960s-era feminist revolution that deeply affected my elementary school classmates.

Life is a mixture of possibilities and very real limitations, she argues. Insofar as we make choices, we are free to act on what we see as our possibilities. But since we are also constrained by physical limits, the disparity of social and economic inequality, and subjugation to the political power of others, we are limited. Personal freedom is enacted within the psychological and philosophical space framed by possibilities and limitation. And it is this condition for which de Beauvoir replaces absurdity with "ambiguity."

In *The Second Sex* she gives the example of women's relationships to their bodies. A woman's body is a condition of ambiguity, for she can use it as a vehicle for her freedom *and* feel oppressed by it. There is no essential truth of the matter: it depends upon the extent to which a woman sees herself as a free subject rather than as the object of society's gaze. Hence, for de Beauvoir, accepting or rejecting a man's advances is always a matter of choice despite social expectations and peer pressure. Marriage and childbearing, too, are no longer norms or forces of "nature" but choices, as de Beauvoir, who never married or gave birth to a child (she did adopt a daughter) demonstrated by how she led her own life.

To characterize the plight of human beings, de Beauvoir prefers the term "tragic ambiguity" to Camus' and Sartre's use of the term "absurd." She chose for an epigram to her book-length essay, *The Ethics of Ambiguity* (1947), a quote from the 16th-century French philosopher Montaigne. "Life in itself is neither good nor evil. It is the place of good and evil, according to what you make of it." Michel de Montaigne emphasizes that life itself is value-free and thus places the individual in the indeterminate condition of a freely acting moral agent. In doing so, he emphasizes the individual's capability and responsibility to make of life what one will. He also recognizes that as self-conscious, reflective beings, humans are aware of both their open possibilities and their finite limitations.

"The continuous work of our life," de Beauvoir quotes Montaigne, "is to build death." For while human beings aspire to touch and be touched by what is timeless and permanent, humans cannot escape awareness that not only is life in general fleeting but one's personal life, one's very consciousness, is destined to come to an end. This duality, bearing within oneself both the finite and infinite, constitutes the tragic ambiguity that every reflective person has to overcome each day. De Beauvoir did not bemoan this tragic ambiguity, rather, as did Sartre with his pronouncement that life is absurd, she celebrated it. This may at first seem counterintuitive.

Sartre asserts that an individual's life is not predetermined or fated, rather that each person is radically free to discover and choose his or her values and goals and in doing so to create meaning. In this sense, the term "absurd" qualifies the individual's realization that his or her life has no intrinsic meaning bestowed by a God, the state, one's family or community, or the historical period in which one lives. Sartre recognized that each person is born into circumstances beyond his or her control ("facticities") such as social class, gender, nationality, and family religion. These empirical facts are the cards you are dealt but, once awakened to your true condition of freedom, they need not determine how you would play them.

De Beauvoir agrees (she frequently quotes Sartre in *The Ethics of Ambiguity*) but perhaps because of her own awareness of the ambiguity of what it means to be female, as well as her experience of the unpredictable life and death conditions under the Nazi occupation, she recognizes that the parameters of facticity are not easily overcome simply by declaring them as mutable "contingencies."

When de Beauvoir wrote her book on ethics and then on women's lives, the field of "women's studies" had not emerged and would not do so in the United States until the 1970s. The very notion that women's lives could be understood in historical perspective would have seemed baffling to most scholars. By challenging the socially accepted and culturally approved meanings of women's lives – creating ambiguity – de Beauvoir and those she inspired opened the possibility of countless new meanings. My female classmates were evidence of this historical revolution.

Reunion Time

The Saturday night high school reunion party was held in the ballroom of a suburban hotel. The organizers had very cleverly worked with the caterer to create food stations that mimicked the decors and menus of popular eateries from the neighborhood of our youth. We bit into succulent Coney Island hotdogs smothered in chili, sampled pizzas with cheese so gooey you had to tug away to claim your wedge of pie, munched on crispy ketchup-dipped French fries, and swallowed fizzy Cokes from pale green bottles. A band of gray-haired musicians thumped and thudded to rouse us onto the dance floor where we whirled, twirled, and dipped in a mounting frenzy as the rock and roll of the late fifties turned into the guitar riffs and wild torso gyrations of the psychedelic sixties.

Off to the side of the dance floor people pointed, laughed and embraced one another. Spouses – first, second or hinted-at thirds, were introduced as well as "partners." Many of the women spoke of their careers as doctors, lawyers and college professors. Among the men there was talk of computers, the Internet and second and third careers. Then suddenly, the music stopped. A hush came over the room. Our former yet still charismatic class president, "Jerry Finkel," took the microphone. "Ladies and gentlemen, class of 1960," he bellowed, "please welcome the one and only, Mr. Paul O'Brien."

To a round of applause, Mr. O'Brien – who, I now knew had a first name, wearing a blue blazer, stripped dress shirt and red bowtie, made his way through the crowd toward the band stand. He paused, turned and beckoned to someone. Another man, sporting a long mane of white hair and attired in an almost identical outfit, skipped forward giving the crowd a two-handed wave. As the two approached the stage, they locked arms. A small riser had been placed in front of the stage. Mr. O'Brien, Paul, stepped onto it and helped the other man ascend. O'Brien gave Jerry Finkel a hug and turned to the crowd. "Great to be here," he sang out. "Richard and I appreciate your kindness." They waved and threw kisses to the crowd. Then they stepped down and were immediately surrounded by former students.

I had to speak with him. Certainly, after these many years, I could not ask for an explanation of what he had meant with his parting words to me that last day of class. He'd never remember. But I wanted to thank him for challenging me and his other students to tackle research assignments that introduced us to worlds that were in so many ways different than our own. I had neither the time nor the ability to explain all this background information to my wife so I just took her by the hand and led her toward the circle of O'Brien's admirers. I told her that O'Brien had been a great influence on me. We reached the circle and for a few minutes, stood there listening to the affectionate teasing and bantering that went on. Then Mr. O'Brien looked at his friend. "Richard is starving," he said. And he took the man by the elbow and guided him toward one of the food stations. My wife and I followed.

I think it was under the neon sign of the Chinese take-out that Paul O'Brien, with a plate of shrimp fried rice balanced in one hand and a plastic fork held in the other, turned to us. "I know you. Or is it you?" he said, looking first at me and then at my wife. "No," he said, "It's you," nodding to me. "She's too young." Actually, my wife (second) and I are only months apart in age but she seems to have been endowed with a youthful gene that enables her to look ten years younger.

"I took your twelfth grade English course in 1960," I blurted out. "I had to compare Camus and Gide. *The Stranger* and *The Immoralist.*"

Mr. O'Brien nodded slowly and gazed off in the distance as if he were thumbing through a huge stack of term papers looking at the names placed in the required upper right-hand corner. Meanwhile, his friend Richard had turned away from the food cart, a piece of eggroll in hand, and burst out laughing. "Paul, how dreadful of you. Your students are ever haunted by those ridiculous tasks you set for them. Camus and Gide for a what, 17 year-old?"

O'Brien smiled at Richard. "I had to prepare them for college."

"Yes, and what else?"

"For the new age that was coming."

"Or so you hoped," said Richard, waving his egg roll. "Wasn't that it?"

"Well," said O'Brien. "Wasn't I proven right? Look at all the changes I helped to prepare them for." And with that he leaned over and took a bite of Richard's eggroll. Then, chewing and swallowing, he asked, "You'll have to tell me your names. I'm sorry."

We made our introductions and I filled in a bit about my career, children, divorce, remarriage, and the places I had lived. My wife, Gail, more adept at connecting emotionally and ever the charmer, told "dear Paul" that she knew how much his class had meant to me and what a great influence he had been.

"Oh, don't flatter him," Richard interjected. "You'll make his fat head even fatter."

O'Brien ignored Richard and pointed at me. "You know, existentialism was just coming into vogue in the U.S. in the late fifties as it was going out of style in Europe. All my students were taken with Camus. He was the literary equivalent of James Dean. *The Stranger* touched a nerve just, as had Holden Caulfield in Salinger's *Catcher in the Rye.*

"Alas, these alienated, misunderstood heroes," said O'Brien, shaking his head. "Harbingers of massive social change, uprisings, demonstrations. Of course Holden was tragically self-destructive. He could see through the phoniness of the adult world but he couldn't turn his anger into something useful. And poor Meursault, he confronts the absurdity of life, the indifferent universe, yet he's so in touch with the elements – the sea, the sand and the sky in which the ever-present North African sun shone so brilliantly. It's a shame he couldn't have become one of those rebels that Camus later wrote about."

"Yes, a terrible shame," interjected Richard. "You know, we've been there. Tunis. Yes. Paul, when was that? 75, 76? Oh, amazing place. And the young boys are still lithesome. No wonder Gide loved it."

"It was in 1979 but I'm not going to say how it is that I remember the year." O'Brien winked at his friend.

Richard smiled. Shrugged. "Hey, Paul? Didn't Camus die the same way as James Dean?"

O'Brien turned to us. "Well, yes, now that you mention it." And looking at my wife he explained. "Car crashes. But James Dean was driving alone. Apparently he was breaking in a new Porsche he had hoped to race somewhere in California. Now Camus, on the other hand, was a passenger. But that was five years later, in France. The driver was his friend and publisher, Michel Gallimard. A few days later Michel died too." O'Brien took a forkful of the fried rice. "Both tragedies. Talent lost to us. And so absurd. Especially, when you think about it, in Camus' case. After all those risks during the war when intellectuals, artists and writers were being rounded up and shot by the Nazis. Then to die in a car crash. Not at all the right ending."

Richard stepped away from Paul and put a hand on Gail's shoulder. "Let's speak no more of death to these lovely people," he said, turning back to Paul. "Anyway, what about Gide? You know, of course, that he was fey long before it was fashionable to be gay. Your husband, Ron, here, he did pick that up back in the old twelfth when he read *The Immoralist*? Hmm. I wonder."

Gail looked over at me with a bemused expression on her face.

"Well, I knew and didn't know," I admitted.

"Do tell," said Richard.

"I understood that Gide's hero was rebelling against the conventions of his social class and of his status as a scholar of antiquity. That he had opened himself to pleasures that he had hidden from himself before his near-death experience. He had denied his body in favor of his mind. Now he loved everything of the senses including an attraction to men and boys whom he found beautiful."

Richard smiled at me. "And that's what made him an immoralist?"

"Now that's the part I didn't understand at the time."

"Well, how could you?" said O'Brien. "You hadn't yet ventured out of the social order, I wager."

"Yet?" said Richard. "Just how much do you know about your former student?"

O'Brien shrugged. "The beard, the wire rimmed glasses, the blond beside him," he nodded and smiled at Gail. "Just a guess."

"No, Mr. O'Brien... " I sputtered, lapsing back 50 years.

"Please, in honor of our mutual gray hair and wrinkles, and God knows what else, Paul will do."

I'm making a fifty-year transition. "So, um, Paul, my point, actually my realization only years later, is that the label 'immoralist' is a judgment that others make about someone."

"Yes, very good, Ronald. In fact, by giving that the title of his book, Gide was putting a challenge to his readers. 'Is my character really immoral?'

he's asking. Or is it you who live a life of suppressed emotion and who know neither ecstasy nor despair that are the immoralists? In contrast, Gide offers up a life of sensuous engagement in which we can truly be ourselves freed from the falsity of conventional norms. It's funny, you know. When that morose Dane, Kierkegaard, shouted from the rooftops that we should all 'choose ourselves' and even 'give birth to ourselves,' he meant become authentically Christian. But for Gide, give birth to yourself, his version of born-again, was to accept, no, to celebrate, his uniqueness as a gay man."

I looked at Gail whom I saw was beginning to get a little uncomfortable with this esoteric conversation. She had been an education major in college and later climbed the ladder in the world of financial services. What she knew about existentialism she knew from bits and pieces of conversation with me about, say, an existential theme in a movie. Still, there would be no repeat performance of this moment. Paul O'Brien, while he looked remarkably hale and hearty, had to be in his 80s. Even were we to attend another reunion in ten years, it was unlikely that he would still be around. Or would we, for that matter? There were no guarantees.

"Paul," I began. "I'm so pleased that you came to this reunion."

"Obviously, you're a hero to many of your former students," added Gail, putting her hand on his sleeve.

Paul nodded to Richard who gave him an admiring smile. There was so much more I wanted to say. How his being there gave me the chance to thank him for having the confidence in us to encourage independent thinking and to make us stretch beyond our comfort zones.

"Reading Gide and Camus helped me see the strangeness of my own situation, a life I pretty much just took for granted," I began. "Sitting there in the Main Library reading all those articles we had to find to supply footnotes to back up our opinions, I began to see the stranger, the outsider and the immoralist in myself. These were just glimmering, mind you, just tiny cracks in the walls made up of everything I accepted as real even though I didn't know I was making any assumptions."

Gail took my arm. She knew this was enough said. Paul O'Brien understood what he'd set out to accomplish. After all, he was one of a very few of our former teachers to show up for the reunion. I reached out to shake Paul's hand.

Paul looked at me for several seconds and looked down at my hand. Then he pulled me into an embrace and, releasing me, held both my wrists in his hands. "I'm grateful for your telling me this story about how you stepped through the cracks to go wandering in the existentialist landscape. Once you've stepped out of the path of the tried and true, you never again know quite where you're going. It's a gift and a burden, as I'm sure you've discovered."

"That's for sure," quipped Richard who pointed to the people gyrating on the dance floor. "From existentialism to women's lib, gay liberation, black liberation, and who knows what other groups are in the queue to get liberated."

"It's amazing what a little consciousness-raising will do," laughed Paul.

"Listen to this," said Richard. "From the mouth of the provocateur himself."

Just then, several of the dancers came running up to us, reaching out their hands to pull us onto the dance floor as the band played the opening guitar chords and drumbeats of the Rolling Stones' "Satisfaction."

I doubt that many of the women who attended the reunion had read Simone de Beauvoir's *The Second Sex*. But I'm sure many had read Betty Friedan's The *Feminine Mystique*, a 1963 bestseller that owed a lot to de Beauvoir. And I'm guessing that few read another of de Beauvoir's liberating critiques, one equally relevant to the crowd of people demonstrating their moves on the dance floor.

AGING TIME

Twenty-one years after publishing *The Second Sex*, with feminist consciousness-raising groups cropping up across the U.S. and Europe, the now 62-year-old novelist, social activist and thinker took up the plight of another oppressed and socially marginalized group. As she had done in *The Second Sex*, de Beauvoir approached this new subject matter from a variety of perspectives including the biological, anthropological, historical, and sociological. In her doorstop-size tome, *La Vieillesse* ("old age"), translated in 1972 as *The Coming of Age*, de Beauvoir argued that the fears and stigmas associated with old age "are imposed" upon the elderly by society and then internalized by older people who come to loath their own existence.

Just as with *The Second Sex*, *The Coming of Age* is divided into two sections, the first dealing with the objective condition, "Old Age as Seen from Without," and the second with the subjective, "Being-in-the-World," an existentialist idiom that aims to capture the experiential point of view. Within the experiential perspective, de Beauvoir focuses on the older person's relation to his or her body, to time, and to the external world. Her existentialist attitude is vividly exemplified in the matter of "temporality," our changing consciousness of time.

Drawing on the insights of the ancient Greek philosopher, Aristotle, de Beauvoir observes that every stage of life exhibits a different relationship to time. Unlike the young for whom the future is a looming horizon, the past a fleeting shadow, de Beauvoir reflects that, "as the years go by our future shortens, while our past grows heavier" (361). The old, she says, echoing Aristotle, "live more by memory than by hope." Beauvoir acknowledges that as we grow older we have a tendency to pile up memories to serve as a bastion "against the deteriorations of age." She looks disparagingly on those who "tirelessly tell stories of the being that they were, a being that lives on inside them" (362). She regards as an act of self-deception the idea that by clinging to the remembered past, "we remain unalterable."

Citing Sartre, she affirms, "It is the future that decides whether the past is living or not." The past of memory is an artifact, a frozen fiction.

For de Beauvoir, it is only when we have "projects" – plans and actions that impel us forward, which enable us to "take off from the past." To live "authentically" (an existentialist's rallying cry), the elderly must continue to have projects and march valiantly on into the future in defiance of ageist prejudices that their lives are over. Even towards the purported wisdom and spiritual inwardness associated with hard won experience and serene detachment, de Beauvoir remains a skeptic. She cites Gide, who said: "I wholeheartedly despise that kind of wisdom that is reached only by weariness or by the loss of all warmth" (486).

More than 40 years have passed since de Beauvoir sought to rouse "the old," as she had challenged "woman," to throw off the mantel of imposed images of how they should look, feel and act. While she was among the first to frame a critique of the social construction of old age, she was soon joined by countless others – psychologists, sociologists, gerontologists and political activists who raced to catch up with the dramatic changes taking place. In 1970, de Beauvoir could document the issues of poverty, illness and social isolation among the still-small percentage of European and American citizens who were 65 and over. But she could only glimpse what was coming next – an unplanned and uncoordinated worldwide "age revolution" exemplified by the very people who had gathered at our elementary and high school reunions.

Beauvoir remarks in *Memoirs of a Dutiful Daughter* that her youthful liberation from middle-class values made her "Free, yes, but free for what?" The same could also be said for the Age Revolution. As in the women's movement, an almost "anything goes" attitude about aging and later life can be both liberating and perplexing. The rules, guidelines and general cultural consensus of earlier times have largely faded away. This situation can precipitate anxiety and a sense of crisis.

Because of the dramatic rise in life expectancy during the twentieth century, most post-industrial societies experienced a historically unprecedented percentage population increase in the later part of the life course. This led sociologists and demographers to describe a phenomenon of the later decades of the twentieth century as the "graying of society." Advances in health care, nutrition, health and economic supports such as government-mandated health insurance and public and private income security, combined with rising levels of moderate affluence and educational attainment created a new stage of life.

With full or partial disengagement from the labor force (a retirement age, for some, as in France, mandated by law) occurring, on average, in people's early to mid-60s, a democratization of leisure became an unexpected bonus for the first waves to reach the shores of this time of life – a "Third Age" or "Second Middle Age." With ten, twenty or even thirty more years to live, the time of retirement brought with it an unprecedented array of choices about how to live, what to do, and with whom to do it. Should one venture into another career, go back to school, pack up and move, find a new spouse, or explore spirituality? For many, these options triggered a kind of second adolescence. For others, such a range of choices felt more like a first-time experience as necessity, more than possibility, was the dominant theme of their earlier life. Austrian sociologist Leopold Rosenmayr called this new stage of life, "the late freedom."

Arising to meet these newcomers and offering a world of choices and challenges, a whole new "retirement industry" generated guidebooks, websites, consultants, advocacy and membership organizations, housing arrangements, wellness programs, and a worldwide network of lifelong learning programs. Retirement, now understood as a term describing a multi-decade period rather than a one-time event, turned into a set of lifestyle issues.

Beneath the surface of organizing one's calendar of activities to find fulfillment in this "second half of life," numerous nagging questions would begin to surface. Apart from one's career and family roles, was there a core identity that provided a sense of continuity or did there seem to be multiple lives and identities that somehow did not coalesce? With increasing awareness of time running out, how did disappearance from the world shared with others challenge one's sense of meaning? For which choices did it feel "too late" to take action and for which "just in time?" To what larger spheres of life did one belong, if any? And what about values that had seemed so comfortable and reliable in midlife but now appeared uncertain and uninspiring?

No longer beholden to an employer, to the requirements of climbing a career ladder, or to the heavily scheduled demands of both work and family responsibilities, the retiree is faced with a lot of newfound discretionary time. Along with unstructured calendars come anxieties generated by rising, perhaps unrealistic expectations, fear of passivity or boredom, isolation due to a shrinking social circle, diminished power and authority, concern about illness, disability, and dependency, and the increasingly real prospects of a final curtain call.

The sense of "not mattering" or purposelessness – the notion of old age as a "roleless role," may conjure up the existentialist's pronouncement that since all meanings are contingent, not fixed, that "life is absurd." Perhaps an overstatement, it is not that meanings are no longer available, but since they are not given or imposed, they require more effort. A reassessment is called for to sustain the structures that buttressed the goals, values and rewards of one's former daily life. Simone de Beauvoir provides a useful approach.

Parallel conditions of ambiguity obtain for the older person. In *The Coming of Age*, de Beauvoir offers a nuanced understanding of sexuality and old age. Against the then widely accepted view that sexual desire should diminish and even disappear in old age, "those moralists who condemn old age to chastity," de Beauvoir asserts that the older person retains his or her longing for sexual experience because he or she is "still attached to the erotic world he [or she] built up in youth or maturity" (319).

Retention of this complex desire that brings the potential, even in old age, to "transfigure" the sense we have of our embodied self and of the beloved other, this desire has the power to "renew its fading colors." Steering clear of either the position that since life is absurd anything is possible no matter what your age or that hard and fast norms apply at each stage of life, including old age, de Beauvoir explores the range of choices sexologists have revealed about the life of erotic desire in later life. She is as sensitive to the limitations as the possibilities.

The many ways of expressing the erotic in later life is an important source of meaning for self-identity and relationship to others. Thanks to plastic surgery, transgendering technologies, hormone replacement therapy, and drugs used to treat erectile dysfunction or low libido, ambiguities abound. Beauvoir is pointing to the fact that most meanings in life cannot be definitively resolved according to fixed, supposedly universal, rules.

As Kierkegaard wrote in his *Journal* of 1843, "Life is lived forward but understood backward." Each new day is a step into the unknown and uncertain. For de Beauvoir, the activity of defining and interpreting meaning is not a singular reflection on what has been. Understanding is always a matter of retrospection framed by the present moment. That's what makes life exciting and challenging. Makes it existential.

READING *THE SECOND SEX* IN LONDON

In 1964, I came across a copy of *The Second Sex* in a bookshop in the Bayswater neighborhood of London. I had been living there for several months following a hitchhiking tour around the British Isles, bunking in Youth Hostels. I was trying to figure out what to do with the rest of my life after graduating from college. I had a few London contacts supplied to me by my former teachers but it was a lonely life and despite all the wonderful museums and parks of the vast city, I was spending a great deal of time in my rented room reading.

As I sat beside the gas fireplace, periodically depositing shillings into the meter that kept a modicum of heat in the drafty room, and struggling to understand de Beauvoir's unique historical analysis, images of my relationship with my first serious lover, Susan, crept into my mind.

I first met Susan at my friend Jerry's apartment near the university campus. She lived across the hall with her roommate, Karen. Both were majoring in art, Karen a painter and weaver, Susan studying ceramics. At the time, Susan went by the name Agrippina X. Agrippa was a Roman consul and architect. Susan was fascinated with the name and constructed the female equivalent while adding the "X" as had the African-American Muslim minister and civil right activists Malcolm X.

I had never met anyone as different from me as Susan. She had grown up in a small town in southern Michigan not far from Battle Creek (home of Kellogg's). Her father was a tinkerer and inventor but mostly, when he was not working as a custodian at the state mental hospital, a man devoted to fishing – from boats, piers, along beaches, in streams and through ice. Her mother also worked at "the home." Both parents were avid motorcyclists.

Unlike talkative and cerebral me, Susan could go for long periods without speaking. She gestured, mimed, exclaimed in single syllables, and smiled or frowned. Several times after we had started to date and I came to take her out, she would take one look at me and shake her head. No, she was not going. There was something in my demeanor, my posture, or facial expression that betokened darkness. Susan's shorthand was "cat's paw." I was "Cat." And when I was the warm and loving cat I could be petted. But when the cat was in the mood to bat around small prey with its extended claws, then Cat was dangerous and not to be tolerated. I would try to persuade Susan that she was mistaken but she always knew there was an element of asperity in me at that moment even when I was unaware until I saw that look of fear in Susan's eyes.

I didn't know it then but Susan and I had completely different notions of time. Mine was linear, marked out by hurdles, courses to complete, a senior thesis to write, graduation, then new horizons, travel abroad, eventually returning to the U.S. for graduate school, an academic career, publishing my ideas, and somewhere, though very far away, maybe settling down with someone and maybe having children. But just how, when and where that would occur remained indeterminate. Susan's experience of time did not involve a deferred future. Hers was not a *bildungsroman*. I was her man, her Cat, and that was settled. We would be together forever. She would teach me how to acknowledge my feelings, to know as much by touch as by thought, to make a place for fantasy and irrationality, and to pay attention to my inner life. More than anything, Susan would teach me how to be free, spontaneous, goofy and irreverent.

Some of my serious-minded friends were appalled that I had taken up with a girl like Susan. It didn't make sense. What could I possibly have found in her, someone so unlike "Us"? I wondered the same thing but I wanted to be with Susan and to open up to the part of life that had remained all but hidden. Still, in the back of my mind, I suspected I was using her. Susan would be a stepping-stone along the path of the coming of age story I was telling myself. I didn't know and I didn't inquire as to what Susan's path might look like or even if there was a path other than making sharp pointed ceramic objects that looked like medieval cudgels.

I don't remember whether we broke up or just that I graduated while Susan was in her junior year. I moved out of my apartment, sold my car, and told my parents I was going to tour English youth hostels for the summer. Susan and I parted. We would probably never see each other again. But I was wrong. We would resume our relationship on the Danish island of Bornholm where Susan was enrolled as a residential student in the Folkehøjskole, studying ceramics and Danish language and literature for the year. When I accompanied her to the island and met him, the school's principal kindly arranged for me to take up residence with the farm family I mentioned earlier. On weekends I would bicycle the 10 kilometers to the folk high school and stay in Susan's room while her roommate went home to her island family for the weekend. Everyone thought that we were *forlovet*, engaged, but really we were more accurately *forelsket*, literally "in love," which in Danish implies something like going steady.

Susan's experience of time, as I perceive it now, was expansive, like the opening motions of a flower or the trickling of water in a mountain stream. That, however, was my version of Susan's temporality, my myth of this Other.

As de Beauvoir laid out a list of myths about women's lives, bodies, "nature," aspirations, competencies and capacities, it still didn't dawn on me that I subscribed to many of these myths. That I should suddenly be classified as one among the millions of oppressors of women seemed unfair. It would take several decades for me to realize I was a product of cultural attitudes that bestowed certain privileges upon me that in actuality I didn't deserve. The fact that my sister chose secretarial school rather than college and married and started having children at age 19 was her choice. I attended college and did not marry until I was 27 and only then commenced to enter the path of fatherhood. But these were all just incidents of personal choice, weren't they?

REFERENCES

Beauvoir, Simone de (1947/1979). *Ethics of Ambiguity*. Translated from the French by Bernard Frechtman. New York: Citadel Press.

_____ (1952). *The Second Sex*. New York: Knopf.

_____ (1972/1996). *The Coming of Age*. Tr. Patrick O'Brian. New York: W.W. Norton & Co.

Descartes, Rene (1968). *Discourse on Method and The Meditations*. Translated by F. E. Sutcliffe. London: Penguin Books.

Heidegger, Martin (1962). *Being and Time,* translated by John Macquarrie and Edward Robinson. New York: Harper & Row.

Kierkegaard, Søren (1980) *The Concept of Anxiety: A Simple Psychologically Orienting Deliberation on the Dogmatic Issue of Hereditary Sin.* Edited and translated by Reidar Thomte. Princeton: Princeton University Press.

Rosenmayr, Leopold (1983). *The Late Freedom: Old Age – A Piece of Consciously Experienced Life.* Berlin: Severin & Seidler.

Sartre, Jean-Paul (2007). *Existentialism Is A Humanism*. Translated by Carol Macomber. New Haven: Yale University Press.

Taylor, Charles (1992). *Ethics of Authenticity*. Cambridge: Harvard University Press.

5. Dwelling

Most of us have lived in a variety of abodes: houses, apartments, flats, dorms, cottages, cabins, barracks, and maybe even a lean-to that protected us from the wind. The way we make a place to call home gives concrete meaning to the existential concept of "being-in-the-world." I hadn't given philosophical consideration to the places in which I had lived until one morning while still a graduate student. I was once again gazing out the Hofstadters' picture window waiting for My Professor. Lying on the coffee table were the page proofs for a new book. I couldn't resist peeking inside the cover. That's when I discovered the fifth star, one that at first seemed remote from the other stars of existentialism, the concept of dwelling.

Awakening to Home

I started to leaf through the author's proof of a collection of lectures that My Professor was translating from German. The book, *Poetry, Language, Thought,* included a chapter called (without commas) "Building Dwell Thinking." Skimming through the essay, originally a lecture that Martin Heidegger had given at a conference in Germany in the early 1950s, I was stunned to discover that there were subtle meanings lurking within the spaces that we call our homes.

My mind wandered to Descartes who, in *The Discourse on Method,* draws an analogy between the work of a philosopher and that of an architect. The philosopher uses doubt to clear away unquestioned assumptions in order to be sure to establish a solid foundation for his step-by-step deductions. He does this by employing "clear and distinct ideas" to build up the edifice of his ideas. The architect does something similar by using his surveying and plumb line determining tools. He too makes sure the ground is level and solid before starting the work. But as I paged through the soon to be published book, I realized that Heidegger's way of excavating the earth was unlike Descartes'. Instead of employing doubt, Heidegger was using etymologies, word origins. He was digging back through layers of accumulated meanings into the remote past to find the most original ideas about what it means to both build and dwell. From Heidegger's point of view, he was "disclosing" the long-forgotten meanings of *Bauen*, the German word for "to build" (144). Unlike the rationally methodical Cartesian narrative Heidegger's account was lyrical, poetic, and at times almost mystical.

As I went on reading, the Hofstadters' living room began to feel more like an ideational space than just a drywall-enclosed box with pieces of furniture deployed about. A new way of looking at the world began to open up. A home should have an organic life. It breathes through its ventilation system, it sees through its transparent openings, it invites through its welcoming portals. When you cross the threshold into a home you're transformed from stranger to guest while the householder now becomes your host. My mind raced on. The home, it's a sanctuary, a temple, and a place for rituals. Then a voice called my name and I had to put down the manuscript. I would buy a copy of this book once it was published.

As Heidegger sounds out the etymology of the German word *bauen*, he finds its origins bespeak "nearness and neighborliness" (145). *Bauen* also implies "to cherish and protect, to preserve and care for." Going further into the philosophical realm, Heidegger argues that the idea of dwelling invokes a "fourfold unity" of earth, sky, mortals, and immortals (148).

To illustrate, he harkens to a favorite place in the German landscape, the Schwartzwald, the Black Forest, and points to the rustic farmhouses erected by peasant farmers who, intuitively drawing on the fourfold unity, in responding to weather and terrain, placed the farm on the "wind-sheltered mountain slope looking south, among the meadows close to the spring" (157). Inside this carefully situated abode the inhabitants erected an "altar corner behind the community table, it made room in its chamber for the hallowed places of childbed and the 'tree of the dead' – for this is what they call a coffin there: the *Totenbaum*" (158). The latter, a hewn log platform on which a casket could be set at the time of a wake.

Few of us live in a setting like the German Schwarzwald, but we glean from Heidegger's example that authentic dwelling is respectful of the environment and sensitive to light, weather, the spiritual, the communal, and the cycle of birth and death. This "fourfold unity," when accomplished architecturally, is what gives a home a special sense of belonging to, rather than imposing upon, an environment. For Heidegger, these peasant dwellers, presumably the "mortals," don't just live spatially inside these mindfully designed and located farmhouses, they are in harmony with them and with the "world." This is their setting.

For Heidegger, everything in the built environment speaks to us through form and materials. In the case of a domicile, the most elementary components – floor, wall and roof, communicate the relationship between inside and outside, above and beneath, within and around, and over and below. Dwelling is the way we orient ourselves. A cosmological act, dwelling is the mental frame through which we look out into the world and invite the world onto our doorstep.

Inspired by Heidegger, I tried to excavate my memories of house and home, searching back through images of college apartments, rented flats, until I reached my place of origin. Unlike Heidegger's Black Forest, I grew up in an urban residential setting of two-story brick houses laid out along a grid of intersecting streets. Maple trees stood before each house and, in summer, they formed a canopy over the streets. The one feature that now stood out for me was not as elemental as an "alter corner" or "community table" but something no less primary and familial, an architectural feature then commonplace in many houses built in the 1940s and 50s.

MILK CHUTE

This square, enclosed hollow in a wall could be opened from the outside to allow bottles of milk, tubs of butter, and pints of cream to be placed on a linoleum-lined shelf to await, from the inside, the hand of the householder or apartment dweller who retrieved these items. In my neighborhood, milk chutes were situated next to the side doors of houses and occasionally beside a backyard door. Perishables were placed there weekday mornings by a man with a bow tie who stepped from the sliding side door of a delivery truck. Standing on the landing of the basement stairs, you grasped the lever of the inside metal door and slid it open to gather in the contents.

By the middle of the 1950s, our milk chute compartment stood vacant, a relic of bygone days. Metaphorically speaking, the milk chute was a way of communicating one's wishes to the outside world, an almost daily reminder of the distant farm and dairy represented by the uniformed official of abundance and of the system of exchange enacted by Friday's placement in the chute of a check made out to the dairy company in recognition of the milkman's faithful service.

Milk chutes do not bear the tradition of the long-hipped roof or the kitchen tiled stove. They are a feature of the automobile age like the drive-in restaurant or drive-through teller. But for those of us who grew up with them, the milk chute is a memorial of a way of life, a form of trust, and a connection with a wider world. I would never have thought of the milk chute in this way without Heidegger's calling attention to this most basic fact of human habitation: dwelling.

HOW EXISTENTIALISTS DWELL

As far as their own way of dwelling, our French existentialist couple, Sartre and de Beauvoir (who never occupied a home together), might seem an unlikely source for insight into the concept of authentic dwelling. Though they grew up in middle-class Parisian apartments, they spent much of their young adulthood living frugally in rented hotel rooms in the then-bohemian Montparnasse neighborhood. In a 1946 article in *Life* magazine profiling Sartre and his "cult," the journalist, Bernard Frizell expresses shock that a man with such literary success should "continue to live like a poverty-stricken student" in a fourth-class Paris hotel. Frizell associates Sartre's way of dwelling with his "bleak philosophy of pessimism" (59). However, things were about to change.

As their fame and fortune grew and they could afford fancier digs, Sartre moved with his twice-widowed mother into a small apartment. De Beauvoir, then 46, with money she received from the 1954 French literary Prix Goncourt, bought a studio apartment a five-minute walk to Sartre's place. For decor, both preferred a spartanly appointed interior. They surrounded themselves with books, a few artworks (most often given to them by artist friends), record players and collections, and a desk and a typewriter. Sartre also had a piano on which he and his mother played duets. While the intellectual duo had little to say about existential decor, their good friend Maurice Merleau-Ponty did write about "at-homeness" and how we are situated as bodies in space and time. His ideas have had considerable impact on architects and city planners.

Merleau-Ponty fell into the company of Simone de Beauvoir and Jean-Paul Sartre when they were students at the École Normale Supérieure and the Sorbonne in the late 1920s. They became lifelong friends who shared the central tenet that philosophy must be grounded in an analysis of the concrete experiences, perceptions, and the day-to-day challenges of human existence. He was, however, less attracted to Sartre and de Beauvoir's fascination with radical freedom, being-towards-death, or the perpetual conflict with the Other that fills the scenes and dialogues of Sartre's plays and de Beauvoir's novels. Instead, he would make his philosophical contributions in terms of what he called the "lived body." Merleau-Ponty gathered information about human perception that was emerging from then-contemporary research in experimental psychology.

Once the trio had completed their degrees, they went off separately to various parts of France to take jobs teaching in high schools. Eventually, they gravitated back to Paris where, like many other Parisian intellectuals, they found places to live in low-cost hotels in the Saint-Germain-des-Prés neighborhood. There they frequented cafés such as Les Deux Magots, Le Dome, and the Café de Flore where they exchanged their latest ideas, flirted, smoked, ate their meals and drank. They also did a great deal of their writing and thinking in what amounted to an office away from home.

When Simone de Beauvoir made extended visits to the United States in the late 1940s and 50s, she found middle and upper middle class homes and apartments overheated and over-decorated. She was most at home in a Greenwich Village apartment where the literati lived. But she also loved the adobe haciendas of the high desert town of Sedona, Arizona, and said she could imagine living there.

Like Sartre, Merleau-Ponty was a soldier in World War II and was likewise taken prisoner. At the end of the war in 1945, he teamed up with Sartre to launch the influential literary, political and philosophical journal, *Les Temps Modernes*, reputedly named after the famous Chaplin film, *Modern Times*. Traveling in the company of his existentialist friends, Merleau-Ponty embraced many of their ideas. But he modified them under the influence of Edmund Husserl, the founder of phenomenology.

Merleau-Ponty realized that while it may be the starting point for philosophical investigation, every act of consciousness depends upon the fact that we are embodied beings and that it is only and always through the body that we comport ourselves as being-in-the-world. For Merleau-Ponty, "the perceiving mind is an incarnate mind."

Merleau-Ponty examined the multiple ways in which visual perception functions as a non-self-conscious mode of engagement with the environment. This orientation made his contributions to the analysis of being-in-the-world fertile ground for followers to elaborate on his ideas. One such investigation runs parallel to Heidegger's notion of "dwelling," that of "being-at-home." In this way, Merleau-Ponty's work was applied to the field of architecture and environmental design.

ANYONE HOME?

Drawing on Merleau-Ponty's theories, University of Maine philosopher Kirsten Jacobson discovered that not only is the body a way that we are "at-home-in-the-world" but that our relationship to actual homes of wood, brick, glass, stone, and concrete can be understood as parallel embodiments; that homes are a "second skin" within which we find not only shelter, privacy and security but also, as she wrote in a 2009 journal article, "a place of self-nourishment and self-development" (359).

When we read Jacobson's description that home is the place where "the outside world can be temporarily set aside," and that it is the location where we not only feel sheltered from outside intrusion but it is a place "to recollect oneself in a space of familiarity" (358), we begin to sense the subtle yet profound meanings of being-at-home.

Jacobson quotes from Merleau-Ponty's French contemporary, Gaston Bachelard's 1964 work, The Poetics of Space, where the author provocatively contends: "The house shelters daydreaming, the house protects the dreamer, the house allows one to dream in peace" (The Poetics of Space, p. 6). Bachelard does not mean literally "dreaming," but rather what we might call communing with oneself in the form of daydreams, fantasies and musings. In other words, our home is a space in which we are not only "inside" a shelter, but where we can go inside ourselves. In this sense, not only does the mind possess a body but also the body possesses a mind.

Merleau-Ponty did not limit being-at-home to a person's domicile. Like his philosophical compatriots, he regarded the neighborhood in which one chose to live as an extended part of dwelling. Cafes, bookstores, bakeries, butcher shops and parks were intimate parts of the psychic landscape. The ethnic diversity of neighbors, their places of worship, the smells and music wafting from their windows were also important aspects of the milieu in which the French existentialists lived. So while a domicile may provide a semblance of at-homeness, one's experience of the wider community one shared-with others, might make one feel connected or isolated.

Surely we have come far from everyday expectations of occupying a house of brick, glass, and stucco, wood and perhaps steel. It's more like occupying a metaphorical house than a real one. And yet if we think about how we talk about our homes we hear existential resonance in words like threshold, footprint, hearth, foundation, illumination, intimacy, privacy, surroundings, and so on. Some people give their home interiors a sanctuary atmosphere by creating small, tabletop shrines with Buddha figures, candles, crystals or crosses. Many Jews affix a mezuzah (a piece of parchment inscribed with certain verses from the Hebrew Bible, enclosed in a decorative case) to the doorframe of an entryway. Even among the secular we often find tabletop or book shelve groupings of ceramic or wood-carved chickens, cats and owls. From an anthropological point of view, they resemble totemic shrines. Also common in households are framed photos and painted portraits of both living and deceased family members along with passed on heirlooms that serve to pay homage to ancestral kin.

Thinking of a home as a haven, refuge or sanctuary brings us closer to Heidegger's fourfold unity and what it means to dwell. In this sense, a mountain cabin may address us more eloquently in the language of dwelling than a brand new mansion in the suburbs. As Alain de Botton puts it in *The Architecture of Happiness,* "We depend on our surroundings obliquely to embody the moods and ideas we respect and then to remind us of them" (107). To de Botton, we want the external surroundings of a home to re-enforce our identities and enable us to bring our values "within."

Heidegger's ideal of dwelling is almost impersonal in following certain austere harmonies that contrast sharply with what, by contrast, would seem the subjective dictates of taste, comfort and self-image that function as the basis for most modern homes. His orientation comes closer to what might be called "sacred space" in contrast to an egocentric style that bears the stamp of the householder's and/or the architect's self-image. If you belonged to a traditional society in which the form and materials of dwellings were prescribed by culturally and religiously derived tenets, you might achieve Heidegger's ideal. For example, Hindu temple architecture conforms to strict religious models that incorporate elements of astronomy and mystically imbued geometry. This is also true of Greek temples of the Classic period.

In Hindu belief, the temple represents the macrocosm of the universe as well as the microcosm of inner space. Related principles found in the Sanskrit treatises on architecture, *Vastu shastras*, have been applied to some contemporary home dwellings whose inhabitants seek to live by transcendent principles rather than egoistic preferences. The recommendations for this type of sacred architecture include where to locate the *puja* or prayer room (northeast), the kitchen (southeast or northwest with the person facing north when cooking), and the householder's bedroom (on the southwest corner of the building). When sleeping, the householder's head should be oriented in a south or west direction. This type of dwelling arrangement is meant to enhance a sense of integrity and right living. This prescribed architecture underscores that being-at-home-in-the-world presents an existential challenge to live a well ordered, spiritually disciplined life.

CHANGING HOUSEHOLDS

Unlike Heidegger's Black Forest residents whose families have occupied the same places for generations, few of us in the United States and in other post-industrial societies live in ancestral homes or even multi-generational hometowns. We move a lot – for work, schooling or family matters. Moving households multiple times makes us more sensitive to how a home is not only a physical place but also a conceptual one.

Once home becomes an idea it tends also to generate certain expectations about comfort, privacy, intimacy, status and identity. One's abode becomes the narrative of "my home." Still, some people struggling to make ends meet experience the vulnerability of homelessness or the drabness of public housing. For others, home can mean the regimentation of an institutional setting such as a prison, an orphanage, or a health care facility. Though at the other end of the spectrum, even the most palatial domain may fail to satisfy a certain longing for a safe and secure place in which to experience peaceful wellbeing.

Changing households at any age can be challenging. Boxing and unboxing our material goods can take a physical and psychic toll. It's not only our "stuff" but also emotions that get transported. For those building or remodeling a home, the long list of choices can be daunting. Selecting drawer pulls, paint colors and even a style of mailbox requires time and research. Owners' decisions are conditioned by factors such as budget, practicality and aesthetic judgment. What we "like" is often a matter of what we are accustomed to, perhaps what our spouse desires, or what we associate with the home or homes in which we grew up. The tiniest detail – a doorknob, a light fixture, or the placement of a picture – is charged with subtle meanings. In mid- or later life, with the accumulation of memories and associations, and with perhaps more free time in which to deliberate on making "the right choices," creating the space to call home becomes a statement about our values and priorities. While some people aspire to a showy "trophy" house, others opt for one that reflects "green" values.

Moving to a new home in the second half of life, whether to a spot on the other side of town or in a distant state, may hold the promise of a fresh start. Or does it? Many people discover that relocating to a new community doesn't automatically produce desired changes. To use a phrase attributed to mindfulness author Jon Kabat-Zinn, "Wherever you go, there you are." A fresh start requires a fresh outlook and possibly a change in demeanor. Perhaps we always carry our metaphorical home and accompanying baggage with us. Feeling truly "at-home" in a new place is sometimes illusive. Just when we might be in a position to make our freest choices about how and where we want to live, we may find ourselves stymied by conflict and confusion. On the other hand, in reestablishing a home we may discover that our new domicile fits us like a beautifully tailored suit of clothes.

I became an observer of home relocation after I moved to Asheville for a career change that allowed me to integrate backgrounds in philosophy and gerontology.

In the late 1970s I started to lead educational programs for older adults at senior centers and public libraries. I then went to work for The National Council on the Aging in Washington, D.C., running their national arts nities programs. When in 1988 I was recruited to establish a ⌐ased lifelong learning program at UNC Asheville, the NC Center for Creative Retirement, my two areas of expertise became united. As director of the program, I helped to develop and lead workshops for people considering relocating in retirement. This enabled me to observe individuals in the throes of a threefold life transition. They were uprooting themselves from a familiar locale while, in many cases, leaving behind a life of full-time work and an identity-defining career.

Another way I have followed the process of how people go about finding an existing home or building a new one is through my wife, Gail, a realtor. She deals primarily with retirement-age individuals and couples considering relocating to Asheville from other parts of the country or who, having bought one home, then decide, perhaps a decade later, to move to another home more suitable to their changing situation.

While confidentiality is sacrosanct, I have on more than one occasion overheard telephone conversations with clients and, on many occasions, met them either during the period of the home search or after, when some of them became our friends. Gail uses a client profile whose thirty-three questions and clients' subsequent answers (from both spouses) help her to present those homes that most closely meet their requirements. I have gleaned some insights from these two sources, insights that reveal various dimensions of what it means to dwell.

A home chosen in retirement is sometimes different from earlier homes in people's lives. Previously, it was the location of and access to work and possibly family of origin that dictated the general area for habitation. With children grown up and often scattered and proximity to the office, plant or lab no longer an issue, these clients are now free to go wherever they please and to live in the part of a newly chosen town, suburb or countryside that best suits them.

The usual factors of square footage, number of bedrooms, asking price, property taxes, and type of neighborhoods are still relevant in the new setting. Yet other factors now command their attention: the desire for acreage, seclusion, or the opposite: close proximity to neighbors as in a multistory condominium or in a mixed-age, single-family home neighborhood. For some, a planned development that might include a commons area, clubhouse, pool and other communal amenities is especially attractive because, for newcomers, these settings provide immediate opportunities to make new friends. For others, the proximity of a local university's lifelong learning program means access to an affinity group of people who are like-minded and value education and the youthful atmosphere of a college campus.

Given our topography, a town surrounded by forested mountains, some people want a scenic view. Long-range views can be taken from on high (mountainside or ridge), looking down (into a valley or town), looking out (across acres of fields dotted with houses and barns), or even looking up (e.g. at ridgelines, hillsides, or woods). To "have a view," as if possessing one, may give the status-seeking householder the feeling of arriving at the top, in command, and looking down on those "below." For others, a mountain or valley view produces states of calm or even sublimity as one experiences being a small part of something greater, a kind of overwhelming grandeur that is not threatening but, rather, reassuring.

Some people seek land to build their dream home, others to remodel or renovate an existing home to enhance its architectural charm while bringing it up to current standards. In building new, we intend to inhabit a future that is yet to be. In renovating, we come to inhabit and partake in someone else's past, recreating it to suit our own personal vision.

Many of Gail's clients have experiences from previous moves when they relocated because of business, service in the military or federal government, or because they tried another retirement location and found it wanting. They know how to assess the real estate market and how to go about integrating themselves into a community where they might not know any other people.

Most of Gail's clients are couples. Some appear relatively harmonious. But some couples are at odds about their needs. Their differences become exacerbated in retirement because they are freer now to consider a wide range of options no longer constrained by practical necessity. Long-simmering differences come to the fore as they once again engage in the drama of making a house a home. These differences are usually resolvable through a series of compromises, the give and take of any relationship. But some couples' negotiations about the place to call home grows contentious as an emotional history of homemaking and remaking reaches a crisis.

HOW COUPLES DWELL

"Susan and Frank" moved to Asheville from a midsize town in the Midwest that was home to a major university. The long cold winters had been too much for them and when work and family were no longer anchors holding them in place, they headed south. Finding them a home was a challenge for Gail because while Frank said he wanted to live out in the country away from people, Susan made it clear that she did not. She wanted to live closer to the amenities that made Asheville attractive to her, including the university's lifelong learning program and the various arts and cultural organizations in the downtown area. Susan, a vivacious woman in her early 60s who had been the head of a hospital's nursing department, was outgoing and cheerful. She wanted to jump right in and get involved in the community.

Frank was reluctant and diffident. Gail found him hard to read. He seemed intent on leading the life of a hermit. How, during the course of a fairly long marriage and raising children, had they managed to stay together? Still, they did a lot of things together like dining out and going to concerts. Frank had been a civil engineer. During a brief conversation, when Gail brought them by our house, he let me know that, as far as work and career were concerned, he'd "had enough of that." Now he wanted to "watch the trees grow."

Where then could they find a home that satisfied both their mutual as well as sharply divergent needs? The home they found that they could both agree on was located in a semi-rural area on a small tract of land but only 15 minutes to the places that Susan wanted to frequent. The front of the house faced other homes in the neighborhood and the back faced a wooded hillside laced by a meandering creek. The basement would accommodate a wood shop, something Frank had dabbled in on and off for several years. As it turned out, Frank would not only set up a wood-working shop, he created a so-called "man cave" in a separate part of the lower level. Susan told us that Frank had his classical and jazz music collection, a sound system, a shelf of books he planned to read, a sleeper sofa, several lamps, a Lazy-boy chair and even hot plate and kettle for making tea or instant coffee. There was also a small toilet area with a sink and mirror. "It's as if he's gone camping inside the house," Susan laughed.

The rest of the house was what we might call suburban modern with a few rustic touches such as a fieldstone surround, wood-burning stove, built-in bookshelves and lots of wood trim around windows and doorways. Susan said it wasn't like their house up north, which was a much older, arts and crafts style home in a neighborhood convenient to shopping, restaurants, the public library and the kinds of coffee houses you would expect in a university town. Still, she could live in this new home, especially since for her it was more of a place from which to head out into the wider world of daytime and some evening activities. Frank stayed home or went for long solitary walks on woodland trails fairly close to the house.

I saw a lot of Susan as she became involved in the lifelong learning program, not only taking classes but also serving on volunteer committees. She was having a great time. When I asked about Frank she would roll her eyes and then chirp, "He's okay." It was probably about a year later that I learned from some other volunteers that Susan and Frank were moving back to their former hometown. I ran into Susan one day and asked if this were true. She nodded. "We miss the old neighborhood. The weather is yucky but we really liked living there. Besides," she sighed, "the way things are, it's like Frank and I are leading separate lives. I'm thinking this will bring us closer together." And then they were gone.

Several years later I heard a follow-up story from a member of the program who had kept in touch with Susan. Not long after they had moved back to their Midwestern university town the couple had separated. Susan was doing okay as she had a good support network of old friends. She had gotten involved in the lifelong learning program at the university and that was helping her to move on with her life. Strangely enough, it seemed that Frank had moved back to our area. Apparently fulfilling his quest for the hermetic life, he was reportedly living in a mountainside cabin about 30 miles from Asheville. Then about a year later we heard that Frank had been found lying dead on his cabin floor. Was the cause of death a stroke, heart attack or possibly suicide? No one amongst his circle of acquaintances knew exactly what had happened.

For Susan and Frank, their house became a metaphor of their relationship. They were living in two separate worlds inside one house. Frank enacted his withdrawal from the world in an isolated setting in the woods and then he vanished. Susan reestablished herself in her previous neighborhood, rebuilding her life on familiar grounds.

Another couple's story also involves a return move.

"Jerry and Helen" moved to Asheville from Manhattan where for many years they owned a unit in a high-rise apartment building with a concierge service and a doorman. Jerry had recently retired from the television advertising business. Helen, who had earlier worked in interior design until their children were born, volunteered as a museum docent. One of their daughters had moved to Asheville with her husband several years earlier and Jerry and Helen had visited them several times. Jerry loved the outdoors, the relative quiet compared with Manhattan and also the clean air and four mild seasons. Helen liked these qualities, too, but she wasn't sure about the local culture. Despite Asheville's eclectic make up and thriving cultural scene, it wasn't, as Helen put it, "like being in the City."

The couple purchased a condo in an attractive gated development of single and duplex units spread out across beautifully landscaped, rolling hills about fifteen minutes from downtown. The majority of the homeowners were retired or semi-retired couples. The gated condo community suited Jerry and Helen because they wanted to be able to "lock and leave" at the drop of a hat to visit friends back in "the City" or go to see their other daughter in Texas.

Not long after settling in, Jerry came to see me in my office on campus. Dressed as if he had just strolled off the golf course in khakis, a stripped polo and loafers, the tanned, youthful looking Jerry could have been a model for a Brooks Brothers catalog. Belying his upbeat appearance, Jerry was unhappy. He explained that he had come to the realization that he had retired "too early." Yes, a corporate buyout had foreshortened his career unexpectedly. Nevertheless, the separation bonus was so significant that along with their life savings and investments, he believed their financial situation was secure for their later years. But he missed work, the challenges, the people and the environment.

As I listened to Jerry, something occurred to me. I had read in our local newspaper that the high school had recently acquired the equipment to establish an in-school video production studio. I knew the teacher who was in charge of the drama and mass communication program of the school. Would Jerry consider having me arrange a visit with the teacher to find out if there might be some volunteer role for him to play? Jerry was intrigued and we set up an appointment.

A few weeks later, Jerry dropped in again and thanked me for the suggestion. The high school teacher was thrilled to have someone with Jerry's wealth of experience and expertise. The teacher was himself just learning how to use the equipment. As it turned out, not only did Jerry have a significant presence in the school, he made arrangements for the teacher, his students and some of their parents, to go on a field trip to Manhattan where, using his prior contacts, he set up tours of some of the major TV studios. The group met with people in the industry, including some well-known TV newsroom personalities.

Jerry's collaborative venture went on for about a year. I would read articles in the newspaper about the students' innovative work and notice frequent mention of Jerry's name. Then one day I heard that the couple had sold their condo and were moving back to Manhattan. Jerry dropped by to say good-bye. "It's been great," he said, "but Helen is not happy here. She just doesn't feel like she fits in. She hasn't found her niche. It's weird," he shook his head. "She walks around this beautiful condo that has twice as much space as our old apartment and she feels... what did she say? Disoriented. She complains the whole set up feels artificial. Like she's part of a stage set. Isn't that funny? I mean coming from Manhattan? What could be more artificial?"

Jerry further explained that they were buying an apartment in the same building where they had lived for over 20 years. Moreover, he was starting an independent consulting business and a trade association for people who specialized in writing TV and radio advertising jingles. In short, they were going back to their former lives and the place where they would both feel at home. What had gone on between the couple in private for them to reach this accommodation? I do not know. What I do know is that they could not find a way to feel at home – together – in Asheville. They found the comfort they sought together in the familiar hustle and bustle of the streets and sidewalks of Manhattan. Gotham was their Black Forest.

Sarah's Story

Gail helped "Sarah," a single woman, purchase a piece of property, which until recently, was the site of a mobile home. Sarah moved to Asheville from New Orleans where she had grown up. Never married, she continued to work part-time from home as a project manager for an Internet start-up, a field she had entered through her background in library science.

Now in her mid-50s, Sarah was an avid fitness devotee who worked out at a local gym and kept to a vegetarian diet, a practice of many years.

Sarah told Gail that she planned to build her dream home following certain criteria. It would be energy-efficient, simple but elegant in design, and it would have several features from the home of her childhood – a breakfast nook with built-in window seats, a butler's pantry for extra dishes and glassware, and a fenced yard big enough to grow vegetables. While these were features from her family's nearly 100-year-old New Orleans home, Sarah's home would be free of ornamentation both inside and out. Additionally, as Sarah was a cat lover (as were her parents), she wanted to have what she called a "catio," a large, wire and wood framed enclosure attached to the back of her house and accessible through a cat door in a wall of the living room.

The house, on almost an acre of land, was at the end of a narrow street of small bungalows that had once been occupied by families of men and women who worked in a furniture factory about a mile away but were now the homes of blue-collar retirees and recently arrived families with young children.

We visited with Sarah and she showed us around her new home, commenting, "This is how I've wanted to live for years. I have finally been able to bring my vision to life." Sarah shared that she had not previously felt truly "at home" in places she had lived before building her own home. Some were apartments in multistory buildings and others in large homes that had been divided up. "Oh, some of them were totally charming, lovely details like ceiling moldings and French doors leading onto porches with wrought iron railings all decked out in bougainvillea."

Almost the entire interior of Sarah's home was painted a soft white, giving the rooms what is called in museum terminology the character of a "white box." With a large sliding glass door opening onto the surrounding pine and leafy woods and the solid doors to other rooms painted in subtle shades of blue, rose and yellow, the house felt colorful and intimate despite having grey-toned concrete floors equipped, as Sarah proudly explained, with radiant floor heating.

On our tour we were followed around by a trio of black and white kittens who would pause to tangle with one another and then scurry to catch up with us. "They're with me for a couple of weeks," Sarah said, pointing to the kittens. "I help to get them ready for adoption from the animal shelter." Just then a large tabby poked its head through the rubber flap of the cat door and cautiously made its way onto the living room couch where it curled up.

"Finally, I feel like I am truly in a place that is mine," said Sarah, reaching down to pick up one of the kittens. "I mean, I belong to this place and it belongs to me," she went on, giving the kitten a careful inspection. "There's just the right balance between feeling safely enclosed but not contained. My house is not the place I retreat to. It's where I... what's the word?" Sarah waved her hand holding the kitten, which didn't seem to mind the ride. "Ah, yes, transcend myself. Do you know what I mean?"

Sarah's account of both replicating features of the home in which she grew up while also opting for a totally opposite, modernist vibe, suggests that in the ways we "dwell" we reenact and revise scenes from our childhoods. Researcher Kirsten Jacobson likens this to "nesting." Inspired by the 1995 work of Claire Cooper Marcus (*House as Mirror of Self: Exploring the Deeper Meaning of Home*), Jacobson, in the previously cited 2009 article, notes that unlike other animals, human "nesting" is not instinctive. Rather we learn how to inhabit through a process that begins in the home of our childhood. As adults, we may seek to replicate the atmosphere of that home or we may rebel against it for a variety of reasons. Nevertheless, our childhood home or homes are the reference points from which we transform a domicile into the place we can call our own. Making a home, asserts Marcus, has its origins in "playing house," something we repeat and rehearse as we move into a dorm room, student apartment, or a place we come to share with a significant other or others. In this sense, dwelling is also an activity of remembering. Dwelling as remembering is often a key ingredient to making a home in later life, even when we experience the spatial diminishing of our nest.

DEPENDENCY

While these examples focus on people in the early stages of retirement years, eventually most will either die while still occupying these homes or make another move to a form of congregate housing or possibly move in with family or friends. If their first relocation or renovation is all about obtaining desired "amenities," the second is to compensate for increasing "dependencies." Apart from family members' homes, these latter settings range from providing minimal support services such as housekeeping, a personal emergency alert system, and some meals, to hospital-like 24-hour assistance and monitoring.

These housing variations include the independent living facility (ILF), assisted living facility (ALF), the skilled care facility (SCF) commonly called a nursing home, and for those who can afford them, the continuing care retirement community (CCRC) that offers entry to and transition across all three levels depending on need. Within this range are many innovative alternatives, most designed to try to make dependency-oriented housing more humane, less institutional and more truly communal while preserving residents' sense of dignity and independence. Infrequently, individuals with major dependencies will move into the home of another family member such as an adult child. In-law apartments and "granny flats" have been around for a long time.

How then does one dwell in a situation defined by dependency? One way is by introducing the familiar into the environment of the unfamiliar. In many ILFs and ALFs, residents bring their own furniture and decorations. Personal mementoes such as family pictures, cherished artworks, books and recordings may remain in the possession of individuals and couples in the space they occupy right up to the time of death. To the outsider, these small gestures towards preserving a semblance of at-homeness may seem trivial. But to individuals whose world is shrinking, a single cherished item may transport them from a cubicle-sized room to a veritable palace of memory.

During the time I served as a hospice home visitor, I would spend about an hour and a half each week with my client "Rosemary." My memories of these visits remain vivid.

A tall woman in her early 80s, Rosemary's pixie-style haircut handsomely frames her tanned, strong-boned face. She lives in an assisted living facility where a number of her friends are neighbors. Breakfasts and dinners are provided, as are chore services. A hospice nurse checks in on her weekly and keeps tabs on her lab results. A social worker, a psychologist and a music therapist are other weekly visitors. "I've got quite a crew attending to me," remarks Rosemary whose tone conveys a mix of gratitude and frustration over the annoying but also necessary intrusion into her domestic space. The long-term effects of Parkinson's Disease and the medication she takes to calm her tremors leave her a bit unsteady on her feet. Some other health problems she prefers not to discuss have landed her with a six-month to live prognosis. Rosemary is remarkably adept at using her walker and maneuvers deftly from room to room.

The facility occupies a four-story building that looks like any other modern condominium except that it has a high porte cochère to accommodate emergency vehicles. A brightly lit lobby equipped with a wall of mailboxes and a check-in office window gives the building the atmosphere of a college dorm. While the building's placement and architecture is far from Heidegger's fourfold unity, the furnishing with which the residents decorate their units do contain indirect evocations of earth, sky, mortals and immortals.

Today, I'm getting a tour of Rosemary's few cherished room decorations. "This is a hammered copper urn I brought back from India," she says, pointing to a table supporting a large exotic looking lamp. "Literally, I had to carry the thing in my lap to get it home," she adds with a laugh. I ask Rosemary about the unusual shade. "Oh," she says, "I had the hardest time trying to find a shade appropriate for such an unusual lamp base. But one day, when I was living in Key West, I went into a store that sold these funny lamps that had shades made of bird feathers. I asked the guys who owned the store whether they had any bigger sized ones. They didn't. But bring in the lamp, they told me, and we'll see about making one. Which, as you can see, they did."

Rosemary's compact apartment holds other unique objects – an incised clay jar that, she tell me, comes from a Peruvian mountain village. Against her living room wall is a "partner's desk" with a side built-in bookcase, something that might once have sat in a mid-nineteenth century accounting office. Above the desk hangs a reproduction of what Rosemary a few weeks earlier told me was a Chinese Song dynasty painting. She suggested that I look at it closely. As I stood in front of the painting, admiring how the artist had captured the craggy peaks just poking through a lacy mist, I noticed there were figures of robed men using walking sticks. They were completely dwarfed by the landscape of huge old trees, rocks, and bamboo forests. And there were also miniature-thatched huts tucked among boulders. Rosemary, who had majored in art history in college, told me these were retirement retreats for scholar-officials who had lost power and sought to find solace by withdrawing into nature.

"They're conversation pieces," says Rosemary, glancing around. "Uh-huh," she smiles, nodding. "They do a lot of talking to me." While Rosemary is recounting the memories associated with the various objects, the head of a black curly-haired dog appears from around a corner. Recognizing a familiar scent, the dog trots into the room, approaches me and rests his chin on my knee.

Important, though thus far missing from the existential-phenomeno-logical consideration of dwelling, are pets. For many a house without a pet is not a home. Enjoyed by over half the households in the United States, pet ownership is especially common amongst seniors who, often living on their own, find the company of a loyal cat, dog, bird or other pet to be of great comfort. The bond they develop with their pets can be deep; indeed, an older person's closest confidants often walk on four legs.

Until fairly recently pets such as dogs and cats were not allowed in dependency-oriented settings except for visits from service dogs accom-panied by volunteers or pet therapists. But that has changed. In the U.S., federal housing laws mandate that publically run facilities cannot prohibit residents' pet ownership provided they are able to care for the animal. While private facilities are not required to abide by these federal rules, many do allow pet ownership on varying levels. Rosemary is fortu-nate to live in one such location.

"Max, mind your manners," says Rosemary, chastising the animal. Max turns and looks at Rosemary and then puts his head back on my knee. "You know," she says, "without a dog to keep me company, my place would seem empty. There's something about having another creature round about the place that is comforting." I scratch Max's head. He raises his eyes to study my face. "Plus it's a relief not to have someone who com-plains about every ache and pain and tells the same story three or four times in the same conversation. Just pure unbounded affection between the two of us."

Max seems to have gotten what he needed from me and now goes over to sit at Rosemary's feet. "Do you think dogs are self-conscious?" asks Rosemary. "I mean, do you think they are inclined to self-reflection or do they only live in the here and now?"

From a psychology class I had years ago, I learned of a study of the emergence of self-awareness in babies. The researchers put a small red dot on the baby's forehead, like the bindi worn by many Indian women. The baby is placed in front of a mirror where he or she can observe. At a certain age, a baby will notice the dot and put a finger to his or her forehead. This indicates recognition that the image in the mirror is that of the child's who also perceives that its own body has a strange, new decoration. So a child's recognition of having a body image is one of the first indications of the rise of self- and body-consciousness. I've had dogs that would growl at a dog appearing on a TV screen and bark at their own image as reflected in, say, the glass doors of a fireplace. Certainly dogs have memory, not only of the visual and auditory world but, even more remarkably, of scent.

Before I can launch into my account of babies and bindi dots, Rosemary offers her view. "I think we project ourselves into our pets. We can't really know what they're thinking. Maybe they're not thinking at all." Rosemary raps on the wooden chair arm. "The main thing is we've made our home here."

Max lifts his head at the sound of knuckles on wood and looks at Rosemary, sniffs a couple of times and lies back down.

Rosemary chortles. "All Max has to do to make himself at home is walk in a little circle two or three times and then flop down. Sometimes he sprawls out like one of those ladies on a couch in a seraglio painting. Other times, he curls up. Dogs are moody. Eh, Maxie?"

PHENOMENOLOGICAL DOGS

Merleau-Ponty must have had dogs and possibly cats. For him, non-human animals count as existential creatures that have "their own style of being-in-the-world." From Merleau-Ponty's perspective, Rosemary's Max displays "gestures of behavior... which [Max] traces in the space around [him]." The sprawl, curl of repose, and incessant sniffing are part of Max's canine way of being-in-the-world. However, says Merleau-Ponty, animals like Max "do not allow the showing through of a consciousness" because, unlike humans "whose whole essence is to know," dogs, though they may receive treats to learn tricks, find even an unexamined life worth living. What we can say about non-human animals is that they have "a certain manner of treating the world," which is their way "of existing."

Of dogs, cats, birds, even fish, our French existential phenomenologist says they are "sentient-sensible beings," like us. We find commonality with them, something Merleau-Ponty identified as a "strange kinship," a mutuality he termed "interanimality" (*Nature*, 278). For example, we too are curious about smells (of food, flowers, perfume) when entering someone else's household. We are sometimes startled by visual changes to the familiar as dogs will take on a frozen posture and perk up their ears when an unfamiliar object (visitor's car parked along the street) appears in their familiar milieu. Unselfconsciously, we may perform a sort of waltz around a newfound or stylishly clad friend to assess the person from every angle. As different species, yet kindred beings, we share with dogs what Merleau-Ponty called the "flesh of the world."

THE SQUEEZE

I was rather slender as a child, a disadvantage when playing tackle football or street hockey but advantageous when summoned by our neighbor, the forgetful "Mrs. Hartman," who occasionally locked herself out of her house. She'd come knocking at our door and ask my mother if I was home and whether she could borrow me for just a minute. She took me by the hand and walked me to her side door and then lifted me into the open milk chute. Fortunately, the inside chute door was left unlatched and I managed to push it open and to wiggle my way through the space so that my head and arms were inside the house while the rest of my body remained lodged in the compartment. I liked briefly to rest in that position, not because of the exertion but because it gave me an entirely different perspective on life. Maybe the position triggered some kind of primal birth memory or a dawning apprehension of being a divided consciousness, an interior and exterior, an insider and outsider.

I was like a thief. I could squeeze my way into any number of neighborhood milk chutes to then walk around, sit at a table, open a refrigerator and make believe that I lived there. Yes, I was playing house. In the midst of this reverie, Mrs. Hartman, still holding onto my ankles, would whisper into the chute, "Hey, there. Are you all right? Can't you get through?" I knew there would come a day when my childhood advantage would disappear. I'd grow broader and thicker. But for the moment, I could wiggle my legs and push with my hands against the inside wall as I let myself down to the landing floor where I would rest my forehead before slithering across the little braided throw rug, my feet sliding down the wall behind me. Then I'd unbolt Mrs. Hartman's back door.

REFERENCES

Bachelard, Gaston (1964). *The Poetics of Space*. Trans. Maria Jolas. Boston: Beacon Press.

Bergson, Henri (1913). *Time and Free Will: An Essay on the Immediate Data of Consciousness*. Tr. F. L. Pogson. London: George Allen & Co.

Botton, Alain de (2006). *The Architecture of Happiness*. New York: Vintage Books.

Descartes, Rene (1968). *Discourse on Method and The Meditations*. Translated by F. E. Sutcliffe. London: Penguin Books

Friezell, Bernard (1946). "Existentialism: Postwar Paris Enthrones A Bleak Philosophy of Pessimism." *Life*, 1 June. Pp. 59-61.

Heidegger, Martin (1971/2001). "Building Dwelling Thinking," in *Poetry, Language, Thought*, translated by Albert Hofstadter, Harper Colophon Books, New York.

Jacobson, Kirsten (2009). "A Developed Nature: A Phenomenological Account of the Experience of Home." *Continental Philosophical Review*, 42:355-373.

Marcus, Clare Cooper (1995). *House as Mirror of Self: Exploring the Deeper Meaning of Home*. Berkeley, CA: Conari Press.

Merleau-Ponty, Maurice (1962). *The Phenomenology of Perception*. Trans. Colin Smith. New York: Routledge & Kegan Paul Ltd.

_____ (1963). *The Structure of Behavior*, trans. A.L. Fisher, Boston: Beacon Press.

Merleau-Ponty, Maurice (2003). *Nature, Course Notes from the College de France*. Tr. Robert Vallier. Evanston: Northwestern University Press.

6. AUTHORITY

For Sartre and de Beauvoir, the role of the writer was inescapably a matter of political engagement. Authority and authorship went hand in hand. In contrast, for Kierkegaard authority was a matter of separating oneself from mass movements and taking up the position of the outsider. Authority for Kierkegaard meant inward appropriation and living by the maxim, "only the truth that edifies is truth for you." To evoke his readers' own authority, Kierkegaard employed techniques of indirect communication, using pseudonyms and fictional characters to engage readers to look into themselves. This polarity of viewpoints is what makes generalizing about "existentialists" so difficult. Encompassing this polarity, however, is the way its authors would resonate with the motto of the 1960s "youth revolt" and its exhortation: "question authority." The legacy of that period lives on in the light of our sixth star. To gaze upon it, we enter a scene from the near present.

JAZZ SCENE

We were out with a couple, "Darlene" and "Barry," who were new to our area. We discovered our common interest in jazz at a neighborhood Halloween party. Seeing Barry sporting a fake goatee, black beret and neck scarf and Darlene striding around in black tights, black turtle neck sweater and black ballet slippers, I at first thought they were dressed as bohemians of the Parisian Left Bank.

"*Les Existentialistes? Mais non!*" Barry laughed, flourishing what turned out to be a chocolate cigarette. "*Nous sommes de grands artistes de jazz,*" he bellowed.

Darlene's get-up reminded me of Audrey Hepburn's costume in the 1957 musical, *Funny Face*, when she does her jazz-inspired "crazy dance" in a subterranean bohemian nightclub. In what is clearly a satirical take on the Left Bank existentialist lifestyle promoting self-expression and independent thinking (and not a little libertarianism), Hepburn plays the type of free spirited female as in other movies like *Breakfast at Tiffany's*. Her character is emblematic of several thematic concerns of existentialism. The Introduction to the *Bloomsbury Companion to Existentialism* mentions eight, among which are: "an emphasis on authenticity" and "denigration of its opposite," and "a rejection of any external determination of morality or value" (3-4). In other words, not ceding authority to others. Darlene and Barry's outfits and his command of French intrigued me. Had they been participants in the youth revolt? I suggested to my wife that we should invite the "grands artistes de jazz" to join us for dinner at the Majestic.

A renovated former single-screen neighborhood movie theater, The Majestic was located on a street where used furniture stores, appliance stores and hair salons had been transformed into coffee houses, yoga studios and boutiques selling handmade clothing. We enjoyed going there on Sunday nights when you could make your dinner reservation to coincide with the jazz sessions.

Setting out water glasses, our waiter stepped back and with a ceremonial bow announced: "I'm Luke, I'll be looking after you tonight." He proceeded to explicate the list of designer cocktails and dinner specials (many compensating for the bad kind of cholesterol with virtuous heaps of kale). Luke then asked if we had any questions. We didn't. He smiled, nodded, and with another bow, moved off.

While the musicians were setting up their instruments on the stage, Gail scooted her chair toward Barry. Over the lively conversations all around and the rattling of plates and silverware, I couldn't make out what she was saying. She must have asked a question because Barry leaned in closer and nodded. The two were immediately immersed in conversation. Meanwhile, Darlene and I sat silently studying the organic chemistry of the cocktail menu. I was desperately trying to think of a good conversation opener but, before I came up with a hot topic like whether she and Barry had found a dentist yet, Darlene took the initiative. Setting down the menu, she leaned over so that her reading glasses slid toward the ball of her nose and in a conspiratorial voice whispered, "Got any weed, man?"

Her jet-black hair pulled into a ponytail secured with a red ribbon and with her gaping white blouse revealing prominent clavicles and an expanse of pale flesh, Darlene exuded the aura of a former hipster. Reading the confusion in my blank stare, Darlene landed a soft punch on my arm and laughed. "Hey man, be cool, be cool." Then she sat back, cocked her head coquettishly to one side and said, "Don't tell me you didn't go to smoky jazz clubs back in, where was it? Detroit? In the sixties?"

"Sure," I said. "We went to a place called The Minor Key." Then in an aside, I added, "But I didn't tell my parents."

"Of course not," said Darlene. "It was in a black neighborhood or you needed fake ID to get in, right?"

"The former, not the latter," I replied. "They didn't serve alcohol. You could get Turkish coffee and baklava. And you didn't need to light up. The air was so thick it stung your eyes."

"Yep," she exclaimed. "Those were the days."

"So you went to jazz clubs? Chicago?"

"The Windy City," said Darlene. "We'd go to the Green Mill. Ever heard of it?"

"Oh," I said. "It's famous. I've been there with my son who lives in the West Loop. Now there you would need fake ID. It's a bar, right?"

"I have a sister who's two years older," quipped Darlene, leaving me to fill in the rest. "The Green Mill's a landmark. A lot of other jazz clubs have come and gone. Rock and roll did them in. But now," Darlene's hand swept the room, "these jazz venues have made a comeback." She raised her water glass. "Hurrah!"

"Yes," I responded and, waving my cocktail menu, added, "And we can order Tequila Mockingbirds and stay out long past our curfew."

"Ha," Darlene snorted. "We can if we can stay awake. Fortunately, the smoking part is out." Darlene put her hand on my wrist and squeezed. "No Marlboro Men. But alas, no Mary Janes either."

"Times have changed," I nodded.

"Some for the better, some worse," said Darlene, in a mock woeful tone. "Say," she brightened up, "what were you reading in that era of Monk,

Mingus and Milt Jackson?" Darlene shook her head. "I don't mean for school. You know, stuff you got onto that fed your soul?"

"Oh," I replied, "some of the Beat poets like Ginsburg and Gary Snyder, and Corso."

"Gregory Corso," Darlene beamed. "You know his poem, 'Marriage'?" Darlene broke into a recitation.

> *Should I get married? Should I be Good?*
> *Astound the girl next door*
> *with my velvet suit and faustus hood?*

"Vintage Corso," I murmured.

"What about novels and highbrow intellectual stuff?" persisted Darlene.

I closed my eyes to conjure up a cinderblock and wood plank bookshelf that leaned against the wall in my campus apartment. "Well," I responded after I had made out some of the titles on the book spines, "I read Camus. You know, *The Plague, The Stranger.*"

Darlene nodded vehemently. "Yeah. Go on."

"Um, that little essay of Sartre's on how existentialism is a kind of humanism. And," I said with a smile, "I bought a copy of Betty Friedan's *The Feminine Mystique.* I think it had just come out. Ah, that must have been 63, 64?"

"Well weren't you the young man ahead of your times," she beamed.

"Actually, I'd just broken up with someone and thought I should know a lot more about, um, I guess back then I would have called them 'girls.'"

"Yes," said Darlene, "we were definitely girls." Darlene scrunched up her face. "I don't think the book would have helped you, though."

A bit taken aback as to what she meant, I gave a neutral, "Mm, maybe not."

Darlene laughed and put her hand on my wrist again. She was one of those women who are comfortable touching other people as if this were just an extended part of speech. "I'm sure you were a very cool dude and charmed the hell out of, you know, the girls."

"Well," I started into an explanation of my sheltered upbringing.

"So you would have been better off with Mr. Corso than Ms. Friedan." Darlene sat up straight and went into another Corso recitation:

And the priest! He looking at me as if I masturbated
asking me Do you take this woman for your lawful wedded wife?

And I trembling what to say...

Darlene paused. "You know how the line ends. Right?"

I nodded and we announced in unison: "Pie Glue!"

Darlene and I broke into guffawing while our spouses turned around and starred.

"What kind of pie did you want, honey?" my wife asked. "I don't know if it's on the menu."

"Pie for me and pie for you," I said, winking at Darlene.

"Oh," said Gail, "I'm happy to share."

Soon our protector, Luke, returned bearing the various elixirs of the night.

I sipped my Tequila Mockingbird and watched Darlene stir her Grey Goose on the rocks. No frivolous fruit juice-laced drinks for her. Setting her reading glasses on the bridge of her nose, she glanced at the dinner menu and then looked up at me.

"Isn't it great?" she announced, her hand making a wide sweep of the tables filling up with people who looked a lot like us.

"It's great that we're here to enjoy this," I replied.

"Uh-huh. There's that," said Darlene. "You know what I did after reading *The Feminine Mystique*?"

Many possibilities raced through my mind but censoring them, I shook my head.

"I changed majors. That's what I did," said Darlene, nodding thought-fully. "I was going to be a schoolteacher. First or maybe second grade. I liked kids that age. But after reading that book I saw the light. Went to my advisor and switched to becoming a business major. You see," Darlene fluttered her eyelashes and drawled, "I'm good with figures. And I did not want to have to lean on no man."

"That was a big decision. How did it turn out?" I asked, since I didn't know anything about what Darlene did before she and Barry retired and moved to Asheville. He, I'd heard, had been some kind of business executive who made frequent trips abroad.

"Oh, you bet your sweet ass it was a big decision," she said. "How did it turn out? Well, I eventually got to running my own accounting business. I had twenty-three people working for me. But that's not the point."

"Not the point of your changing majors?"

"Not the main point of my life decision. No, accounting was secondary. The main point is that I was defining myself as the kind of woman I wanted to be." Darlene counted with her fingers. "Independent, successful and a risk taker. Really," she added, "I think that was the first decision of my life. I mean one where I didn't consult my parents or some other authority figure."

"You were a pioneer."

"I was existentially inspired to take charge of my own life," declared Darlene. "Friedan's book made me realize I was taking the path of least resistance. One that had been laid out in front of me. Don't get me wrong. Teaching children is an honorable thing to do. But it wasn't my dream job. And I could see myself drifting into that passive female role. You know, just going along. Teacher, marriage, kids, the suburbs. And I'd be dependent on my husband. He'd call the shots. Friedan shook me. I woke up."

"You know, Friedan was influenced by Simone de Beauvoir. Did you ever read *The Second Sex*?"

"Read it?" Darlene laughed. "I was it!" She made a sharp jab at the table to reinforce her point. "That French woman. Beauvoir. I remember her name. She's one of your heroes?"

"Yes, de Beauvoir. That's the one. So, you've read her too?" I nodded. "You know, she also wrote a book about growing old."

Darlene's eyebrows went up. "Haven't read it. I don't feel I need to be reminded about wrinkles and age spots." Darlene studied the back of her hand that held her glass. "Or do you think I need Mademoiselle's advice?"

I paused to consider how I should respond. After I ran through my options, I decided to change the subject. "Isn't it amazing," I began, "that here we are a number of decades since we discovered the existentialists and we're still talking about them."

"And digging jazz, too," Darlene interrupted.

"Yes, and jazz, too. And here we are like right back where we were, as in the days of our youth."

"Well, that's very poetic. The days of our youth," she repeated. "Sounds like a soap opera. Anyway, they were more than a few decades ago and I for one have no desire to return to those times." Darlene picked up the dinner menu and studied it.

"What about the existentialists?" I asked, putting my hand on her wrist. "Do you think they're still relevant? I mean, to us. Today?"

Darlene regarded my hand, which I quickly withdrew. "You're imitating me," she laughed.

I'm sure my face turned red. Fortunately, the lighting in the music hall part of the restaurant had just been dimmed.

"It's okay," said Darlene, patting my hand. "I'm flattered." She turned to watch the musicians assembling their instruments, and then turned back to me. "Yes," she said. "Look, aren't we asking ourselves the same questions we asked in the days of our youth? When you're no longer the boss of an accounting firm, who are you then? Why are we still around when so many others we've known have already passed into the great unknown. What's our purpose? We don't have to pretend to be nice anymore." She leaned over and whispered, "Not that I ever was."

Again she grabbed my wrist. "What's our place in the universe? What lies on the other side of the grave, if anything?" Darlene threw up her hands. "We're right back where we were. Except for one thing. We're a lot smarter." She paused and stroked her chin. "Well, at least we're more experienced. What did we know about life, sitting in the student union with a copy of *Fear and Trembling* in our hands or walking around town feeling superior because we're toting a copy of *Being and Time?*"

"I guess we had some premonition that we should do something different with our lives."

"We were privileged thinking that we could." Darlene held her glass to her nose and then took a sip. Noticing that I was observing her, she

commented, "The sniff test. Just making sure they're using my vodka."
She took another sip. "And they are."

Setting her glass down, Darlene pointed toward the stage. "You know
why I love jazz?" she asked. By this time in our conversation I knew it was
a rhetorical question and that my role was to await her answer.

But, wanting to keep up my part in the conversation, I offered: "When
I first heard Coltrane playing a 15-minute improvisational solo of "My
Favorite Things" I was entranced. I didn't know you could take a song
from a Broadway musical and evoke such complex emotions." I counted
on my fingers: "Joy, despair, hope, anguish. It was thrilling. No, more than
thrilling. Transporting," I enthused.

Darlene narrowed her eyes as if she were making an appraisal of my
credibility. "Yes," said Darlene. "Those are all the things I love about jazz,
too. But there's something more, something that's underneath all that.
Something philosophical." Darlene smiled. She knew philosophy was my
academic domain. Was this a test?

"What you're describing, what Coltrane was doing, it's all about
freedom, about rebellion, about taking a tune from the pastel world of
the bourgeoisie and coloring in the dark shadows. That whole existentialist thing." Darlene closed her eyes as if she were picturing something. The
glistening sweat on Coltrane's brow toward the end of his solo? Or was
she hearing the other three members of the quartet, McCoy Tyner, Steve
Davis, and Elvin Jones, backing Coltrane with a sweetly intense, thrum-
ming wall of sound?

Darlene opened her eyes. "Sure," she announced, as though I already
knew what she had conjured up in her mind's eye. "Sure, that incredible
improv. Doing your own thing. Individualism." Darlene nodded as if that's
what I was thinking. "Freedom," she asserted, rapping the table. "Fucking
taking charge of your life. Declaring that you're your own authority. That
you're not just going to go along with all the nonsense you've been fed in
school and at home and on TV." She jabbed her finger toward the stage,
"Jazz, made in America but an African import. I love its defiance."

Darlene folded her arms. She had staked out her side of the table. As I
sipped my cocktail my mind drifted off to a literary character who medi-
tates on a style of music that led up to jazz.

EXISTENTIAL JAZZ

A famous scene in Sartre's novel *Nausea* occurs near the end when the protagonist, 30-year-old Antoine Roquentin who, returned from years of knock-about world travel, has settled in the fictional French seaport town of Bouville (Mudville) to finish his research on the life of an 18th-century political figure. It's three years later and he's again ready to venture on.

In this scene, Roquentin is waiting for his train. He goes for the last time to his hangout, the café *Au rendez-vous des cheminots*, (The Railroad Workers Meeting Place) and asks the waitress, Madeleine, to play his favourite record, the ragtime tune *Some Of These Days*. In the novel, Roquentin muses on the song, believing it was born out of the "worn-out body of this Jew with thick black eyebrows" (172) and sung by a "Negress." In this, Roquentin, and his creator, Sartre, were mistaken. Sartre had probably noted on a record the name of Shelton Brooks and, lacking more precise information and associating Brooks with composers like Irving Berlin and George Gershwin, he assumed Brooks was Jewish. Sartre knew that jazz and the American music-hall owed a lot to the collaboration of Jews and Blacks. Under the German Occupation, the collaborationist press regularly denounced ragtime or jazz as Judeo-Negro music.

In actuality, the composer and lyricist, Shelton Brooks, was the son of Native American and Black parents whose ancestors had crossed the frozen Detroit River to escape slavery and ended up in the southern Ontario town of Amherstburg, where Brooks was born in 1886. His family emigrated to Detroit when Brooks was 15. A self-taught pianist, Brooks was most well-known for his tune, "Dark Town Strutters' Ball." As for the singer, that was the flamboyant Sophie Tucker, born Sonya Kalish to Russian-Jewish immigrant parents who settled in Hartford, Connecticut, just after the turn of the century, where they opened a restaurant.

Roquentin and presumably, Sartre, are transported by the music's "glorious little suffering," as the singer proclaims. "Some of these days, you'll miss me honey." Roquentin fantasizes about the composer who is the conduit through which the song springs into being, and the singer whose own emotion serves as the medium of the music's poignant and angry sorrow, that the "two of them are saved: the Jew and the Negress. Saved! Maybe they thought they were lost irrevocably, drowned in existence. Yet no one could think of me as I think of them, with such gentleness."

Sartre's earliest contact with American popular music came when, with his mother and her second husband, the engineer Joseph Mancy, the family moved to La Rochelle, a French port on the Atlantic Coast. There, in 1917, the 12-year-old Sartre would have heard disembarking American soldiers singing music hall tunes as they made their way through town toward the Western front. Thirty years later, Sartre became personally acquainted with many of the jazz artists who found Paris a more hospitable or at least less racist place than the United States. Sartre shared his enthusiasm for jazz with de Beauvoir.

Though she uses the term to cover a wide swath of popular American music, Simone de Beauvoir captures the impact of "jazz" on the youth of France in her memoir, *The Prime of Life*. "We were passionately moved by negro spirituals, by work songs and blues," she says. What spoke to her generation was the musicians' expression of "a voice that had brutally sprung up from the heart of their night and shaken with revolt."

In the travelogue of her postwar visit to the United States in 1947, *America Day by Day*, de Beauvoir writes extensively about jazz clubs and musicians from New Orleans to Chicago. She focuses especially on "real jazz played by black musicians." What she most admires is a spontaneity and depth of feeling that conveys "a way of life and reason for being." Authentic jazz to de Beauvoir expresses "a kind of ferocity of rhythm, a violence which they call 'swing,'" which she senses grows out of the hardship of life for black people in America (*America Day by Day*, 222-226). In distinguishing inauthentic from authentic jazz, de Beauvoir notes not only the bond of warmth between players and audience in authentic jazz but also the tendency towards commercialization in white jazz that has turned superficial to satisfy a mass audience (38).

Knowledgeable about racism in the United States she understood how the music of black entertainers broke with the politeness of conventional music and, while deeply personal, "was born out of vast collective emotions – the emotions of everyone, of all people – these songs touched us all in that most intimate part of ourselves that is common to everyone; they inhabited us, they nurtured us in the same way as certain words and certain rhythms of our own language, and through them America existed in our inner selves."

Sartre, too, had traveled extensively in the United States, first as a guest of the State Department in 1945 and then again in 1946. He wrote about the jazz haunt called Nick's Bar in New York for his French compatriots who were fascinated with things American in the aftermath of the war. The well-known opening line of the essay, "Jazz, like bananas, has to be consumed on the spot," was Sartre's way of capturing the immediacy of jazz as an art form uniquely based on spontaneity and presence. Even recordings, Sartre noted, gave the date and time of the session because each performance would always be slightly or radically different from another recorded session of some of the same tunes. Consuming the ripe bananas of jazz tunes, "on the spot," was Sartre's way of evoking the listener's being-in-the-moment as the combo stamped their own distinctive interpretive authorship on a well-known tune or fresh composition.

In 1949, on the occasion of a jazz festival in Paris, he was introduced to famed bebop saxophonist Charlie ("Bird") Parker and trumpeter-composer Miles Davis. He perceived in their style of playing, with each musician cultivating a unique sound, and in the unusual, to him, innovation of the extended, improvisational solo, an affirmation of the freedom and autonomy of the individual players that was so unlike the relative anonymity embraced by the classical musician who strove for fidelity to the score.

Just as for Sartre and de Beauvoir, jazz became a medium of liberationist expression on the American scene of the late 1950s and on into the 60s until people like Chuck Berry and then The Beatles and the Rolling Stones pushed it to the sidelines. By then, the so-called youth revolt was in full swing.

AUTHORITY AND THE YOUTH REVOLT

The philosophy of existentialism as it was understood, and probably just as often misunderstood, by a generation of young Americans is only one of the many influences that fed into the liberation ethos and life-style experimentation of the youth culture of the 1960s and 70s. Other factors include access to birth control pills, increasing distrust of government leaders following revelations such as those brought to light in *The Pentagon Papers* and later the Watergate scandal of the Nixon administration, organized opposition to the war in Vietnam, intensification of the civil rights movement, and then the movement for women's equal rights.

In following the Sixties' edict to "do your own thing," many experi-
mentations with sex, drugs, political protest, communal living, and rock
and roll could just as easily lead to disappointment, if not disaster, as
to insight and creative productivity. The problem was (and still is) that
as you chose to suspend or overthrow social conventions and to defy or
ignore prevailing cultural mores, you also had to put something else in
their place as a way to guide and govern your life. Also, it's easy to get
swept along by peers and new currents of a subculture in the making that
give one a sense of belonging and affirm the value of pilot testing features
of a new identity.

Proto-existentialists had already been warned by Dmitri's claim from
his debate with Rakitin in Dostoyevsky's *The Brothers Karamazov*: "But
what will become of men then?" I asked him, "without God and immortal
life? All things are permitted then, they can do what they like?'" In other
words, without transcendental limits based on commandments issuing
from an absolute power, human being would run amuck, letting loose
anarchy and chaos upon society.

As early as 1956 psychologist Robert Lindner in his book *Must You
Conform?* had the premonition that the youth culture was no longer in a
predictable state of adolescent rebellion "but in a condition of downright
active and hostile mutiny" (4). Writing in the midst of the 1960s turmoil
on college campuses, the American existentialist, Sartre translator and
commentator, and University of Colorado classics professor Hazel Barnes
praised those student activists who "refused to sacrifice purity of principle to ideological commitments" (*An Existentialist Ethics*, 200), and
who could not be accused of "quietism or of standing aloof from history."
She chastised those other young activists who took delight in "fomenting trouble and undermining democratic institutions." Insisting on high
standards of ethical responsibility, Barnes would not accept the behavior
of students who used a "teach-in" as an excuse for failing a test in a course
that did not interest them.

Looking back at student ethos of the 1950s, Barnes reminded her colleagues that they could "no longer complain that students as a whole were
apathetic and showed no interest in the world around them." After years
of prodding their students to play a part in needed social change rather
than just conforming to the status quo or focusing singly on advancing
their own happiness, now many a professor, says Barnes, secretly longed

"for the days when he could feel that he was ahead of his students instead of dragging along in the rear."

Defying authority and staking your own claim to live and believe as you choose is laudable in young persons, insisted Barnes, yet she struggled with the kind of role models that were attracting youth in revolt. While a great admirer of Sartre's mind, she could not follow him into supporting the use of violence and armed uprising which he advocated as a means for people to cast off the yoke of colonialism as well as that of imperialist, repressive governments that Sartre regarded as exemplifying capitalist oppression of workers.

Barnes' concerns were justified as numerous offshoots of non-violent protest organizations began to emulate militant anti-colonial groups. For example, a militant faction of the activist organization Students for A Democratic Society (SDS), known as the Weather Underground, took to bombing government buildings and banks to protest against specific governmental acts connected with ramping up the war in Vietnam. The Symbionese Liberation Army (SLA), a self-described black power revolutionary group, also committed acts of violence in the form of bombings, bank robberies and kidnappings (most notoriously, abducting 19-year-old heiress Patty Hearst).

Barnes strove mightily to erect an existentialist moral philosophy in the void that Sartre had left after ending *Being and Nothingness* with the promise of a forthcoming work on ethics building on his analysis of the human condition. Sartre abandoned that project half way through. Instead, he veered sharply to the left in reaching the conclusion that only through one's commitment to a social and economic revolution, as evinced by the Soviets and the Maoists, could talk about how individuals should conduct their lives have any real meaning. In this same period, he repudiated his earlier belief that the socially committed writer could effect social change, henceforth declaring such an assumption an example of bourgeois false consciousness.

Clinging to her belief in the democratic values that motivated the American founding fathers and (though she does not yet in 1967 dare to use this language) mothers, Barnes argued that those student activists who had strengthened their determination and convictions through careful study of the novels and essays of Albert Camus had the likeliest chance of effecting social change without ushering in a new period of ideological demagoguery. Camus, the perpetual rebel, not Sartre, the Marxist revolutionist, was the role model Barnes hoped her students would follow (205-206).

The students would call themselves "existentialists," not "Marxists" or "Socialists," because they chose to identify with the causes of social justice (e.g. opposing racism, bigotry, class prejudice) and were willing to put their lives on the line to advance these causes (e.g. joining the voter registration drives then taking place in the South), yet sought to avoid coming under the thumb of any political party that demanded loyalty and adherence to whatever its leaders declared as the current creed.

What those whom she dubbed "the New Radicals" were trying to do, she gleaned through conversation with her students, was to realize the ideals of democracy and freedom that they had learned in grammar school. This form of idealism, channeled into immediate and practical actions was, for Barnes, the positive direction she believed superior to the still fashionable role models of the Hipster and the Beatnik whom she dubbed "the negative rebels" (*An Existentialist Ethics*, 152).

The Hipsters and the Beats were, for Barnes, as unsavory choice of role models on whom young people might base their sense of authority. Barnes was ahead of her time in pointing out that lurking under the "regressive neo-primitivism" of writers such as Norman Mailer, William Burroughs and Jack Kerouac was a repugnant swagger of male superiority and covert misogyny (167).

One would not find this type of feminist critique of radical male social activists until the courageous writing of women who had been in the midst of the social activism of the 60s and 70s. Bettina Aptheker tells her story of being relegated to the status of the "second sex" while passionately involved in the Berkeley Free Speech Movement. In her 2006 memoir, *Intimate Politics: How I Grew Up Red, Fought for Free Speech and Became A Feminist Rebel*, she describes being forced into subservient roles and overshadowed by male co-activists. She goes on to reveal an earlier background of abuse from her father, the Marxist historian and outspoken American Communist Party member, Herbert Aptheker. (More about how my path crossed with his in a moment.)

Barnes' commentary on existentialism and the social activism of American youth was based, in part, on her direct observations of and conversations with her students. Serving, in retrospect, to chronicle the influence of various existential figures on specific young leaders of the period, George Cotkin in his *Existentialism in America* (published in 2000) emphasizes Camus' attractiveness as a political role model for many African-American activists of the 1960s. Cotkin highlights Robert Moses who was one of the founders of the Student Non-violent Coordinating Committee (SNCC). Moses devoured Camus' *The Rebel* and his novel, *The Plague*, even when serving time in a Mississippi prison for carrying out SNCC organizing as part of the voter registration drive. The credo that Moses found in Camus, says Cotkin was the choice to live, take responsibility and act in a hostile world while refusing to cling to absolutes (*Existential America*, 232).

Not unlike Camus's situation during the Algerian crisis, Moses also became caught in the ideological crossfire between those who wanted the civil rights movement to proceed slowly and non-violently and those who proclaimed "freedom now!" and, like the Black Panthers, were ready to take up arms. Struggling to hold on to Gandhian principles of non-violent direct action, Moses felt agonizingly responsible for young black and white student coworkers murdered by racist fanatics while under his charge. Put on a pedestal as a Biblical-type Moses, the soft spoken but no less charismatic Robert despaired of the infighting among black and white SNCC volunteers and staff. He sought to avoid the cult of personality that, he believed, would detract from the ideal of "participatory democracy." Moses' non-leader leadership style frustrated many SNCC workers and leaders. They felt he was undermining the organization's need to build a more effective structure.

Robert Moses saw the connection between racism and the United States' involvement in the war in Vietnam. He broadened his activism to include protesting against the war and then sought to challenge the all-white delegation to the 1964 Democratic National Convention. Eventually Moses withdrew from the fray, avoided the draft by moving to Canada and then to Africa where he became a math and English teacher. Under the amnesty program of the Carter administration, Robert Moses returned to the United States and developed a math and computer skills program for inner-city youth in Cambridge, Massachusetts.

Cotkin profiles a second figure influenced by Camus, the radical student activist Tom Hayden, later and better known as the husband (for a time) of Jane Fonda. Hayden had served as editor of the University of Michigan campus newspaper in his senior year in 1960. In an editorial he advised incoming freshmen that in a world of vast confusion, cultural change and the nearness of total war, they would need to "grope" as they moved along their educational path and searched for ways to take responsibility for their lives and for that of their fellow students. A year later, in an article for *Mademoiselle*, Hayden apparently tried to reach style-conscious coeds with the message encouraging young activists to pursue "calculated rebellion" by turning "the impulse of outraged protest" into practical programs for social change.

This tentative, muted radicalism was the hallmark of the influence of Camus' writing on the young Hayden. Two years later, Hayden helped to write the founding document of the Students for a Democratic Society (SDS), known as the Port Huron Statement. The Values section of the Port Huron Statement reads as through it could have been written by a committee of humanistic existentialists. Hayden and his SDS compatriots proclaimed that "men have unrealized potential for self-cultivation, self-direction, self-understanding, and creativity" (Quoted in Cotkin, 245). Finding a meaning in life that is "personally authentic" should not lead to "egoistic individualism" but to "having a way that is one's own." Confrontations between student demonstrators and local police forces and, in some instances, the National Guard, would increasingly radicalize SDS and Hayden.

The story of the rise and demise of SDS is well chronicled in, for example, Kirkpatrick Sale's 1973 book, *SDS*. In his 1980 memoir *Reunion*, Hayden has revisited those years in which he moved from a Camusian rebel to a more Sartrean revolutionary and later into more conventional political forums. Hayden served for 18 years as a California State Senator.

NIGHT THOUGHTS

The quintet opened with the rising and falling base line of Dizzy Gillespie's "Night in Tunisia," a long-time jazz standard. Flashing through my mind was the first time I had heard it. The Minor Key in Detroit on a wintery night in 1964. The band was Art Blakey and the Jazz Messengers. The moment was especially memorable because, unlike a lot of jazz musicians,

Blakey liked to talk to the audience, telling them more than who was on bass and who was playing drums and then announcing the title of the next tune. Sometimes he'd launch into a little discourse on jazz history.

Looking down from the club's narrow balcony at Blakey in the spotlight, I listened to him tell a story about how he was present when Dizzy wrote this tune, using for a writing surface "the bottom of a garbage can at a gig in Texas." I pictured the musicians taking a break around back of the club, maybe having a smoke and a couple of pulls on a bottle. Then Gillespie borrows a pencil and pulls a cue sheet from the inside pocket of his suit, folds it over, sets it down on the lid of the garbage can and, turning it into a desktop, jots down the musical idea that he will later flesh out.

My conversation with Darlene had set my mind whirling. It was impossible to talk while the quintet picked up the pace and the trumpet player stepped forward to demonstrate his chops. Instead I ordered a second cocktail and continued my side of the conversation in my head, figuring that one day or night, if we became friends, I'd share these thoughts with her.

In 1964 I was a senior at Monteith College, part of the sprawling Wayne State University campus. I lived in an apartment nearby with a fellow student, Jerry, a loose-jointed, zany guy with red hair who was a fraternity brother. We had both dropped out of the all-white, almost all-Jewish chapter as we drifted further and further into the multicultural campus world where university professors mixed with undergrads and graduate students at parties and where the talk was about trade unions, demonstrations and the underground press, not about booze, broads and sports.

Of course there was lots of gossip about who was sleeping with whom, who had a poem or short story published, who had gotten busted for using or selling dope. The music on the stereo might be bassist Charles Mingus's 1959 release, "Mingus Ah Um," with its mix of civil rights protest songs ("Fables of Faubus,"), blues, gospel, and bop, and the John Coltrane Quartet playing "Softly as in a Morning Sunrise." Coltrane's going into this hypnotic soprano saxophone solo as if the tune had morphed into an Indian raga. Or it might be Dylan or Joan Baez if the party hosts were more folkies.

I was the president of the university SDS chapter. Recently, we had organized a demonstration about race prejudice in campus housing, not the dorms but the campus list of recommended private apartments. There was de facto segregation. We'd done the research. In fact, Jerry and I discovered, after a little prying and teasing of our building manager that she'd been instructed by the owner not to rent to black students. We marched with hand-drawn signs around the university administration building. The press covered the event. Early the following morning the ringing phone in the living room wakened me. It was the dean of students.

"Did you know your picture was in the morning paper?"

"No."

"What was all this about segregated buildings on the campus housing list?"

"It's a fact. I found this out about my own apartment building."

"Hmm," he said. "We'll have to look into this." Then a pause. "By the way, you're about to graduate, right?"

"Yes."

"I guess you have plans to attend graduate school? Where would that be?"

I started to answer then it hit me. He's figuring out a way to do me harm. "Um, I haven't quite decided yet."

"Oh," he said. "Okay. Well, good luck. Thanks. Good-bye."

I had also been involved with SNCC but, thanks in part to the actions of Robert Moses, all the white folks had been asked to withdraw. This was now going to be an exclusively black-led, black-run organization. That was a shock. At first, I didn't get it. But when I went up to Ann Arbor for meetings with Tom Hayden and Dick Flacks, the big honchos of SDS, they explained. Black pride. Whites have a tendency to take over. They're used to being in charge. Young blacks are just learning the ropes. Don't take it too personally.

SDS, in its Camusian phase, was staunchly opposed to communism but friendlier to Scandinavian-style socialism. I'd already had a brush with the Party. A few years earlier, when I was chair of the college's student activities committee, I had been approached by a man by the name of

Herbert Aptheker (yes, Bettina's father) who offered to give a free lecture on the tyranny of the U.S. government's House Un-American Activities Committee (HUAC). The committee had been established to investigate alleged disloyalty and subversive activities of private citizens, public employees and organizations suspected of having ties to Communism. Many of my peers were opposed to the McCarthy-like actions of HUAC, so this seemed like a good opportunity. Plus we wouldn't have to pay the speaker. I agreed. Then, as the event was publicized, the dean of the college called me in.

There was a campus ban on communist speakers. Did I know that? No. Should I withdraw the invitation, knuckle under to the forces against free speech or challenge the ban? I was caught. I hadn't known of Aptheker's notoriety. Naïve. I didn't want to bring more trouble to the college, already frequently under attack for encouraging its students to think for and express themselves. Bunch of useless Beatniks, Pinkos, declared the college's detractors. So I knuckled under and apologized to Aptheker who said he understood and hoped I fully realized the implications of my actions. I didn't. But I did arrange to have the college sponsor a screening of a new documentary on the evils of HUAC. The auditorium was packed. Men in dark suits circulated around taking pictures of the audience.

Politics, I was learning, was a serious business. It would get even more serious in the years to come. In fact, it would turn into street violence with tear gas, rubber bullets and troops in combat gear marching ten abreast up the Berkeley streets toward the demonstrators. It would turn into Kent State and the bodies of students lying dead on the quad.

THE WAITER

Luke tucked plates of appetizers amongst our glasses and silverware. He stood back as if to appraise the arrangement while we pulled our chairs closer in toward the food. "There," he said, rapidly glancing at our faces. "That should get you started." He bowed, pivoted on his heel and strode off.

"He seems like a nice kid," said Barry as he reached hairy knuckles towards the tomato topped brochettes.

"They have a very attentive wait staff here," said Gail, reaching for her glass of wine. "Plus it's the South. Kids here are more respectful towards adults."

Darlene leaned forward to scoop a spoonful of tapenade, waving her spoon in Gail's direction. "Do you think they genuinely feel respectful or just act like it so they can get a bigger tip?" Taking a bite of olive oil dipped crust, she fluttered her eyelids. "I hate it when waiters play act at being waiters, through and through."

"But that's his job," Gail shot back. "To be our waiter."

Barry gave me a conspiratorial smile accompanied by raised eyebrows. He sensed some competition between the women. Then he broke the brief silence. "Well I for one am a waiter, too. Could someone please pass me the salt?"

RIDING HOME

"You and Darlene seemed to be getting along famously," said Gail as she snapped on her seatbelt.

"Uh-huh," I murmured as I eased the Subaru out of the restaurant parking lot. "We reminisced about jazz clubs."

"Oh," said Gail. "That's nice." Ever the driver's alert assistant, Gail turned to peer out her side window. Facing away, Gail muttered, "She looks like she's seen the insides of quite a few clubs."

"Mm," I replied, drawing up to a traffic light.

"I found Barry quite interesting," said Gail. "His career was in pharmaceuticals. A French-owned company but he's worked mostly in New Jersey."

"Ah," I said. "That would explain his French."

"You'd think. But actually he said he learned French in college and then on a Fulbright to study in Paris."

"Well, that worked out nicely, then."

"Yes," said Gail who rummaged in her pocket book and extracted a tissue. She wiped at something from under her eye. She set the bag down on the floor and folded her hands in her lap.

"Barry and I talked about careers and how many times we had to start over. And I told him about how I had never really held a job outside the home until my divorce at 31. And about selling women's shoes and then, taking a friend's advice, and jumping into the chilling waters of the financial services industry. "I was one of the few in the early group of women recruited in the 80s, you know?"

"Yes, you've told me. Very few women. You were brave."

"Yes, that's what Barry said. Well, actually he didn't say brave. He said I was courageous."

"Not the same?" I asked, glancing toward Gail.

"No," said Gail. "Barry said when you're brave, you're fearless. Which as a matter of fact I wasn't. But when you're courageous, you act despite your fear because you know you have to succeed."

"Determination," I said, launching the car down the freeway on ramp.

"I had to protect my children," said Gail.

I nodded and accelerated to merge into traffic.

"I had to become someone." She turned toward me. "Myself."

REFERENCES

Aptheker, Bettina. (2006). *Intimate Politics: How I Grew Up Red, Fought for Free Speech, and Became a Feminist Rebel.* Berkeley, CA: Seal Press.

Barnes, Hazel E. (1967). Especially Chapter VII, "The Negative Rebels," in *An Existentialist Ethics.* New York: Knopf.

Beauvoir, Simone de (1952/1999). *America Day by Day.* Tr. Carol Cosman. Berkeley: University of California Press.

Cotkin, George (2003). *Existential America.* Baltimore: Johns Hopkins University Press.

Corso, Gregory (1960). "Marriage," in *The Happy Birthday of Death.* New York: New Directions.

Lindner, Robert. (1956). *Must You Conform?* New York: Rinehart

Sartre, Jean-Paul. (1947/2013). "Nick's Bar: New York City," *We Have Only this Life to Live: Selected Essays of Jean-Paul Sartre, 1939-1975.* Ronald Aronson and Adrian Van den Hoven, eds., New York: New York Review of Books.

7. Authenticity

Kierkegaard and Nietzsche, to whom dual paternity is often attributed for bringing forth the philosophy of existentialism, each invoked what in the mid-nineteenth century was a new norm and is our seventh star: authenticity. Though perhaps without the anguish and intensity of a Nietzsche or Kierkegaard, the felt imperative to "find oneself" seems to have become a cultural norm in contemporary society. But this is rarely an easy task.

As the 22-year-old Dane wrote in his journal dated August 1, 1835, "The thing is to find a truth which is true for me, to find the idea for which I can live and die." (*Papers and Journals: A Selection,* I A 75.) Kierkegaard's "truth" put him at odds with both theological and philosophical trends of his time and in opposition to certain conformist or crowd mentality traits he observed in the rise and empowerment of the middle classes as Denmark moved toward the status of a constitutional monarchy. His truth to self also centered on an inward and highly experiential interpretation of Christianity that, for him, ran counter to a comfortably encultur-ated form of religiosity he labeled "Christendom."

For Nietzsche, the term signified resistance to the "herd mentality." Nietzsche drew a distinction between "the common human being," a creature confined by motives of greed and morose seriousness and those possessing more noble natures who live life heroically and bequeath to posterity "the signature of their most authentic being" (*Unfashionable Observations,* II, 2). For Nietzsche, that act could be one of outstanding courage in battle or an artistic creation on the level of a Wagnerian opera.

For both philosophers it was not enough to pretend to be an individual through bombastic behavior and an inflated sense of ego. Rather it took one's "signature," a committed stroke of action that often required standing apart from the crowd and risking social castigation, something that, in fact, befell both individuals.

Nietzsche and Kierkegaard would have been shocked to observe how "being true to oneself" had turned into a socially adopted existential norm. They would have been equally surprised to see their books, translated into a multitude of languages, mass-marketed in both print and online editions.

Indeed, the advent of the secular society and the broad dissemination of scientific knowledge have led millions of people into conflictive situations with the faith traditions and cultural values in which they were raised. Lightened from the burden of imposed state religions and traveling to other countries for education and employment, countless numbers accepted the challenge to find their own guiding beliefs and moral principles.

Authenticity was no longer an issue primarily for the highly educated, intellectual elite but increasingly for the average person. By the time the counterculture movements swept the United States and many other countries in the 1970s and beyond, it was all about the quest for authenticity. It had become a search that could focus on anything – the type of clothes you wore, the food you ate and the demonstrations and protest movements you chose to join. Among the hotbeds of the counterculture movement was the City by the Bay. No better place to observe the quest for authenticity could be found than in the counterculture milieu of late 1960s San Francisco.

LOAF OF BREAD

San Francisco is a city renowned for its rumbling cable cars, the soaring arches of the Golden Gate Bridge, and for the smoked ducks and chickens hanging in Chinatown's windows, "their heads," as San Francisco Beat poet Lawrence Ferlinghetti put it, "a block away." My fondness for SF goes back to my graduate school days when I was enrolled at UC Santa Cruz in the late 1960s. Then car trips over the mountains to "the city" usual led to the Mecca of the emerging counterculture, the Haight-Ashbury District. There our entourage would take in art happenings and impromptu street theatre performances staged by the Theatre of the Absurd and the existentialist-inspired anarchist group, the Diggers, who championed liberation from the evils of capitalism and the repressive conventions of social conformity.

The Diggers were the progenitors of many new communal ideas such as baking whole wheat bread in one- and two-pound coffee cans to distribute from their Free Bakery. The Diggers established a no-fee medical clinic, which inspired the founding of the Haight-Ashbury Free Medical Clinic. And they revived an ancient African art form, the making of tie-dyed clothing. The Diggers also put on celebrations of natural planetary events, such as the Solstices and Equinoxes. And they coined various slogans, "Do your own thing" and "Today is the first day of the rest of your life," among the most memorable.

Over the decades, The Haight, as it was called, has turned into another of San Francisco's high-rent districts and rectangular or cylindrical loaves of whole wheat bread can be found on the shelves of hundreds of "artisanal" bakeries dotting the Bay Area. Still the spirit of social and personal experimentation envelops the hills and valleys of San Francisco. Hundreds of organizations aiming to achieve social justice through solidarity with the oppressed vie with those devoted to practices focused on self-actualization and mindfulness to attract the attention of the up and coming generation. Which is the truer path to enlightenment: political or spiritual liberation? And can there be one without the other?

Passing through the city of the Beat generation, the Diggers and, more recently, the New-Agers, one never knows what might occur in the most commonplace of San Francisco locales. For me, one such spot was the lounge just off the lobby of a downtown hotel where the 1998 annual meeting of the Gerontological Society of America (GSA) was being held.

Sanjay

Gathered in a cluster of heavily padded leather armchairs in the hotel lounge, we had been discussing a paper on neuroimaging and brain plasticity as related to characteristics of wisdom in later life such as equanimity and tranquility. As friends in the "aging business," we would see each other a few times each year at professional conferences. The group was just breaking up and members were conferring on which sessions they would attend next. Nearby, another animated bunch of conference attendees were saying their goodbyes. That's when I felt a hand on my shoulder from someone who must have been sitting directly behind me, our lounge chairs almost touching. That began my conversation with an

Indian-born endocrinologist and a discourse on being true to oneself in a context I had never before considered.

"Are you going off or staying?" asked the man who, after a handshake, introduced himself as "Sanjay." There were some sessions that mildly interested me but something about Sanjay's earnest and intelligent face made me decide otherwise. So I told him I was going to wait until the 11-o'clock seminars. "Good," he said. "May I join you?" I nodded, pointed to the empty chair, to which he dragged his briefcase and sat down.

"Very interesting stuff, that neuroimaging of the brain," he said, tapping his own forehead. "For myself I'm more interested in the hormonal secretions. You see." He pointed to his conference badge that showed his affiliation with a major U.S. hospital research institute. "I am an endocrinologist by trade. And you?"

I explained that I was the administrator of a university-based lifelong learning program and a member of the university's philosophy department. "Ah," he exclaimed. "A warm-hearted humanist among the brainy scientists." I commented that many of the scientists seemed to have warm hearts.

"Oh, Ronald," he said. "They're just putting on a good show."

Though I told Sanjay he could call me Ron, he said he preferred the sound of Ronald. "It suits you better," he commented. "You see, Ronald, that while we scientists go around with a big smile and are most capable of what you call chit-chat, all the time that we're exchanging pleasantries, we're thinking about some small nine-amino acid peptide."

"Is it necessary to do this?" I asked. "To keep this peptide in the forefront of your mind?"

"Actually," he replied, giving me a wide grin, "although it's produced in the hypothalamus, it's stored in the posterior pituitary gland. Have you ever heard of oxytocin?"

"Yes," I said. Wasn't it was some kind of party drug? He waved his hand, nodded and then launched into a discourse that I will just summarize.

The hormone on which Sanjay was conducting research plays an important role during women's labor. It seems that large secretions of oxytocin help to promote the birth process and stimulate the mother's supply of breast milk. In recent decades a great deal has been learned about the hormone and its role in men's erections and ejaculation in lovemaking and in women's orgasms as well. Clearing his throat, Sanjay said, "It's the hormone of love and maybe even the hormone of bonding between the sexes."

Taking my raised eyebrows as a sign that I wanted to hear more, he continued by explaining the case of the prairie vole. It seemed that research on this highly sociable rodent that is found widely in Europe and parts of Asia, led scientists to discover that the prairie vole is one of the mere three percent of mammal species that form monogamous bonds for life. And that it seems when these voles mate, large amounts of oxytocin are released. "Now," he said, "you take their cousin, the montane vole, which is 99 percent genetically alike." Sanjay shook his head. "Just a few genes different and their endocrine system just does not put out oxytocin. The result? A vole that favors the one-night stand."

"Does that mean that it's simply because we humans have oxytocin in abundance that we're monogamous?" I asked.

Sanjay smiled but then pursed his lips and looked around at the pre-noon bar crowed. Professionally attired men and women, some already nursing beers and cocktails, patted, hugged and jostled against one another. "Yes, Ronald. But apparently not quite enough."

Our conversation up to this point was informative. I enjoyed hearing how Sanjay described his fascination with the nine-peptide amino acid. He clearly was a bench scientist type but to his subject he brought both a sense of humor and something else I couldn't quite identify. The way he held his body, his shoulders a bit sunken so that he didn't seem to quite fill out his suit jacket, his glances assessing the people around him as though their banter, laughter and eager interrogations about their latest research was a scene out of an absurdist drama. Maybe that's what impelled me to utter something that came out of my mouth before I realized what I was saying.

"You've given up on humanity. Is that it?"

Sanjay sat up. Looked at me and laughed. "Wow," he said. "Am I that transparent?"

"Well," I said, "there's something a little despairing in your tone of voice. I don't mean to pry."

Sanjay presented the profile of his face and I noticed for the first time the tiny crows' feet beside his eye, the stringy muscles of his neck, a few hairs growing from his ear. I guessed then that Sanjay must be in his early 60s. He turned his head to face me.

"Ronald, you seem like a good listener type. May I divulge some personal information?"

I nodded and took a sip of my now lukewarm coffee. Was a complete stranger going to reveal his innermost truths to me and, if so, how would I respond? The situation reminded me of some comments of Sartre's that I had read years earlier. For Sartre, being true to oneself also meant revealing that truth to others.

SARTRE'S TRANSPARENCY

Addressing the virtues of transparency in an interview conducted in 1975 on the occasion of his seventieth birthday and published in the *New York Review of Books*, Sartre reaffirmed his philosophy of radical openness. "I think transparency should always be substituted for what is secret," he said. He projected a future authenticity-oriented social world in which, "no one will have any more secrets from anyone, because subjective life, as well as objective life, will be completely offered up, given." Sartre acknowledged that this ideal of interpersonal transparency would not be easy to accomplish. Something holds us back, which he identified as "a depth of darkness within me that does not allow itself to be said." One of the causes of this residual secretiveness, said Sartre, is "material scarcity," which, he added, "is for me the root of the antagonisms among men, past and present."

Sartre was referring to social inequality caused by the establishment of a class structure that makes some dominant and others subservient. As long as there are societal differences of power and control, people will be guarded in what they say and how the act towards others. In his Marxist-inspired vision of the future, Sartre argues that the eradication of material scarcity ("a real revolution") will change the economic, cultural and emotional relations among people. Without a necessary struggle over scarce resources, people will be more inclined to reveal themselves to one another. And while unanticipated antagonisms may persist, nevertheless, Sartre said, he awaits a "form of sociality in which each person will give himself completely to someone else, who will also give himself completely."

Giving oneself completely in a reciprocal relationship sounds like unconditional love, erotic abandon, or both. Sartre was well known as a generous person and, enjoying success as an author and playwright, he was an easy touch for money. He was also a notorious womanizer, as has been well documented in the posthumous publication in 1992 of his correspondence with Simone de Beauvoir, *Witness to My Life: The Letters of Jean-Paul Sartre to Simone de Beauvoir: 1926-1939*. And also in books recounting candid interviews with de Beauvoir in the last years of her life such as Hazel Rowley's 2005 *Tête-à-Tête: Simone de Beauvoir and Jean-Paul Sartre*. While they conducted a remarkable open amorous relationship over many years, sharing information about their various lovers and in their early years indulging in shared third partners, they also kept many secrets from each other. Perhaps this is what Sartre meant by "a depth of darkness."

Equitable redistribution of wealth and the abolition of material scarcity might help to create an atmosphere conducive to self-transparency and genuine camaraderie, which is certainly one kind of cultural revolution. Indeed, the "social revolution" associated with the May 1968 uprising, which sought to bring down the conservative de Gaulle government and usher in more participatory conditions in industry, higher education and cultural institutions, was an example of the greater transparency that Sartre would have had in mind. Sartre, and indeed de Beauvoir, would also play key roles in revolutions of transparency that were fomenting at the time of his birthday in 1975 – the feminist and LGBTQ rights movement and activism around the conditions of older members of society were also on their radar screens.

An important dimension in Sartre's comments about transparency was his insistence that in interpersonal engagement, while we may keep our thoughts hidden, "we yield our bodies to everyone." Not just in sexual relations, clarifies Sartre, but by the ordinary practice of gazing, gesturing and touching. For Sartre, the physiognomy of consciousness puts us in communion with one another. Sartre and de Beauvoir were very keen on how ideas are embodied in such gestures as the "caress," and in the role of the other person whose "glance" penetrates, as it were, our defense against self-revelation. We can try to give whatever appearance we may choose and to withhold our secrets but we cannot prevent "being seen" by another in the way the other, as we say, takes us in.

In confirmation of this theory, I had read neurological imaging studies that have shown we intuit a great deal more about other people in the ways their faces, torsos and gestures "speak" to us than we realize reflectively. Maybe that's what induced me to open this conversation with the endocrinologist, one that veered in a direction I could not have anticipated.

SANJAY'S DILEMMA

Sanjay's interest in endocrinology was not only professional and scientific but also personal. While the effects and uses of oxytocin was his current research, he was newly venturing into the use of another drug, vardanafil, which, he explained, is called Levitra in the trade. It's used to treat male sexual problems. "Erectile dysfunction, to be exact," added Sanjay to make sure there was no ambiguity. Given the widespread use of ED drugs, this did not seem like an earthshaking matter. Sanjay did not miss the shrug of my shoulders, commenting, "Yes, in today's world, no big deal. Right?"

A complicated recent love affair was the reason for his ambivalence, which was about much more than increasing blood flow to his penis. Sanjay had been divorced for over ten years. His first wife was from an arranged marriage that occurred in his parents' town located about an hour's distance from Kanpur in Uttar Pradesh.

"You know Kanpur?" asked Sanjay. I responded that I've never been to India. "Oh, too bad. Well, it's really quite populous. Leather. A huge tannery industry, you know. The Ganges, you see," he began, and then hesitated. I thought for the moment we were going to verge off into a lecture on the economics of modern-day India but Sanjay waved his hand as if to set aside this topic for another time – if there was to be one. He continued.

His marriage did not survive the couple's tenure in the U.S. where Sanjay had a post-doctoral fellowship. Sanjay explained that while his wife conformed to Hindu dietary traditions and prayer rituals, and continued to wear a sari, she had a modern outlook about women's roles. Still, she had a hard time adjusting to the permissiveness of American life. To her, what she called the "degenerate" culture of the U.S. was a constant source of disagreement between them. Two children, a boy and a girl, were born in this country. The kids were now in college, one in the U.S. and the other in London.

The wife, whose name I did not learn, had gone back to India over a decade ago, initially to help take care of her ailing mother. But after the mother died, his wife remained in the household of the extended family. She became involved in the family business. Though she did not favor a divorce despite their unlikely reconnection, his wife recognized that Sanjay should be free to get on with his life.

Sanjay stayed on and became an American citizen. He channeled all of his energy into his research and vowed that he would lead a celibate life.

"Ronald, do you know about the four Ashramas?" I shook my head.

"Okay." He showed me his left hand and counted with his right. "Brahmacharya, you're a student; Grihastha, now a householder; Vanaprastha, gray or no hair, so retired; and Sannyasa, that's the life of the wandering beggar who lives in complete renunciation of the pleasures of this world."

"This does not sound like Piaget or even Erik Erikson," I said, referring to the names of two prominent developmental psychologists, the first who mainly studied cognitive development in children and the latter who became famous for his eight stages of the life course. According to Erikson's schema, the last stage, old age, was framed by the tension between achieving a sense of completeness or integrity and reconciling oneself to the disappointments and shortcomings of one's life. Erikson called this a struggle between integrity and despair.

"No, of course not. Western developmental psychology is optimistically oriented. Even now about people in their last decades." Sanjay shook his head and laughed. "Perpetual happiness. Something better is coming right until you're taking your last gasp. But this is not the Hindu outlook. Not at all. And so what I am telling you? You see what I am driving at? I figured, well, Sanjay, you've done your job of producing a next generation and soon you could retire on a small but sufficient pension. So why not just skip over Vanaprashta and go all the way to Sannyasa?"

Sanjay threw up his hands and waved them dramatically. "No, no. Not exactly a hermit dressed like Gandhi in his loincloth. You know what Churchill called him? The 'half-naked Fakir.' Well, actually that's important. You know, sartorial integrity? Gandhi was sending a message. He would attire himself in the garb of the impoverished millions. But I digress. I'm just saying that I looked ahead in my life and thought that what I wanted was to devote myself to a pure and uncomplicated bachelor life and explore some of my Hindu roots that I had ignored, lo these many years." Sanjay gave out a great sigh.

"Plans didn't work out or they're still to be realized?" I asked.

"Something like that. You see, I met someone. A professional woman. Yes, in fact, a child psychiatrist. Sandra. No, she's not here at the conference. I won't bore you with how we met. Well, actually, it was at one of those international food markets. We were standing in front of the spices and she was trying to remember something she liked to put in a tandoori dish. She looked me over and figured, well, he looks Indian so he must be an expert. Actually, the tandoor, a clay oven, is used primarily for chicken and beef, and, oh yes, bread. You know, naan? But wayward Hindu that I am, I did know the answer to her spice question. That got us talking about Indian food and by the time we reached the checkout Sandra knew I was alone and so she invited me to come help her make dinner. Yes, I can see the look of doubt on your face, Ronald. Had she, as you say, picked me up?"

I don't think I wore any such look. This sounded like a delightful love story. I wasn't going to interrupt.

"I will sum this up because we both have to go in a short time." Sanjay shot his sleeve and peered at this watch. "Okay, ten minutes. Sandra and I did not have sex. We began to see each other by inviting each other over for Indian food. I was not a great chef but I was competent and I could make some Indian dishes that Sandra had never heard of before. She was a very good cook and she had a splendid kitchen. It was spotless, well lighted, totally organized. With all the stainless steel and bright lights, it could have been a surgery center.

"After dinner, we sometimes went for walks in the neighborhood. We held hands and occasionally did a little, you know, making out. Well, this went on for several months. So why, you might ask, did I not invite her into bed? I had every reason to believe that she would welcome me. The answer is a bit complicated. You see, I was afflicted with this condition. Erectile dysfunction. Not too serious though it had already presented during the latter stages of my marriage. But I was preparing myself for Sanyaasa, not sexual satiation. Not, Rama help me, to start over again with adolescence. Finally, one night, I just had to tell Sandra what was,

up." Sanjay gave a little cough. "Or, rather, was not up with me. If you get my drift." He gave a little wink and a half smile.

"I must say she was not very understanding. 'Sanjay,' she said, 'you of all people know that your problem is easily remedied. Besides,' she said, 'you treat other mature adults with hormone replacements and other drugs to help regulate practically every gland in the body. And what about insulin? It's not like you're contemplating an organ transplant, though there's nothing wrong with that either. 'Yes, I told her, but this is an artificial modification of my natural process. Who would I be kidding? Am I to become like a teenager again? At my age and stage of life?"

Sanjay sat back in his chair and touched his fingers to his forehead. The issue he had brought up was very much in debate among my gerontology friends.

The Politics of Sexual Rectification

Cosmetic surgery, mood enhancers and anti-aging facial treatments would seem antithetical to Sartre's ideal of self-transparency and authenticity. Still, with longer life expectancy and the emergence of a huge aging middle class in post-industrial countries, the options to stay, look and even act younger and more youthful were becoming increasingly available. When the Baby Boom generation (born between 1946 and 1964) came of age, the "modernization of the life course" (as my gerontologist friends called the phenomenon) accelerated this trend. Mainly the more affluent and more educated benefited the most from a "late-life freedom" of continued or revitalized self-actualization. In book titles and magazine articles authors exhorted older people to "reinvent" themselves. Traditional cultural norms for the elderly would drop away as the American Association of Retired Persons would change the name of its highly circulated magazine from *Modern Maturity* to the organization's new name, the acronym, *AARP The Magazine*.

But some of my friends would argue that this so-called "age liberation" was mainly a "freedom away from" conventional roles and norms, much less a "freedom for" personal and societal improvements. They worried it was contributing to age denial, self-deception and a kind of youthful disguise presented to others. Especially controversial was the sexuality revolution of later life. Historically, sexual decline was assumed to be an inevitable and universal consequence of growing older. Aging individuals

:xpected to adjust to it gracefully and to appreciate the special moral benefits of post-sexual maturity. However, iconic celebrities like Jane Fonda, Richard Gere and Michael Douglas (AARP magazine cover stories) had changed all that.

As sociologists Stephen Katz and Barbara Marshall pointed out in a 2003 academic research article, we now live in a "culture of obsessive self-improvement where these assumptions have been completely reversed" (4). Katz and Marshall argued that what had been considered normal patterns of declining sexual capacity have been relabeled medical dysfunctions. And once reframed as a category of disease, the clinical door had been flung open, inviting older people to avail themselves of prescription drugs to reverse or ameliorate the aging process.

They viewed this radical reinvention of the aging body as, in part, a postmodern capitalist conspiracy. The pharmaceutical and medical industries had jumped on the aging advocacy bandwagon that regards "active aging" as a moral imperative. Reversing sexual decline, insisted Katz and Marshall, is not just a personal choice, rather it is part of a "neo-liberal political agenda" that exhorts individuals to take responsibility for their sexual wellbeing "as part of their commitment to the collective health of the aging population" (4). In other words, older people have a social obligation to keep performing sexually. To fail at aging successfully is a betrayal of the social good.

Katz and Marshall may be correct that all the hype about "success-ful aging" is replacing one stereotype – the disengaged, declining and dependent older person – with another – "the active (including sexually active), mobile, autonomous, experimental, knowable, networked, and consumer-niched" Third Age adult (12). Katz and Marshall noted that three decades earlier, highly regarded sociologist Bernice Neugarten pre-dicted that the U.S. was moving towards a norm-liberating "age-irrelevant society" in which an older person's abilities, skills and experience would trump earlier assumptions about chronological age. While acknowledg-ing the benefits of perceiving and judging people by their abilities, not their chronological age, they worried about the negative effects of creat-ing yet new norms for trying to achieve agelessness.

So, one might ask, what is the alternative to this age and life stage blur-ring of identity? Taking advantage of the "true resources of time" (13), argued Katz and Marshall, puts older people in touch with their folkways and cultural traditions, their accumulation of wisdom and the ability to pass that wisdom on through storytelling as they draw on a rich repository of memories. In addition, these more authentic, less "socially constructed" older persons can benefit society through their awareness of change and the cycle of generations. These qualities would enhance their continuing capacity for leadership. Clearly, for Katz and Marshall the "new aging" brings a high degree of inauthenticity while the potential roles of the more traditional wise elder do the opposite.

Still, I countered, when discussing this subject with my friends, isn't it good to have this newfound freedom of choice where, previously, the biochemistry of the aging body and seemingly irreversible wear and tear of joints and tissue set limits to personal initiative and activity? To some, a facelift is a masking of identity; to others it is simply a way to preserve the attractive face we have long presented to others and to ourselves.

Now I saw that Sanjay's newly kindled romance placed him in the midst of this modernized life course debate. Something, I speculated, was drawing him back to the traditional values of his childhood upbringing in India. But living in a multicultural society with many contesting ideals about how to live well and happily put a different frame around his self-questioning than if he had been residing in Kanpur and walking daily down to the banks of the Ganges. Here in America, living according to your own ideas of the good life was supposed to be a great freedom. But how many of us were capable of taking on the challenge of working our way through all these complicated issues?

SANJAY'S CHOICE

Taking the pause in Sanjay's soliloquy to see if I was following him, I asked: "Do I understand correctly that you were ambivalent about getting involved with someone you really liked because you didn't want another round of earthly suffering?"

Sanjay stroked his clean-shaven chin. "I know it sounds odd to you, Ronald. It is terribly old-fashioned. At least in this country. I mean, living in accordance with certain quite ancient ideas about virtue and purity. Believe me, I was all done with that years ago after I'd finished my postdoc in Texas. My wife, well she continued to recite prayers and burn incense and to wear Indian garb. I wasn't very interested in all that but I felt she

was attending to the traditions on both of our behalves. And then... "
Sanjay gave a deep sigh. "And then she wasn't."

"And that is how it ended with Sandra?" I asked.

Sanjay shook his head. "Oh, no. You see, I was quite torn. To Sandra's
questions all I could do was give a shamefaced nod. Yes, of course she was
correct about these matters. And did I really want to become a holy man?
What? You're smiling. You see my plight, right? So then Sandra gives me
a gift. A piece of paper. Script. A prescription for you know what. It was
up to me. Well, Ronald, I tell you. I did not become an adolescent all over
again because I was never that adolescent in the first place. No, no. I was
a quite suppressed, well-behaved Indian boy of the middle class whose
first and only sexual partner was a childhood playmate who had become a
young woman. And she, too, rather modest and sexually repressed though
keen on her duty to produce her parents' grandchildren.

"But now this, this sex for its own sake and now with an entirely different kind of partner, a mature woman who knew her bodily needs and
knew how to satisfy them and, um, mine as well. I will tell you, Ronald,
this was a profound education. And, of course, the oxytocin did its work."
Sanjay put a hand to his mouth stifling a laugh. "The bonding hormone.
All I wanted to do was bond with Sandra – frequently. Naturally, given my
background, I thought that if we were going to have sex then we should
get married. You know, it's interesting. Sandra had never been married.
She only lived with male partners a few years at a time. A very independent woman. Remarkable. At least to someone like me."

I caught a glimpse of Sanjay's watch and saw that it was soon time for
us to go our separate ways. Perhaps we could arrange to meet later. He,
too, took note of the time.

"So, before we decamp, you want to know how it all turned out?"

I nodded enthusiastically.

"Mmm. Well, Sandra did not want a marriage. She did not feel the
need for an exclusive marital-type relationship. She did not want us to
live together. She needed a lot of solitude and could not abide having
another embodied self, stumbling around in the dark looking for the
toilet or shouting into his cell phone on long distance calls. To be herself,
she needed to live mostly apart. She insisted that in this way she would
have more to offer me, would in fact be able to give herself completely to

me when we were together in bed or out for a stroll. Still, there might be contingencies. You know? Other people, other Sanjays standing in front of bins of spices. So therefore, we should each retain our separate lodgings but we could stay over with each other on weekends and occasionally in the middle of the week. We would go places together and introduce each other to strangers as 'my soulmate.'

"Isn't that something, Ronald? Soulmate. It's beautiful. Still, this arrangement is difficult for me. And why, you ask? Because I am not comfortable with this postmodern lifestyle. You see, here I have this lovely and intelligent person in my life, someone to whom I can fully share myself, someone I long to be with day and night. But her needs are different. She already feels complete. For Sandra, I'm ... what? The cherry on top of the sundae? No, better, a dash of saffron, the most expensive of the Indian spices. The one she was trying to remember at the grocery store. I'm her saffron man. Don't get me wrong. I love being her saffron man. But is this the right way to live? It's so, what do you call it, topsy turvy?"

Sanjay put his conference program back in his briefcase and snapped it shut. I grabbed my conference tote bag. We both stood facing each other. Then we embraced. "Thank you, Ronald," he said. "I wish we had taken the time for me to ask you a few questions. For example, do you use a vasodilator and, if so, which one?"

Given everything Sanjay had divulged, it was a fair question. Maybe we were practicing Sartre's ideal of transparency. We did make arrangements to meet that evening for dinner. I certainly had a lot to think about in the meantime about my own oxytocin-producing experiences. It puzzled me to think about where we draw the line on the increasingly common medical interventions that give us a new heart valve, hip joint or knee. Who would refuse? But then what about skin tightening, lifting or tucking, stomach banding for weight loss, or drugs to improve memory, cure late-life depression or rejuvenate our sex life? Are these unnatural ways of growing old, our war against the inevitability of decline and death?

For his part, as he got older, Sartre took huge amounts of Corydrane, a mix of amphetamine and aspirin to keep his writing productivity in high gear. Continuing to smoke and drink alcohol, he persisted in leading an unhealthy lifestyle. But it allowed Sartre to continue to embrace the projects that made life worth living. Adages for the elderly like "acceptance," "letting go" and "graceful aging" were anathema to him. Consequently, Sartre's last decade was marked by intermittent medical emergencies.

THE DISCOURSE OF AUTHENTICITY

The challenge of authenticity has been around for centuries. "To thine own self be true," pontificates Shakespeare's Polonius to his son Laertes. Advice coming from Polonius, the character who, we remember also served to spy on Hamlet for King Claudius, reveals that such platitudes can just as easily disguise calculated self-interest as courageous honesty. For the existentialists, authenticity is centered on moral authority.

It would seem a matter of common sense that being oneself is inescapable since whenever we make a choice or commit an act, we are the ones doing these things. Yet, we all know that there are times when some of the thoughts, decisions and actions we undertake are not really our own and are not genuinely expressive of who we are. The pressure to fit it, not make waves or avoid stirring up controversy or conflict may cause us to go against our personal values. In one sense, the issue of knowing who we are as a unique and enduring identity leads us into the most ancient of metaphysical quandaries.

The Athenian gadfly Socrates' exhortation to his fellow Athenians, "Know thyself," contains within it the provocative suggestion that the individual subject, rather than communal custom and received opinion, becomes the ultimate arbiter of moral authority. Yet even when we take possession of this authority, we still might speak and act in ways that violate our integrity or contradict the inner voice of better judgment.

My conversation with Sanjay had brought out how being true to oneself is not something that goes on in a vacuum. The self that one might be true to has always been part of a family, a neighborhood, perhaps a religious or cultural tradition. Kierkegaard and Nietzsche's philosophical reaction against the currents of their times would make no sense without those forces pressing against them. Even the Socratic exhortation, "Know thyself," only makes sense when an individual has the option to do otherwise – i.e. go along with the crowd. Sanjay did know himself, but that didn't eliminate the conflicts that pulled him this way and that.

For those in the existentialist tradition, being true to oneself is a major and ongoing challenge, since a variety of temptations such as cowardice, self-deception and envy require persistent vigilance. "Only the truth that edifies is truth for you," we recall Judge Wilhelm proclaiming in Kierkegaard's *Either/Or*. To be edified, for the Socrates of Copenhagen, means to appropriate those truths that enable one to "build up" in character and spiritual development. "Choosing oneself," "giving birth to oneself," are frequently repeated exhortations in Kierkegaard's writing. Not to do so, by implication, would be to fall down into an inauthentic existence by simply conforming to received opinions and popular views of how to lead the good life.

On American shores the French existentialist virtue of being "authentic" had an indirect influence on public discourse in the late 1950s and early 1960s through widely read books such as David Riesman's sociological analysis published in 1950, *The Lonely Crowd*, William H. Whyte's study of corporate America that appeared in 1956, *The Organizational Man*, and Sloan Wilson's 1955 novel, *The Man in the Gray Flannel Suit*, which was made into a highly popular movie of the same title in 1956.

The theme of these works was that American society had declined into conformism and consumerism, in part as a byproduct of successful industrialization, rising and widespread affluence, and as a retreat from the lingering memories of the horrors of World War II. While Whyte's extensive interviews with business managers and CEOs led to his conclusion that the corporate system was dominated by risk-averse executives who faced no consequences and could expect jobs for life as long as they made no egregious missteps, Riesman's study described a post-war middle class increasingly dominated by a certain cultural type, the "other-directed" person who identified him or herself through references to what others in their communities earned, owned, consumed and believed.

More recent versions of this social critique are reflected in the 1998 comedy-drama *The Truman Show*, about a character, Truman, who, from birth, has been trapped in an illusory, white-picket fence world and whose always on-camera existence is like a cross between the 1950s popular TV show, *Candid Camera*, and today's grueling and mock-heroic reality shows. Discovering the charade, Truman longs yet fears to break out. Another comedy-drama of 1998, *Pleasantville*, takes film viewers into a flashback, virtual 1950s black and white TV show version of a middle-class town dominated by false cheerfulness, stifling routines, and fear that any change (sudden splashes of color) signifies a conspiracy. Clearly, the challenge of being true to oneself and honest in dealings with others, major themes of the existentialist camp, hasn't become passé.

For the existentialists such as Sartre and de Beauvoir, the norm of authenticity entails recognition that each of us is a being who *can be* responsible for our actions as we avoid absorption in the anonymous "we" that characterizes our everyday engagement in the world. Authenticity thus indicates a certain kind of integrity – not that of a pre-given whole, an identity waiting to be discovered, but that of a project to which we can commit ourselves and thus "become" what that project entails.

Rousseau and the Diggers

The existential ideal of transparency – I am authentically what I seem to be – has some of its roots in the eighteenth-century social philosophy of Jean-Jacques Rousseau, who argued that the conduct one chooses should come from a source within, not in conformity to norms from without. In his colorful, sometimes painfully candid autobiography of 1770, the *Confessions*, Rousseau extolled the importance of inwardness, self-reflection and introspection as he described how the uncorrupted nature of childhood is the foundation of sincerity and integrity that is so easily deformed by the influence of mannered and socially pretentious adults.

Rousseau would have admired the Diggers for their exuberant non-conformity and their rebellion against social and economic inequality. Differences that made a few masters of the many were not built into the cosmic order. Rather, inequality for Rousseau was a function of certain social and historical developments. These could be changed – indeed, overthrown. Proclaiming this view made Rousseau a dangerous man. His books were frequently banned and he was hounded from one country to another. His published works helped pave the way to the French Revolution.

The Diggers, too, wanted a revolution and maybe their street theater, free bread and healthcare clinics helped to popularize ideas for food co-ops, volunteer doctors' clinics, and even an organization like Habitat for Humanity. Somehow the Diggers managed to make the leap from the absurdist's view of life to collective action directed toward positive initiatives for social betterment.

Existentialists like Sartre and de Beauvoir tried ardently to link individual authenticity to social welfare. "For me to be free," says de Beauvoir, "all others must be free." Not, as in Rousseau, because of an inferred social contract of mutual protection and benefit embodied in the form of the state, but for de Beauvoir because without the freedom of others to valorize the projects to which she, through her actions, assigned value, her freedom, the freedom of *this* individual, would remain a meaningless abstraction. In this sense, authenticity is both an individual and a social virtue. And because authenticity is situated in a relational context, it brings with it the elements of risk and vulnerability.

In other words, while striving to be the legislator of your own life, what Kant called practicing "moral autonomy," is central to being an authentic person, it's a heavy task not easily sustained by the average person. And if you don't accept certain commonly held social values and conventions but you do embrace the moral autonomy that belongs to every person, you would then be hard pressed to explain what guidelines or principles you do follow in your relationships with other human beings.

SANTA CRUZ, 2015

Thinking back to my graduate school years at UC Santa Cruz and the trips we made to the Haight Ashbury neighborhood, I recall another slogan from the period – "Question authority" – made famous by LSD enthusiast Timothy Leary. Not to do so, Leary declared, was to fall into an inauthentic lifestyle of marching to the drumbeat of others and following goals and values that the individual had never chosen to make his or her own.

It's perhaps ironic that on the occasion of its 50th anniversary, my graduate school alma mater, UC Santa Cruz, laid claim to a theme that its promoters believed distinguished the school from others: "The original authority on questioning authority." Claiming that this imperative went back to its very founding in 1965, the school's website insisted that while the exhortation may seem a bit dated it was still relevant. Whoever wrote the website copy warned, "We live in an era of increased conformity and risk aversion." All the more reason for college courses on existentialism.

REFERENCES

Ferlinghetti, Lawrence (1955). "The dog trots freely in the street." *A Coney Island of the Mind: Poems.* New York: New Directions.

Katz, Stephen and Marshall, Barbara (2003). "New sex for old: lifestyle, consumerism, and the ethics of aging well." *Journal of Aging Studies,* 17 (3-16).

Kierkegaard, Søren (1996). *Papers and Journals: A Selection.* Tr. Alasdair Hannay. New York: Penguin.

Nietzsche, Friedrich (1995). *Unfashionable Observations.* Tr. Richard T. Gray. Stanford: Stanford University Press.

"Sartre at Seventy: An Interview," (1975). *New York Review of Books,* August 7. Acquired at: http://www.nybooks.com/articles/archives/1975/aug/07/sartre-at-seventy-an-interview/

8. Identity

Identity is often linked with the concept of what it means to be an individual, a person. Among the existentialists there is a strong divergence of positions. For Kierkegaard and other religious existentialists, each person possesses an innate uniqueness, in classical Greek terms a *daimon*, one's ideal possibility. The Kierkegaardian challenge is to "choose oneself," that is, to seek to actualize and remain faithful to this unique and emerging self.

For thinkers such as Sartre and de Beauvoir, the quality of subjectivity that is the person in potentiality is, in a sense, a void that the emerging bearer of self-consciousness is challenged to regard as his or her freedom to shape an individuality. While Kierkegaard exhorts his readers to resist the leveling forces of social conventions, the drama of personal identity is more inward than outward. Ultimately, for Kierkegaard, a God must enter into the picture. For Sartre and de Beauvoir God, or at least their conception of a supernatural being, has long been left behind. The emergence of personhood is always seen as a social drama with the Self and the Other being the main players.

This dialectic plays a major role in existential dramas, novels, short stories and philosophical essays. For example, in Sartre's play *No Exit* three characters are locked into an afterlife enclosure where they discover their punishment for earthly misdeeds is to see themselves reflected from the viewpoint of another consciousness – forever. Each character's attire – sexy, dowdy or dapper – underscores his or her self-image and how each wants others to see them. For the existentialists, intrusion of the Other (often capitalized) into our conscious or, rather, self-conscious life can either affirm or destabilize our sense of who we are, our identity, the eighth star in our existential sky.

Clothing may seem a trivial example of identity and yet the apparel of no less a figure than Kierkegaard played a strange and ironic role in how he was regarded by the public for he appeared to wear trousers of short and unequal lengths, a topic for political cartoonists in the Copenhagen popular press. For his part, Kierkegaard, the master of parody, satire and the paradoxical, had much to say about literary style and the journalistic sensibilities of his day, but that discussion is beyond the scope of our present inquiry.

How vulnerable we may be to the influence of others varies at different time of life. For example, adolescent style conformity and the risk of not looking cool is the subject of many young adult movies and books. Dressing for success became a big deal in the 1970s, ushering in books, magazines and workshops that emphasized that how you dressed could determine whether you would be taken seriously in a business deal or seeking a promotion.

Devoting a half chapter to the subject of dress in *The Second Sex*, Simone de Beauvoir equated elegance in women's clothing with dependency and even bondage. The "woman of fashion" who "has chosen to make herself a thing," did so, she insisted, to showcase her social status and to please her affluent husband (550). Nevertheless, Simone's friends, the playwright Jean Genet and actress, singer and theater director Simone Berrieau, complained her clothes were too drab and failed to do justice to her figure and stature as a successful writer and thinker. As a quasi-Marxist existentialist, she countered, "Elegance implies a system of values which is foreign to me."

Age-wise, the period of transitioning to retirement is another time of reconfiguring identity and attire. For many, more leisure wear comes in as business attire goes out. The change of social roles is equally if not more decisive, as I learned when conducting weekend Life Transitions workshops for people considering what they want to do, and perhaps be, in the next stage of life.

THE WORKSHOP

"Pauline," dressed in a pantsuit, had been one of the quieter among the thirty or so participant in the group. From the first day of introductions, we knew this slender, studious looking woman with silvery short-cropped hair was among the few attendees who had already made a break with a full-time career. The majority of the participants were six months, a year, or longer from informing their employer or colleagues about their intention to depart from the workplace. When someone asked Pauline why, having already retired, she had chosen to attend the seminar, she said she'd encountered some surprises that required her to rethink her plans. She hoped to get some fresh ideas from hearing about the experiences of others. But on the second day, Pauline opened up about taking, as she put it, "the leap into the abyss."

Pauline was the founding director of a small non-profit foundation in Washington, D.C. that advocated for people with disabilities. Besides raising money for research, the organization conducted periodic seminars and workshops for families with disabled children. Pauline had designed many of these events during her career with the help of her staff and dedicated volunteers. In the last weeks before she was to turn in her office keys, Pauline let it be known that she would be willing to volunteer to lead some of the future workshops or, if not lead, then play a supportive role in them.

For Pauline, keeping a toehold in the organization was part of her plan to, as she put it, "create a soft landing into retirement" by making a contribution to the ongoing success of the organization. She recognized this would depend on the discretion of the incoming director. "I was told by a third party, a member of our foundation board, that the director would not welcome my participation," said Pauline, shrugging her shoulders and looking around the circle of attentive faces. "So much for my soft landing," she murmured.

Making what she thought was a generous offer as a dedicated, soon to be former, employee, only to be rebuffed by the new director, deflected Pauline's gently arcing trajectory into her new life. With eyes expectantly turned toward her, Pauline continued to tell her story.

"I knew that I was going to be asking myself a lot of questions about who I was and what my role in life was going to be when I was no longer, you know, the person in charge," Pauline explained to the ten people sitting around the conference table. "I'm a reflective sort of person, so, naturally, I looked forward to exploring new territory or, well, territory I hadn't thought much about since ... what? Since maybe when I was in college. I assumed I'd have control over that process."

Pauline gave a half smile and continued. "I hadn't expected to get knocked off course."

Pauline's puzzlement was not entirely unfamiliar to other members of the group. Mary, an investment advisor working for a large financial services company, chimed in. "I've heard this from other people who were in leadership positions. They thought they would be doing the company a favor to stick around for a while to help new leaders make the transition. Instead they were treated like unwelcomed intruders."

Then another voice chimed in. "This happens to a lot of people. Especially in do-gooder non-profits and even places like my own school," said Gerald, a biologist at a large state university who was in its phased retirement program. "The arrangement at our school gives you the option of gradually fading into the sunset over a two-year period. After that, you're invited to join the retired faculty association and attend monthly luncheons where one of the deans or the fundraising people come to tell you how well the school is doing now that you're not around. It's great to see long-time associates but pretty quickly it feels like you're in a room full of – um." Gerald gave a nervous laugh. "Well, ghosts. And you're one of them."

Pauline nodded thoughtfully and picked up where she'd left off. "I'd never seen myself as an intrusive person. I was always a team player. I had no intentions of overshadowing the new director," said Pauline in a voice that made it sound like she was apologizing to us. "I mean, I understood that when you're the new kid on the block, you want to establish your own turf, your own credibility. Especially if you're the new CEO. But I thought, maybe, given that my replacement was another woman, well, that would make a difference."

Pauline then launched into a bit of soul searching. She said she wondered if she was deceiving herself that she was an unobtrusive and supporting type of person. Was the director's perception of her more accurate? Maybe she was a more dominating figure than she realized. Occasionally, she'd heard through the grapevine at work that some of her staff members thought she was too "bossy" or that she didn't offer praise often enough. Perhaps she was one of those people who pretend to be team players but who end up always stealing the limelight and taking the credit? Pauline understood that the board had little choice but to support the new director. Their loyalties had already shifted. Despite this understanding, she still felt, as she put it, "a little crushed." Worse, the situation threw her into a state of confusion. Others were contesting her sense of self-identity.

HOW OTHERS SEE US

From Sartre and de Beauvoir's point of view, who we think we are invariably brings us into conflict with others, as identity positioning is equally a matter of relationship to others as to oneself. As Pauline put it and the existentialists confirm, try as we may, we cannot control how others, especially significant ones, perceive us. Fundamental to human consciousness is not only our capacity for self-consciousness but the inescapable fact that we exist in a social world in the condition of "being-for-others."

Being-for-others is not a matter of role playing or what sociologist Irving Goffman called "presentation of self." Rather, as part of what might be called our "relational consciousness," being-for-others is intertwined with our awareness that other people are centers of self-creating subjectivity just as we are. And while we may see other people as projections of our consciousness, as objects, we also come to the realization that we must also be seen as projected objects for them. In this sense, we are that being who is vulnerable to the consciousness of "the other."

Sartre and de Beauvoir's depiction of relational consciousness may seem tainted by an excessive emphasis on how two or more consciousnesses wrestle with one another in negotiating issues of domination and subordination, control and submission, self-definition and definition by the other. Were they stripping away the veneer of everyday social relations to expose the bare conflictive nature of what transpires between people, or did they have a distorted, even maudlin take on how people interact? After all, we might ask, what of love, compassion, empathy?

If the world of human relationships were like the state of limbo in which Sartre's two women and one man are isolated in *No Exit*, ours would be a sorry existence of continuous alignments and betrayals. The drama unfolds as each character tries to persuade, seduce or coerce the others to see himself or herself as he or she wants to be seen. The result is a perpetual ontological struggle as each one's attempt is stymied by the other characters' holding up a mirror that requires each one to see himself or herself as an object in the world of another consciousness. This psychological torture forces each one to confess his and her moral failures.

Conflict with a significant other is a major theme in their novels and in Sartre's plays. And the intrusion of a third person into a couple relationship ratchets up the drama of affection and betrayal, one that rarely ends in a happy outcome for any of the fictional characters. On the positive side, readers or playgoers are challenged to reassess their assumptions about relationships. Perhaps they (and we) reach a higher level of consciousness?

Certainly de Beauvoir attempts this demolition of two-dimensional stereotypes on the larger social scale when she analyzes, in *The Second Sex*, the situation of "woman" as Other and then, in her subsequent book, *Coming of Age*, older adults as the Old People. Still, we ask, are the existentialists correct that adult relationships are inevitably power struggles in which each person tries to usurp the very ground of freedom on which the other stands, whether the other is a friend, a coworker, or a competitor for the affections of another?

PAULINE'S QUANDARY

Pauline was compelled to see herself as an image reflected back to her in the eyes of her board members and former workers. As part of a relationship triangle, her board members, while neither confirming nor disconfirming the new director's perceptions, were compelled to take the new director's side. For her part, Pauline had to consider whether she had been deceiving herself all along about her leadership style?

Pauline told us that at first she got angry. She wanted to try to get to the bottom of this identity conundrum. Maybe if she met with the director and some of the board she could get things sorted out, she speculated. But she quickly came to the realization that this course of action would only make things awkward for all concerned.

"I backed away from anything that might seem confrontational," she said. "I tried to be as graceful about leaving as I could. I realized that in a situation where people have different perceptions than you have of yourself, you're in a no-win position. I felt hurt but maybe, seeing it in retrospect, I probably needed this jolt. I was going to have to take some major steps forward. Trying to continue to play even a very minor role with the organization was a step backward."

"True," said Mary. "You might have been trying to cling to your work identity more than you realized. You don't see how much that defines you until you give it up. I suspect we all do that."

As facilitator of the group, I wondered what Pauline had learned from the experience and whether any insights she may have garnered would be helpful to those who had not yet entered the transition period. So I asked her.

"What I learned? Well, I figured out that you should probably not go where you're not wanted," said Pauline. "You can't control how other people see you. You might discover something about yourself that you hadn't realized. But the take-away for me is to accept there are going to be differences in how we see ourselves and how other people see us. Usually, you don't realize there can be such a gap. But in situations like this, you can really get a wake-up call. All of a sudden, you're forced to look at yourself from someone else's point of view. Maybe you don't like what you see. They're holding up a mirror."

"Yes, and you're holding one up to them," quipped Gerald.

"You are," Mary jumped in. "But they've got all the power."

Pauline's strategy was to try to accept the conflict of clashing viewpoints. She saw it as a way to learn something about herself. "I've decided that when I get back home, I'm going to check out this aspect of my personality with my friends and my partner," said Pauline on a hopeful note.

"Good luck," said Mary, shaking her head. "I wonder if they'll have the guts to be honest with you."

Pauline's dilemma shows that despite thoughtful planning, the transition to retirement can take a person by surprise. Long-dormant questions may arise about who we are separate from our career and workplace identity. Most of the articles and books that offer advice on dealing with these challenges focus on helping us identify acquired knowledge and skills that we might apply to a post-retirement part- or full-time job or in volunteer service. Earlier passions and interests that were set aside under the pressures of earning a living and supporting loved ones, may also be revisited for fresh exploration, as the experts recommend.

These constructive activities help us to maintain a sense of continuity and self-worth. But taking a close look at who we are in the eyes of others is an invitation to a self-reevaluation. The English author Iris Murdoch, for a time quite taken up with French existentialism, was a master at depicting egocentric characters who, suddenly discovering themselves in the eyes of another person, are shocked at the real and independent status of the other person's reality. Often, in the case of infatuations, this revelation comes too late.

Trying to ascertain how co-workers and colleagues might have perceived you is one thing, but being caught in the midst of a social upheaval that forces all parties to take a position and to put their values on the line is a challenge to identity in the larger public arena, as was the case with the French existentialists in the post-war period.

CONFLICTS AMONG THE EXISTENTIALISTS

That there could be conflicts among the existentialists – who had a great deal to say about identity – should not come as a surprise. While Camus had been lumped in with Sartre and de Beauvoir as a key figure in the existentialist camp, he publically disavowed his membership. Camus, the quintessential "rebel," did not want to belong to or be labeled as part of any political or even philosophical group. But he could not detach the label "existentialist" that literary critics had pinned on him.

His fictional and philosophical works did have in common with his Parisian-born colleagues the theoretical claims that existence precedes essence, and that we are born into a world of culturally constructed but not intrinsic or naturally determined meanings, ones that we are free to overthrow. Moreover, our awareness of finitude and of our mortality awaken and intensify our capacity for self-determination.

But when it came to the notion that authentic individuality was inextricably linked to solidarity with others and that the role of the writer must include commitment to the cause of social justice, Camus balked. When Sartre and de Beauvoir publically espoused a kind of Marxist-Socialist-democratic positioning that often aligned them with the camp of the French Communist Party, Camus sought to distance himself. And when it came to the nationalist uprising in Algeria, their friendship was stretched to the breaking point.

Like most of their fellow intellectuals, all three writers and thinkers were torn by the struggles for ideological supremacy between vying

political groups. On the one hand, the Americans had been their liberators and the GIs they had encountered were mostly very likeable young
men. However, they felt that America's democracy-based capitalism was
tainted by an exploitive influence on European countries like France and
Germany and after battling fascism, they felt betrayed that the U.S. government supported certain European dictatorships as well as their own
country's efforts to retain control over their pre-war Asian and North
African colonies.

On the other hand, while promulgating the coming of a classless
society, communism of the Soviet type carried with it the tyranny of a
hierarchical bureaucracy with supreme power vested in a dictator. The
drama of the Cold War was then played out as activist groups in the
various colonized countries such as India, Vietnam and Algeria began to
agitate for independence. In this historical moment, a person's identity,
especially for individuals who played a large public role, was closely connected with how they positioned themselves within the debate between
freedom and tyranny. The eight years of the Algerian uprising was one
such context.

The period of the French-Algerian War of Independence (1954 to 1962)
saw major rifts in French society over whether its long-time colony should
gain its independence from France. Over one million citizens of French
ancestry (the so-called *pieds noirs*, black feet) had lived for generations
among the predominantly Arab and Berber populations,

Not surprisingly, that conflict deeply touched the lives of Sartre and
Camus. Sartre, who favored the Algerian cause and advocated for independence through his newspaper and journal articles and in public
speeches, became an assassination target. His apartment building was
bombed twice and his office once. Born and raised in Algeria, Camus'
course of action was different but no less agonized. His attempt to find a
neutral or middle way led to literary paralysis. In the end, the two friends
became estranged over the Algerian War and the role of the French
Communist Party. Each identified with the liberation struggle in different ways, reflective of their backgrounds and philosophical orientations.

Camus was born into a poor family that had settled generations earlier
in French Algeria. His father died a year after his birth in 1913, and Camus'
illiterate and deaf mother, who worked as a cleaning lady, raised him. His

intelligence and literary acumen (he was a journalist before becoming a novelist) would deliver him from that world of poverty. Camus' North African birthplace permeated his thoughts and shaped his writing. His two greatest novels, *The Stranger* and *The Plague*, were both set there, in Algiers and Oran.

During World War II Camus joined the French Resistance against the Nazis and served as editor-in-chief of the underground newspaper *Combat* from 1943 to 1947. His novel *The Stranger*, which would fascinate many young Americans in the late 1950s and 60s, was published in 1942 and brought him international acclaim. In 1947 came *The Plague*, regarded by many as a classic of existentialism. In 1957, at the age of 43, Camus won the Nobel Prize for literature.

Camus was deeply divided about the war. He sympathized with the Arab insurgency to reclaim their country but could not avoid feeling protective of his friends and family whose fate, should the uprising be successful, might mean forced exile or worse. Readers of *The Plague* may recall the famous scene in Part Four in which the novel's chief protagonist, Dr. Bernard Rieux, goes for a swim in the sea with Jean Tarrou, a visitor who has become trapped in the plague-ridden town.

Tarrou decides that instead of trying to find a way to escape, he will throw in his lot with the inhabitants in trying to contain the plague and help the afflicted. Sharing the stories of their lives, the two men articulate two strong convictions about politics and medicine. First, that since every ideology seems, ultimately, to justify violence in the suppression of others, it is best to avoid binding oneself in loyalty to groups that seek to dominate others in the name of some supposedly utopian ideal. Second, the pledge of the Hippocratic Oath, that above all else the physician should "do no harm" when coming to the aide of another person. Like his remarkably humble doctor hero, Camus sought to avoid supporting either side in the conflict where violence was justified as a necessary tool of liberation or containment. The war was extremely violent in both Algeria and in France where bombings, kidnapping, assassinations and the use of torture were widespread.

For Sartre, the ambivalence and relative neutrality of his former Resistance comrade to the Algerian Arabs' struggle for independence was inexcusable. It was the writer's role, Sartre argued, to demonstrate commitment to the causes of the oppressed even if those causes were pursued by means of violent acts. In the case of the Algerian "question," Sartre cast his lot with the Parti Communiste Française (PCF), which supported the revolution since its leaders regarded Algeria as a glaring instance of the suppression of the rights of the working class. The Arab Muslim and Berber populations of Algeria were predominately poor and illiterate. Camus had written about the country's horrifying poverty in his 1939 series of articles on "The Misery of Kabylia." So he knew first-hand what life for the downtrodden was like in Algeria.

Sartre had little tolerance for Camus' inner dilemma or divided loyalty. Sartre and de Beauvoir supported a version of communism under Stalin despite their awareness of the "show trials" of suspected deviants from the party line, the purges, the stories of thousands murdered or sent to the Siberian gulags. It wasn't until the bloody suppression of the 1956 Hungarian Uprising that Sartre switched to becoming a critic of the Soviet government. Why he and de Beauvoir stuck to this self-deluding belief in the virtues of the Soviet Union is hard to fathom. In part, it may have been due to their resistance to the position of the French government that sought to retain control over its prewar colonies in Asia and North Africa. In part, it was their belief in an ideal of social justice that, they thought, could be better realized through communism's aim to bring about a classless society.

As historian Tony Judt comments, in *Past Imperfect: French Intellectuals, 1944-1956*, on Sartre and his friend and colleague Merleau-Ponty's attraction to the post-war communist upwelling, "They seem to have been waiting for some such moment all their lives, so enthusiastically did they welcome the chance to be part of a romantic commitment whose scope and meaning would transcend, transform, and give practical effect to their earlier writing."

Not so Camus, asserts Judt, who admires the author of *The Rebel* and his famous critique of "progressive violence" (Judt, 126), the cycle of retribution that Camus believed could not lead to an equitable and harmonious resolution.

Sartre, however, saw matters otherwise. He argued that the status quo domination of colonized countries was already a condition of violence, though perhaps perpetrated more subtly and quietly on an entire population. Sartre wanted Camus to adopt the position of a revolutionary but Camus insisted on maintaining his literary and personal identity as the rebel.

So Sartre and Camus went their separate ways. Any possible surmounting of their differences was cut short when Camus was killed in the unfortunate car accident in 1960. What the two freedom-seeking authors did share, however, was the view that one's identity, even when situated within affinities to culture, nationality, family and political ideals of social justice, is the ongoing process of "becoming," not an idealized completion of selfhood or being. But if identity is dynamic and is constituted, according to Sartre, by the sum total of our actions, then establishing a sense of continuity would be a distinct challenge.

Simone de Beauvoir does a brilliant job of describing various individuals' shifts in political affinity and class identity in the post-war years in her novel, *The Mandarins*. Her characters' allegiance to an ideal of individual and social liberation divides them into warring camps while their love affairs and literary pursuits further complicate their interactions. All of the novel's main characters are in their 30s and 40s except for a troubled teenage daughter. Clearly, the political struggles of the Cold War era seriously impacted the French intellectuals' self-image and self-presentation to others.

IDENTITY IN CRISIS

In the midst of the Cold War struggle that engulfed the existentialists and just a year after de Beauvoir published *Le Deuxième Sexe*, certainly a work about women's identity, on the American scene arrived Erik Erikson's surprisingly popular psychoanalytic study of adolescent identity, *Childhood and Society*. Erikson coined the term "identity crisis" to characterize an adolescents' struggle to come to terms with physical growth, sexual maturation, and the integration of images of themselves and perceptions that others have of them.

Erikson's initial focus on adolescence reached towards a more comprehensive theory of human development. As mentioned in Chapter 7, Erikson identified eight stages during the lifespan, each of which, echoing a Hegelian type of dialectic of maturation, presents us with a core psychological need and psycho-social conflict that the individual must resolve in order to be ready for the next stage of growth. But if we stumble we are likely to move forward with an earlier need left unresolved.

As mentioned, Erikson characterized the stage of late adulthood as a struggle between the counter forces of "integrity and despair." The task of old age, given this Eriksonian formulation, centers on the individual's acceptance of the life he or she actually lived and the attempt to formulate a meaningful coherence in one's life story. The very real challenge that Erikson makes apparent is that in conducting a review of one's life the individual is going to have to revisit past accomplishments and triumphs as well as failures and disappointments. For Erikson this is a worthy inner struggle because wisdom, the ideal product of this conflict, is not easily won without honest self-appraisal. It can be perplexing to feel that our life story doesn't add up to a coherent last chapter that might bear a title celebrating the sum of choices we've made.

Unlike most of us who are not highly visible public figures, Sartre, de Beauvoir and Camus played out their private lives in the limelight of public scrutiny. Their actions and words were constantly subjected to criticism in the press. Their actions not only affected close friends and associates but thousands of people who they would never meet.

Those of us who only occupy a small, dimly lit corner of the world stage also affect the lives of others. Our quest, though narrated by a single author, nevertheless includes a cast of characters, social groups, places, times and moments shared with others. These situations bring out how an individual's identity crisis can draw in many other people. Ethicist Alasdair MacIntyre says this process reveals that each of us is engaged in pursuing "the unity of a "narrative quest" (219). The search for a sense of unity in our lives is not based on the chronological arrangement of facts about what we have done and been but is more like a literary work that yields a dramatic form with a beginning, middle and, as of the moment, an end whose telos or aim is our conception of the good. We are responsible, says MacIntyre, for the history of which we are the authors.

CASE STUDIES IN IDENTITY

Before we return to Pauline's struggle, it would be good to examine some other examples of identity challenges in later life. Most of the participants who attended the Life Transitions weekend workshops revealed during discussion periods that, as they evaluated what they wanted in their next

stage of life, they were compelled to revisit how they had made many previous life-changing choices. What lessons had they learned from these
experiences about values that had withstood the test of time?

One participant, "Don," a business entrepreneur, shows us how difficult it can be to reassess our identity. Don guessed, he told the group as
he looked around assessing his fellow participants, that he was probably
older than all of them. He then explained that he had chosen to remain
the head of a large real estate network in California well into his 70s
because he loved the challenges.

He said he already had "all the toys" that some people seek to acquire
in their later years. He owned and operated a helicopter, small jet, and
several boats, and possessed homes in three idyllic settings. In other
words, he had everything that one could want in order to compensate for
giving up a work-based identity. Don then announced to the group that
he had recently retired. The result, he said, was like "crashing into a brick
wall," a collision that left him feeling like he had "broken into pieces."

Don did not appear any the worse for wear after what sounded like a
near-fatal accident. Trim, white-haired and otherwise looking well preserved, Don was like a military general trapped among a bunch of civilians who had never been in a war. He wasn't haughty or arrogant, rather
he gave the impression that he rather pitied the others in the group for
not knowing what life was like at the very top of the mountain or, for that
matter, down in the trenches with bombs bursting overhead.

We got the impression that his somewhat younger wife, who accompanied him to the event, had encouraged Don to sign up for the seminar and
that he was making a reluctant appearance. Later she explained that she
was Don's second wife and that he had children from his first marriage
scattered around the country with whom he had infrequent contact. To
which, Don added that he had "never been much of a family man."

Don is an example of that small group of aging adults who simply
cannot retire. And while some have no other choice either because they
cannot find work or because a disability precludes continuing in what
they had been doing, Don did have a choice. He hadn't been forced out;
though later he admitted he wasn't bringing the same degree of drive and
ingenuity that he felt was characteristic of his middle to late career. For

Don there was no path untrodden, no reward unreceived. He had won all the medals. Now what?

During the course of the weekend seminar, Don loosened up a bit, chatted during break time with others, mostly the men, and could be heard to laugh on occasion. For his wife, as she put it, there was no problem about retirement. She had her book club, a daughter from a previous marriage with whom she enjoyed weekly outings, there were also grandchildren she kept up with and made sure to visit several times a year. Retirement was Don's problem and this seminar was, she said, her "last hope." In his ennui Don was "taking her down with him."

For his part Don said he was determined to find a solution. His seminar peers were eager to help restore the shattered businessman to wholeness. Suggestions flew. What about religion or spirituality? Couldn't he find peace in the pew or on the yoga mat? Don was an Episcopalian, he declared. Thank you very much. How about volunteering for a cause? Favorite ones were suggested such as Habitat for Humanity, Big Brother-Big Sister, even the Peace Corps.

Don said he'd already practically given away hundreds of houses and did some *pro bono* consulting for housing developments in South America. These were great projects but, still, not the same as being commander-in-chief and seeing his portfolio continue to grow, giving Don a dual measure of self-importance and financial self-worth.

The participants seemed to have read the Eriksonian account of the contest between integrity and despair and were determined to help Don gain the former and defeat the latter. And though they grew weary of the task, as a side benefit they took note of some of the ideas that Don had deflected. They wanted to make Don into their own image of a successful retirement transitioner, but he was reluctant to play the role. The seminar ended with Don and his wife embracing in front of the group and telling us all what a great time they had had. Would he report back at some later time? I asked. Don nodded.

When Don signed up to attend the Life Transitions weekend he very likely knew that the seminar would have little influence on his eventual decision. But by attending, he would appease his wife and would suggest that he was open to an alternative future – which, in all likelihood, he was not. Still, he could say to his wife, "See, at least I gave it a shot."

Several months after the workshop, I received a letter from Don on handsome stationery embellished with his initials. Don had found a solution but not one that any of us "civilians" had offered. The year was 2008. The housing market was going to hell. The company in which he still held considerable financial interest was in a battle for survival. In other words, a new war had broken out that required the services of a seasoned general. Don went back to part-time work. For Don the role of the warrior hero was the only one worth playing, even if he could only do it two or three days a week. How his decision affected his wife and his marriage I do not know. What Don's decision underscores is that historical events, such as a downturn in the economy, can influence how we play our part in the late acts of our lives.

Identity, as Erikson so famously proclaimed, is a matter of both one's psychological make up and how the person is situated in what he termed "the historical moment." We don't always recognize just what the historical moment consists of when we are in the midst of it. Simone de Beauvoir had her wake-up call when the German army came marching through the Arc de Triomphe in Paris, thus inaugurating a six-year occupation of France and completely changing how she had planned to conduct her life. Before that moment, she had thought of her personal life choices as primary, and political matters, "history," as secondary. She was wrenched from her individualistic worldview and learned another powerful lesson about "contingency" than the one that framed her amorous arrangement with Sartre.

Personal history can be swept away by world history. Events that are outside our control can overwhelm our hopes and expectations. Cultural norms and social restrictions can do the same, as de Beauvoir came to realize. She had a similar epiphany several years later when she began her research on the history of women's lives and discovered that though she had believed herself an equal to men and to have been treated accordingly, nevertheless, she had not, in truth, escaped being a part of "the second sex."

Regarding oneself as situated in history is not always experienced as a limitation to identity. It can also be an enhancement of it. A sense of history and a commitment to family tradition can play a profound role in how one perceives his or her identity in later life.

When I knew him in the late 1980s Arthur Flemming was a member of the board of The National Council on the Aging, where I worked in Washington, D.C. NCOA is a non-profit association of professionals in the field of aging and an advocacy organization that lobbies for legislation to improve the lives of seniors. Flemming saw himself as a part of history. He was the kind of person who could say, as Tennyson has his figure of Ulysses proclaim in the poem of the same name, "I am a part of all that I have met." The causes and values that had defined Flemming's career had defined him as a person.

From 1974 to 1981, Arthur Flemming, a Republican, had served as chairperson of the U.S. Commission on Civil Rights. Before that he was Secretary of Health, Education and Welfare during the Eisenhower administration. In an activist-oriented retirement, Flemming was deeply involved in campaigning to defend the national retirement income support program through an organization called Save Our Social Security.

In 1987, at an annual banquet that would honor his outstanding contribution to improving the lives of older persons, Flemming was to receive an award and with it a token of esteem from the NCOA board and staff. I was assigned the task of finding some suitable gift for him. It was mentioned that he was a liberal Republican who had great love and admiration for Abraham Lincoln. The budget was set and I proceeded to make my selection, tracking down a two-volume first edition set of Carl Sandburg's *The Life of Lincoln* that I purchased from a rare book dealer.

At the banquet, it was my job to rush to the dais when then-president of NCOA, Jack Ossofsky, congratulated Flemming on the award he was receiving and then mentioned a token of the Council's appreciation for services rendered. On cue, I handed the gift-wrapped package to Flemming who promptly removed the paper and examined the leather-bound, gilt-edged books. He held them up to the audience and said: "Thank you. This is something my family will cherish in the years to come."

By then I'd returned to my seat at one of the banquet tables where a half-eaten slice of pie beckoned to me. Fork poised, I found myself in a stop action moment. What had Flemming just said? His family? Years to come? I put my fork down. Here was a person in his 80s with a distinguished career in public service who chose to carry on in support of social causes he believed in. He, too, was a type of warrior but his battles were on behalf of others. Flemming's immediate and unrehearsed response to the collector's-item gift was to see it not as a personal possession but already as an heirloom. It was as if he had already passed on and the two-volume *Life of Lincoln* now stood on a bookshelf in the home of a son, daughter or grandchild.

Flemming's father, I later learned, had been a judge in upstate New York. He'd also been active in the local community as the head of various civic organizations. His son Arthur had followed in the same family tradition.

PAULINE REVISITED

At the time of the weekend seminar, Pauline was still finding her way. About a year later, I took a call from her. She told me that she had added something to her main tenet – "Don't go where you're not welcomed." The new imperative read: "Do affirm opportunities that arise in the form of invitations."

"My participation in the weekend seminar helped me to take a deep breath. I realized I was going to have to give myself some time to allow new possibilities to come percolating up to the surface. I'm not good about being patient," Pauline laughed over the phone. "Things are going better now."

Pauline explained that rather than resolving to take some single perspective of truth about herself, she decided to accept both her strengths and weakness. Meanwhile, she found outlets for her need to serve others by volunteering for a free medical clinic as a part-time office manager. She and her partner had taken a long overdue vacation. Gradually, messages began to arrive via emails and through her network of professional colleagues and friends about ways in which her talents were needed.

"Some of these invitations were kind of far out," said Pauline. "I mean, like coach the little league team that my cousin's daughter played on? I'd been on a women's softball team in college but I hadn't picked up a bat in probably thirty years."

Still, following her determination to consider all options that showed up on her doorstep, Pauline said yes. As it turned out, she loved coaching and it renewed her interest in baseball and attending home team games. In Sartrean parlance, she was acquiring new projects. In MacIntyre's perspective, she was utilizing her moral compass to charter her moral integrity. In de Beauvoirian terms, she had resisted the imposition of values that others might have held and braved the task of finding her own unique way.

REFERENCES

Beauvoir, Simone de (1977). *The Force of Circumstance.* New York: Harper and Row.

——————————— (1949/1997). *The Second Sex.* London: Vintage Books.

Erikson, Erik H. (1977). *Life History and the Historical Moment.* New York: Norton.

Judt, Tony (1992). *Past Imperfect: French Intellectuals, 1944-1956.* Berkeley, CA: University of California Press.

MacIntyre, Alasdair (2007). *After Virtue. A Study in Moral Theory.* Third Edition. Notre Dame, Indiana: Notre Dame University Press.

9. DESIRE

Desire, our ninth star, is not a uniquely existential category, yet it is the central driving theme of every piece of existential literature. Manifestations of desire – love, hate, greed, the will to dominate or to be dominated – pulse through the existentialist novel and short story. Existential thinkers inherited the concept of desire from a long line of predecessors.

Plato, in the *Symposium*, traces an ascending arc of desire from the carnality of lust to the pursuit of the ideal of the beautiful soul. Moving from the corporeal to the incorporeal, Plato links the ultimate goal of desire to the quest for immortality. Central to Plato's formulation is that desire originates within us as a feeling that something is missing, has been taken away, and that we experience ourselves as incomplete beings.

Likewise Sartre and de Beauvoir's contemporary, the psychoanalyst Jacques Lacan, delves into the philosophical implications of Freudian theory, arguing that desire is the never satisfied difference between need and demand. For Lacan, even the possession of the object of one's love leaves an abundance of unquenchable desire such that desire always begets desire. A great body of philosophical writing is devoted to exhorting readers to squelch desire by living according to reason. But that is not the path of our French existentialists, for whom desire is the momentum of life.

The springboard for existentialism's fascination with desire derives, in part, from Hegel who begins his exposition on desire in *Phenomenology of Mind* with the assertion that "self-consciousness is the state of desire in general" (212). For Hegel, consciousness of self is a restless movement through which the self seeks to complete itself through becoming self-identical. This notion surfaces in Sartre's theory of consciousness as the illusory quest, manifested at the deepest ontological level, that humans seek to become masters of their own destiny or God-like beings. Sartre tries to capture this idea in the term that represents inert objects, "being-in-itself."

The complexities of human desire unfold throughout Sartre and de Beauvoir's plays and novels. Their characters are mainly young or in early middle age but as we all know, desire, whether as hunger, thirst, greed, need or passion, though it may dim, stays aflame as we grow older. Next we find our way into the relationship between age and Eros at the cinema where, in a contemporary film, passion erupts among the elderly.

MARIGOLDS

The night we went to dinner and the movies was in celebration of our second anniversary. We had both been married previously and often discussed the ups and downs of marriage and the changing nature of romance and a couple's erotic life. Perhaps such candid talk is easier in later life when you have more perspective and, hopefully, more self-knowledge. Also, it may be a time when you're less driven by physical needs and passions and when having kids – you had and have them, or you didn't and don't – is no longer an issue. As the rates of divorce and remarriage continue to rise for Americans, Britons and Europeans over age 60, the persistence of the erotic element is a frequent topic for discussion and debate among gerontologists and the general public. We had heard that the romantic comedy, *The Best Exotic Marigold Hotel*, dealt with love, sex and fidelity among the elderly, so it seemed like a fitting choice for the evening.

The 2012 movie follows the trials and tribulations of seven English retirees who trade an unaffordable and bleak British future for the chance to reinvigorate their lives in an economical retirement hotel in Jaipur, India. Arriving at their destination, they discover their anticipated haven is itself in need of rehabilitation. As for Jaipur, the promised sun-dappled paradise, the city turns out to be hot, humid, crowded, noisy, and rife with the odors of an unfamiliar cuisine and a malfunctioning sanitation system. Discomforted, displaced and despondent, the couples and singles of this septet struggle to adapt to their new environment. The film follows their growth and transformation as they move from shocked immobility to resourceful action. It turns out the shabby hotel and its colorful surroundings not only hold the promise to spark renewed romance but also to bring one marriage to a breaking point. There's a lot of humor in the movie along with some poignant shedding of tears.

When we were leaving the theater, I observed it had attracted mainly an audience of people who could easily have played minor character roles in the film. For most of us, I think it was comforting to find a reflection of our own lives acted out against the background of another cultural setting. But why was the hotel named for a flower, the marigold? Having never been there, I didn't know whether they grew marigolds in India. The significance of this detail would not be revealed until sometime later.

I read in the paper that the film had been a huge box office hit. This got me to thinking about the comparatively smaller number of people, mainly documentary film buffs and scholars attending feminist and gerontologist conferences, who had found their way to Deidre Fishel's topically related film, *Still Doing It: The Intimate Lives of Women over 65*. Fishel's 2004 documentary (and subsequent 2008 book) profiles nine women (straight, gay, single, partnered, black and white) who candidly describe their feelings about their bodies, their sexuality, their desires and their loves. The take away of both films and a host of other box office hits such as the 2012 comedy, *Something's Gotta Give*, is that it's increasingly common for people in mid- and later life to pursue romance and sexual gratification despite ageist attitudes, chronic health problems and, in some instances, the disapproval of family members and friends.

Recent gerontological studies of sexuality and aging (summarized in John DeLamater and Sara M. Moorman's 2007 study, "Sexual Behavior in Later Life") corroborate the premise of these films that mature adults continue to experience the desire for the touch of another body. And while the frequency of lovemaking does decrease with age, at least one-third of those over 65 engage in various forms of sexual intimacy well into later life. Further corroborating this point, are articles on sex in later life appearing with some frequency in *AARP the Magazine*, a publication that reaches the households of some 40 million AARP members and other readers over the age of 50.

The cover of the August/September 2015 issue invited readers to turn to page 56 where they would discover "Best Sex. Ever! Even in Your 70s. We Show You How." Some will be disappointed not to find any compelling visuals and nothing in fact on sex after 70. But AARP's "love and relationships ambassador," Pepper Schwartz, does answer several practical questions from readers about the joys and perils of lovemaking, including one from a 65 year-old woman, "celibate for four years," who is now involved with a younger (61-year-old) man and enjoying the proverbial "amazing sex." The woman writes that she and her mate describe their relationship as being "friends with benefits." She admits that she's "a little scared," wondering whether her newfound eroticism is "normal at my age?" Schwartz reassures her "it's quite normal," but cautions whether the woman might find that in having "great sex," she might begin to wish for "great love." The need for "emotional connection" can lead to her need for a "bigger commitment than the other," and therefore the possibility of "some heartbreak in your future."

Ambassador Schwartz's concern reflects issues that surface on TV and radio talk shows and in self-help books about love and desire "after 50." From these we glean that, as in earlier stages of adulthood, sexuality and romance always seem to entangle us in issues of control, fidelity, self-image, trust, vulnerability and emotional triggers of past joys, hurts, and losses.

Philosophers have long been aware of and sought to understand these issues. Returning to Plato's *Symposium*, we hear a series of speeches from an all-male cast of characters about the true nature of the Greek god, Eros. References to homoerotic love swirl around the wine cup-laden table. The playwright Aristophanes' discourse features a semi-comic account of sexual desire. According to legend, once there were four-armed, four-legged creatures, precursors to human beings, who were also dual-sexed, including both same-sex and opposite sex natures. The gods considered their powers threatening and so Zeus agreed to cleave them in half, leaving each unisexual. The unhappy creatures longed for their missing part and desperately sought them out in order to be reunited. And that, said Aristophanes, is the human plight -- the quest for one's missing half.

Though they are often characterized as having their heads in the clouds, philosophers like Plato demonstrate both their fanciful and realistic insights into the nature of human desire. Take, for example, Kant the most influential philosopher of the Enlightenment. In his *Lecture on Ethics*, Kant cautions against those (presumably men) motivated by lust, since it "makes of the loved person an object of appetite." Once that hunger has been sated, says Kant, "the person is cast aside as one casts away a lemon, which has been sucked dry" (163).

Sartre in Love

By his own account, Jean-Paul Sartre comes close to fitting this lemon-sucking description. How do we know? Our knowledge of Sartre's love life comes from works published after his death, such as de Beauvoir's *Adieux: A Farewell to Sartre*, the 1981 book which recounts the progression of an aged and infirm Sartre to his death, and *Letters to Castor and Others* published in 1982, and her own correspondence with Sartre in *Letters to Sartre* published after her death in 1990. From these sources we learn that while he coveted quite a number of women, he did not always discard them. In his later years, he kept several chilled in small Parisian apartments to which he would make weekly visits. Comparing himself to a physician, the dutiful Sartre says he continued to make the "rounds." He did so almost to the last months of his life.

Sartre was probably more empirically acquainted with lust than most philosophers. As for love, his views are not all that far apart from that of the *Symposium's* Aristophanes who identified desire with lack. Most of what we know about Sartre's philosophy of love, sex and desire comes from works written when he was in his late 30s.

Sartre's depiction of love is based on his phenomenological analysis of the primacy of desire, which he outlines in *Being and Nothingness*. The problem with love and sex, according to Sartre, is this. The motive of loving another person is the desire to be loved. While we may presume that it is our attraction to another person that kindles the spark of romance, actually we are already, in a sense, in love with love and are simply seeking a way to manifest this impulse. Sartre outlines the criteria for the chemistry of attraction to the beloved.

Since we are creatures perpetually in the process of becoming, we live in a state of uncertainty, anxiety and insecurity. What we long for is a greater sense of permanence or being self-grounded and, in that sense, God-like. That, we believe, is what our lover can do for us by making us their "whole world" through his or her spontaneously given adoration (*Being and Nothingness*, 364 ff).

From his or her side, while the beloved thrills in the attention of the lover who affirms the freedom and independence of the beloved, the beloved needs to continue to feel that the lover's attention is both emotionally spontaneous and willful. While basking in the certainty of this knowledge, the beloved needs to feel the excitement of constantly discovering and winning this attention. The result is that the beloved gains a sense of meaning and value through feeling important in the eyes of the lover. Sartre puts a lot of emphasis on the "look" or "glance" that communicates this bond between the lover and the beloved. Sartre says, "This is the basis for the joy of love when there is joy: we feel that our existence is justified."

However, this huge investment in the love relationship depends upon its permanence which, given the vicissitudes of human emotion, is always uncertain. Risks are involved. A reversal of affection means that the beloved is thrown back into a state of anxiety and insecurity. He or she is no longer "justified" and reverts once again to the status of a half-being. We cannot force someone to love us. That would defeat the whole point of the requirement that we feel the lover's love is spontaneously and voluntarily given rather than compelled, fated, or motivated by some other external factor such as wealth or social status. Therefore, says Sartre, the lover must always be seeking to "seduce" the would-be beloved who will, in turn, become a reciprocating lover.

Both lovers seek to retain their freedom and independence, yet each feels an element of threat. In taking possession of the beloved, the lover makes of the beloved a "thing," or objectified other who, in a sense, now belongs to us. But the other never ceases to be the creature that is "for-itself," an independent consciousness. Yet giving oneself to another in love means allowing the beloved to engulf one's independence and vice-versa. It is only when two lovers are prepared to give themselves to each other – mutually making "things" of one another, that what we call recip-rocal love occurs.

If each lover seeks in the other's gaze the affirmation requiring the other to serve as the ground of his or her being, which entails a sacrifice of freedom, then each experiences a state of dependency. But with depen-dency comes a loss of freedom. Thus, we have the ongoing conflict and the perpetual ambivalence of the love relationship. For Sartre, loving and, similarly, lovemaking always involves a contest of mastery and enslave-ment, of dominance and subservience.

Sartre is hardly the originator of the conflictual formulation of sexual love. He would have been quite familiar with the discussion of sexuality in Kant's 1797 work, *The Metaphysics of Morals*. There he would have read:

"A human being makes himself into a thing when he or she, motivated by lust, makes use of the other's sexual organs," or likewise gives themselves up to the other, doing so strictly for erotic enjoyment. This commodifying of one's body, Kant argues, conflicts with something inherent, some "right of humanity" (62), which is our intrinsic worth as a sovereign being. But this use of others and of oneself, as if each were like properties that could be acquired or disposed of, is a violation of human dignity since it means using the other person as a means (to gratifying oneself) and not as an end in him- or herself. There is, however, for Kant, one morally permissible condition for the give and take of genital sex beyond the purpose of procreation.

In marriage, says Kant, both partners may acquire one another sexually, "for in this way each reclaims itself and restores its personality" (62). Since in marriage each spouse has committed to a vow of duty to the other, they are able to give and take of one another in a mutuality of sexual gratification. Not only this aspect of genital pleasure is involved, says Kant, since to be a human being is to exist as a "whole unity," taking and giving some part of oneself means taking and giving the whole person.

Not surprisingly, given Kant's stricture for genital sex, infidelity is not morally permissible because it means breaking the covenant of marriage, which has been entered into voluntarily under a rationally grasped principle to will a universal good. Like Kant's, Sartre's formulation places the moral agent at the core of ethics and locates the will or volitional capacity within that core. But Sartre insists that the will is defined as freedom of self-determination. That there are no laws of human nature to fall back upon and that rationality is not what makes human beings unique, rather it is the inescapable condition of self-creation, which also means the creation of values. That these values may sometimes lead to conflict with the values of others is inevitable.

If Sartre's version of the lovers' dilemma sounds like the plot of hundreds of movies, novels and plays, it is. Only, in most cases, the conflictual narrative is resolved through union or marriage (in comedies), the death of one or both lovers (in tragedies), or self-sacrifice (in religious morality tales). These outcomes change the situation but, from a Sartrean point of view, they don't change the dynamics.

Consider the number of movies (e.g. Bergman's *Scenes from A Marriage*), plays (e.g. Ibsen's *Hedda Gabler*) and novels (e.g. Tolstoy's *Anna Karenina*) that begin with a seemingly happy marriage only to disclose the dissatisfaction of one or the other partner. Variations on the theme of dissatisfaction include a perceived absence of freedom in the relationship, a weight of dependency, subservience, or the lovers' triangle. The latter plot is based on interruption of the marital relationship through the appearance of a third party. It is the intruder's beguiling glance that causes one of the partner's to reassess the relationship as seen from outside, triggering awareness of fresh possibilities. It would seem that there is no end of lovers trying to out-transcend one another in the game of domination-subservience.

Sartre's bleak version of desire as manifested in love and sexuality certainly has its critics, including Simone de Beauvoir, to whom Sartre admitted that he tended to withhold himself at the moment of orgasm, a reflection of his urgent need to remain in control of relationships. However, the account in *Being and Nothingness* was not his last word on the subject. In that vast tome, Sartre hints that there are "other ways of loving" if both parties alter their pre-reflective fundamental projects – i.e. the way in which they are in love with love. Curiously, for an atheist philosopher, he looks to something that at first sounds vaguely religious.

CONVERSION

Sartre accumulated a large collection of notes toward writing a follow-up work to *Being and Nothingness,* a promised treatise on "ethics," that would include revisiting the topic of love. He was dissatisfied with his progress and set it aside. *Notebooks for an Ethics* was published posthumously by his adopted daughter, Arlette Elkaim-Sartre, in 1983 and translated into English in 1992. The latter work provides what some scholars consider a sunnier account of love relationships than the conflictual version found in his magnum opus of 1943. In the *Notebooks* account, Sartre points to the possibility of an authentic love relationship in which both lovers reflectively recognize, care for, and affirm each other's freedom. But they can only achieve this quality of relating if they are able to undergo a process he calls a "conversion."

To overcome what Sartre dubs the "perpetual dissatisfaction of the lovers" would be to achieve a kind of love relationship in which each participant becomes a being that has a fixed, yet free, ontological identity. Viewed in terms of Aristophanes' legend, this would amount to being complete, self-identical and free of the desire for a missing half. However, says Sartre, this is an impossibility. Precisely by consciously accepting the futility of this quest and abandoning the project, individuals may take a step forward toward a new possibility for a mutual love relationship that allows the freedom and independence of the other to remain intact and even affirmed.

The Sartrean conversion is nothing less than holding as one's utmost conviction that freedom is our highest ethical goal. This entails the realization of our fundamental ontology that as free beings we create ourselves out of a vast abyss of nothingness.

"Conversion provokes a transformation in consciousness's view of and relation to the objectivity of its body, world and other people," says Sartre (*Notebook for An Ethics*, 12). Though his account is highly convoluted, the gist of his theory is that it is possible for two individuals to recognize the ways in which they each benefit from the objectification of being seen by the other, an objectification that does not need to be experienced as a threat (domination) but as an affirmation that enhances each one's way of being-in-the-world.

Since, as the saying goes, it takes two to tango, clearly for a conversion of consciousness to manifest itself in a love relationship, the lover who first converts must appeal to the beloved to also undergo a conversion. Only then will the reciprocal love relationship be attained in celebration of the "we" of two mutually affirming free subjectivities. Intimacy, in this post-conversion love relationship, consists in not only a sense of closeness but also the feeling that the beloved will support the lover, and viceversa, in their attempt to achieve their independent projects.

Readers of *Notes* might begin to wonder whether what Sartre is describing as the post-conversion form of love is the type of amorous friendship he had with Simone de Beauvoir throughout their adult lives. Did Sartre and Simone de Beauvoir achieve this type of converted love relationship? Both embraced the same ontological views of human freedom as emerging from the nothingness of self-becoming. Neither sought an escape into withdrawal or inwardness or the illusory permanence of marriage. They supported one another's projects even into the realm of the erotic – i.e.

affairs with other partners. They could be critical of one another's literary and philosophical works in progress and certain forms of behavior and yet remain dedicated to one another's welfare. They even ensured that they would be buried together. Sartre's ideal was perhaps influenced by Kant's depiction of an ideal friendship.

In his *Lectures on Ethics*, Kant defined moral friendship as "the complete confidence of two persons in revealing their secret judgments and feelings to each other, as far as such disclosures are consistent with mutual respect" (471). This kind of friendship is not dependent upon feelings that can be inconsistent over time. The friendship provided by a confidant fills a need we have to express our innermost thoughts to someone. However, would having secret sexual affairs with others be consistent with "mutual respect?" Clearly, for Kant, the answer is No. Ironically, Sartre and de Beauvoir might give the same answer. Living up to this ideal of the lover-confidant proved to be elusive for them. But perhaps not for other existentialists.

THE CONVERTED

In 1961, the English translator of *Being and Nothingness*, University of Colorado philosophy professor Hazel Barnes, began recording the first segment of a ten-part, half-hour television series to discuss her favorite topic, Existentialism. Produced by the Denver affiliate of National Public Educational TV, the show was called *Self-Encounter,* a fitting title for authenticity-scrutinizing philosophers and for Barnes, too, since she had successfully managed to break the glass ceiling of academic philosophy, whose departments at that time included few if any women.

Barnes was also leading what was for the 1960s an unconventional lifestyle. In her 1997 autobiography, *The Story I Tell Myself,* Barnes acknowledges and lovingly portrays in a matter-of-fact way, "my longtime companion, Doris Schwalbe." Barnes had earlier, in 1967, dedicated her book, *An Existential Ethics,* to Schwalbe. Since the topics of sexuality, love, eroticism, lesbianism and the general category of desire are well-explored in the writings of Simone de Beauvoir and Jean-Paul Sartre, on whom Barnes was an expert, it is perhaps not surprising that Barnes would see her own sexual liberation reinforced in their ideas.

Barnes acknowledges that in writing an autobiography she felt the obligation to be self-disclosing about some aspects of her personal life.

"Public discussion of private matters" is appropriate, says Barnes, when a relationship has been an important part of both one's intellectual and emotional life. However, Barnes quips, "It does not grant license to bring all the household goods outdoors for a yard sale" (272).

Barnes admired de Beauvoir's courageous insistence on shaping and living her life her own way and for making a major contribution to 20th-century intellectual life. While she did not consciously model herself after de Beauvoir, Barnes says Beauvoir "represented for me in many respects the apotheosis of the type of woman I wanted to be – even before I read *The Second Sex*" (185). Barnes is not uncritical of some of the manipulative sexual liaisons in which Sartre and de Beauvoir engaged, revelations which came out after Beauvoir's death and, therefore, subsequent to all of Barnes' scholarly articles and her own books on existentialism. She conducted a deeply reaffirming interview with de Beauvoir in her Parisian apartment in the summer of 1984.

In discussing the quality of her relationship with Doris Schwalbe, Hazel Barnes says that when they met neither had wanted to play the traditional roles of wife and mother. Though they had both experienced very similar forms of social conditioning with respect to gender roles, neither had any sense of having failed "in not achieving a recognized social status in marriage," which would have undermined the personal satisfaction they experienced in their companionship. Having no models for how their relationship should, by convention, be conducted, they had to work out their own version of a lifestyle. The couple sought a completely egalitarian relationship. As Barnes notes: "Nothing but strict equality would have been workable for two strong-willed persons who regarded individual freedom as the fundamental indispensable value on which all other goods are based" (273).

Barnes says the couple did work out a division of labor based on skills and inclinations. Doris did the cooking, Hazel, the cleaning up. Doris took charge of home repairs while Hazel did the bookkeeping. Each of the couple developed friendships through separate interests – fishing and stamp collecting for Doris, film viewing for Hazel. Over the years they became the equivalent of "relatives of one another's relatives, close friends of friends one or the other of us knew first" (274).

As for what it is that held them together for more than three decades, Barnes says it was their shared enthusiasm for the humanistic philosophy of Sartre and de Beauvoir. The liberationist emphasis on freedom from convention, freedom for self-definition, responsibility and personal value making were crucial. In addition, certain homespun, middle-American qualities gleaned in childhood also pertained, such as independence, self-sufficiency, individualism, concern for others, justice, accountability, honesty and integrity. While these admired and aspired to qualities persisted, Barnes and Schwalbe subtracted from the mix their fathers' political conservatism.

ROLE MODELS

Reflective in the relationship of Barnes and Schwalbe, Sartre and de Beauvoir's well publicized, open relationship and emancipatory views about gender and sexuality had a profound influence on many European and American young people during the heady years of social experimentation in the 1960s and 70s. In the way they were purported to balance fidelity to one another with the freedom to experience "contingent" love affairs, their openness and persistent intimacy, mutual intellectual and artistic support and honest criticism, the lifelong friends, sometime lovers, and political and cultural collaborators served thousands of youths as role models for the new liberated lifestyle of the post-1950s.

When Sartre died in 1980, an estimated 50,000 people, mainly of the younger generation, followed the processional. Six years later, a more modest but still sizable crowd of 5,000 people gathered to watch as de Beauvoir's ashes were interred in the same Montparnasse cemetery plot as Sartre's. A small square in the Saint-Germain-des-Prés quarter was subsequently named Place Sartre-Beauvoir.

A few years later, the publication of collections of their letters and several new biographies that included interviews in the last years of their lives, brought to light many surprises about less than transparent and sometimes secret love affairs, betrayals and conflicts among the "family" of acolytes that belonged to the couple's inner circle. Long-time critics, especially those on the right, pointed to these transgressions as evidence of the moral failure of the couple's brand of existentialism and of their left-wing politics. Those with a more left-leaning political and social orientation were perplexed at these revelations, admitting, in the words of biographer Hazel Rowley, that Sartre and de Beauvoir might have "strained at times against their own philosophy," while partially excusing them on the grounds that "few people have lived life more intensely."

There are few notable philosophers whose political, social and especially sexual behavior can be measured against the tenets of their philosophies. This is because our knowledge of their private and even public lives is, compared to Sartre and de Beauvoir, relatively scant and because their idiosyncrasies are regarded as neither supporting nor detracting from the conceptual products of their minds. However, when philosophers take the position that how one lives, acts and puts his or her life on the line is a manifestation of their philosophy, then assessing the "strain" against the philosophy is meaningful and important.

TYPES OF LOVE

Not unlike most philosophers with an original mind, Sartre took from his predecessors only what he needed to advance his own philosophical ideas. He took Kierkegaard's starting point, the "existing subjective thinker," and made it into the "for-itself" mode of consciousness confronting its own finitude, corporeality and mortality. Kierkegaard's "angst," the feeling of a "yawning abyss of freedom" (*Concept of Anxiety*, 61), which, said the Dane, is like imagining that you are swimming over a depth of 60,000 fathoms, this vertiginous dread Sartre turned into a slightly different kind of deep-sea qualm. His protagonist, as mentioned earlier, the 30-year-old Antoine Roquentin, describes the queasy feeling that results from his confrontation with freedom in the face of the indifference of the universe as "nausea." Sartre had no use for Kierkegaard's God whom he considered ontologically superfluous. He did take note of Kierkegaard's portrait of the seducer in the pseudonymous work, *Either/Or*.

The seducer was a role Sartre played in real life, almost to the end of his days. Kierkegaard, on the other hand, for all his eloquence in "Diary of A Seducer," and "Quidam's Diary" (from his *Stages on Life's Way*) merely managed to charm a 14-year-old girl from a wealthy family, Regine Olsen, into accepting an engagement ring and a wedding date set four years hence. He would later break off the engagement using the ruse that he was an irresponsible dandy, incapable of committing to monogamy and a fellow over whom it was pointless to shed any tears.

In his writing, Kierkegaard would repeatedly return to the suffering and self-sacrifice that was necessitated to break off the engagement and exclude himself from the ranks of the marriageable. Faithful in his own way, Kierkegaard left his meager estate to his former fiancé, now Mrs. Regine Schlegel. Sartre also was a fugitive from the marriage vow though he had several close calls. While Kierkegaard, as far as most scholars can determine from his diaries and journals, had little to no sexual experience with women, Sartre had a great deal.

Perhaps this comparison is unfair. After all, Kierkegaard and Sartre lived in vastly different eras with different standards of sexual behavior. Sartre belonged to a "liberated" crowd of artists, intellectuals and writers for whom sexual encounters in and out of marriage were commonplace. Kierkegaard grew up in a pietistically religious household and associated mainly with highly educated men. During his student days at the university, he did carry on like many of his peers with excessive drinking and high jinx. But his singular human love object was, like many other writers of the middle 19th century, a figure of impossible conquest not, in his case, because of unrequited love, but because of his depressive nature, unsuitable disposition for matrimony, and his sense of destiny that made his a preferential love of the eternal, not the temporal.

For Sartre love was *eros;* for Kierkegaard *agape.* As Kierkegaard compares the two forms of love, the erotic and the Christian, he says the former is selfish, is aimed at the lover's desire, is built on visual objectification of the beloved and is limited to a relation between two people. Agape is spiritual duty to serve the neighbor without discrimination or preferentiality; it is selfless, requires self-sacrifice, humility and transparency, as far as motive is concerned. Agape, for Kierkegaard is the fruit of the work of love, known only through faith that animates the individual's relation to others. In this sense, love involves God as the "third" in the relation. In other words, God, or more accurately, Christ, is called into presence through agapic acts of love. The requirement of the Christian lover in seeking to help the other experience salvation is to become invisible. For if the beloved sees that he or she is dependent on another for coming into faith, then the relationship becomes an impediment.

Secrecy, for Kierkegaard, is a requirement of the helper. That, presumably, is one reason he chose the strategy of indirect communication, using pseudonyms to disguise his authorship, and ironic or paradoxical arguments to draw readers into his "enabling dialectic." Kierkegaard, in emulating Christ, was a secret and self-sacrificing lover of the "individual" who, he hoped, might become his reader. The ideal of love toward which Kierkegaard pointed was beyond any ethical principle supported by an appeal to universality and reason. It required a leap of faith. Love is a duty, a divine command. It cannot be carried out as the logical conclusion to a series of postulates.

For his part, Sartre's work of love was that of an enabler who created emotional and financial dependencies in his women. For example, he wrote certain roles in his plays for several of his mistresses. He encouraged them to broaden their minds and gave them books and records, took them on vacations and gave them money. He ended up financially supporting three women at one time besides adopting a young woman who, for a brief time, had been a lover and to whom he left his estate.

But, like his analysis of erotic desire in *Being and Nothingness*, he sought to love in order to be loved. He basked in the warmth of admiration. In the conflict between fidelity and freedom, he chose the latter and struggled to balance the former, sometimes by maintaining secrecy among his lovers so that one did not know he was also visiting the other on a weekly basis. Much of this would come out after Sartre's death through interviews with de Beauvoir and others and through the publication of collections of Sartre's letters. Many felt hurt and misused though, in truth, they played a role in their own plight through self-deception and passivity. Simone de Beauvoir was the only beloved who did not fall into this pattern. As she and Sartre pledged early in their relationship, they would leave room in their unconditional love of one another for "contingencies." Fortunately, neither had children except by adoption – one apiece, both girls.

THE EXCEPTION

"The greatest souls are capable of the greatest vices as well as the greatest virtues," says Descartes in his *Meditations*. Sartre and de Beauvoir might qualify as such "great souls." Perhaps because they chose to live life to the hilt, to boldly assert their truths, and to allow the public more than a glimpse of both their acts of wisdom and of folly, Sartre and de Beauvoir exposed themselves to accusations that their lives were in contradiction to their philosophies. They might have done a better job of keeping their public image intact. Whether they were exhibitionists determined to ensure the longevity of their fame or committed public intellectuals willing to bare their secrets (which probably would have come to light anyway), remains to be seen.

Kierkegaard, who, wearing the mantle of Socratic irony, led a life of "hidden inwardness," used his literary strategy of indirect communication to keep the reader's attention on the text as a mirror to the self rather than on the narrator as an authority whose life outlook they might try to imitate. A man with a divided public and private persona, Kierkegaard gave a name to those who discovered that in some way or ways they could not mold themselves to conform to ideals of ethical perfection. He asked if we all aren't, in some ways, "exceptions" to personally held ideals of moral perfection.

A person who could write brilliantly about "The Aesthetic Validity of Marriage," in the second volume of *Either/Or*, while simultaneously in the process of renouncing the possibility of marital bliss, Kierkegaard was a self-proclaimed exception. And yet Kierkegaard, too, made sure that the suffering he incurred over breaking off his engagement with Regine Olsen would eventually come to light with the posthumous publication of his massive collection of journals and papers.

For Kierkegaard, exceptionality was not a badge of honor, rather it was a burden of guilt, understanding guilt as the consciousness that one remained powerless to achieve one's own ideal of perfection. In this sense, the person who acknowledges that he or she is an exception also acknowledges being "unacceptable" in his or her own eyes. For Kierkegaard, guilt opens the way toward salvation and the possibility of forgiveness – being accepted despite being unacceptable. Not surprisingly, Sartre and de Beauvoir seem impervious to pangs of guilt or, for that matter, to those of regret. They are simply fallible human beings whose only redemption was literary immortality.

Tillich

Perhaps it is fitting to round out this exploration of desire with reference to another major figure of twentieth century existentialism, a German-born theologian who fled Nazi Germany to take up academic posts in the United States, first at Union Theological Seminary in New York, then at Harvard where he was made University Professor, and finally at the

University of Chicago. In a well-regarded and then (1951) quite popular book, *The Courage to Be*, Paul Tillich embraces existentialism as the philosophical outlook that demands involvement and participation in society and in how one conducts one's life.

For Tillich, existentialism best addresses the conditions of society in the aftermath of World War II. He points to the rise of a modernized and secularized international culture, the collapse of spiritual certainties, and the inescapable awareness (fed by the prospects of nuclear annihilation) of death. In the geopolitical realm, he notes the costs of acquiescence to the demagoguery of leaders who champion social conformity and who seek to chastise and even punish divergence from strict codes of behavior. For Tillich, the antidote to the mid-twentieth century malaise of anxiety, doubt and meaninglessness is a type of deep-seated or "ontological courage" that resides in each of us and which can be accessed through a type of "self-affirmation" facilitated through the symbolic language of Christianity.

One of the impediments to courage, says Tillich, "is uncontrolled desires that create masks and put them over men and things" (14). Some desires, Tillich explains, drawing on the Roman Stoic philosopher Seneca, are natural because they are "limited by objective needs." Think of hunger, thirst, shelter, and safety. These can be satisfied.

Other desires are limitless, distorted by imagination to project wants that can never be satisfied. Though Tillich doesn't name them, we assume he is alluding to desires stemming from lust, greed, avarice and the will to domination. Only by gaining control over these types of desires by "participation in universal reason," can the Stoic achieve the "courage of wisdom." Stoical courage is, as it were for Tillich's historical analysis, a stage along the way towards the ultimate "courage to be" that Tillich believes is accessible through "the ground of being" that is the Christian God.

Tillich was one of the most admired of public intellectuals of the 1940s and 50s. Academic philosophers and theologians pondered his scholarly works and millions of soul-searching non-specialists sought his spiritual inspiration in books like *The Courage to Be* and *Dynamics of Faith* (1957). Tillich died in 1965 at the age of 79. Eight years later, Tillich's second wife (his first marriage ended in divorce in 1921), Hannah Tillich published her autobiography, *From Time to Time*. In that candid and often poetical work, she revealed that from the beginning of their marriage her husband

insisted on having an open relationship so that, not unlike Sartre's agreement with de Beauvoir, the two of them could pursue contingent love
affairs. This Hannah Tillich apparently begrudgingly accepted although
in her autobiography she celebrates her ideal of a configured love relationship, that of two couples in a foursome. "It meant more than a quick
copulation," she says of this arrangement. "It was a break with the whole
concept of monogamy, it was the new concept of participation without
losing one's identity, of becoming more and not less in a foursome." The
foursome, says Hannah Tillich, did not include Paul.

Still the love of Hannah's life, Paul traveled to lecture in Europe and
throughout the United States and so was away a great deal until the later
part of their lives. Then, when his deteriorating health and frailty kept
him closer to home, he and Hannah experienced closer bonds of intimacy
and trust. Nevertheless, she chose to tip the pedestal on which her husband's bust, his public persona, stood perched.

Hannah Tillich shocked her husband's admirers when she also revealed
that Paul had a weakness for pornography and that he was fascinated by
images of crucified-emulating female nudes. Feminist scholar Mary Daly
says of Hannah Tillich's revelations that male "theologians have always
fantasized a female hanging on the cross" (94). Daly argues as part of her
critique of homocentric and misogynist tendencies in Christianity that
"sadomasochistic fantasies," and "torture for 'higher causes,'" have always
been a part of the Christian cross-bearing theology.

Should one think less of Tillich's scholarly and popular works in light
of his wife's revelations? Or is it the case that, as Descartes observed, even
great minds and wise sages may fail in certain ways to live up to their own
principles and ideals?

MORE MARIGOLDS

If *The Best Exotic Marigold Hotel* was considered a "sleeper" success,
critics dubbed its 2015 sequel, *The Second Best Exotic Marigold Hotel*,
variously as tiresome, tedious and over-long, but on the positive side also
tender and poignant. Most of the same distinguished cast of veteran actors
comes to life again in sunny Jaipur, India, but now the characters hold
salary-generating encore careers instead of living on fixed-income retirement funds. The characters are now involved in a number of work-for-pay
enterprises such as managing the hotel and planning for expansion to a

second restorable edifice, buying textiles for an exporter, serving part-time as a local tour guide, and so on.

Romance is still in the air as plot lines from the first movie extend into the second. The threat of illness and death still looms on the horizon, lending dramatic tension to the movie as the characters strive to make each day count as a reprieve from the inevitable. A new personality, an American visitor purportedly recently divorced and working on a novel, Guy Chambers, played by Richard Gere, winds up in a romantic rela-tionship with the young Indian comic character Sonny's hard-driving businesswoman mother. The movie ends in the great tradition of both Shakespearean and Bollywood comedies. Viewers are treated to a color-ful, noisy, family healing, and community solidifying dance party cele-brating the marriage of the young Indian couple whose difficulties had served as the subplot to the unfolding stories of the expat seniors.

There's little overt sex (a kiss, a closed bedroom door) in *Marigold* One and Two, though adultery, coming out as a gay man, and romance with multiple partners are, not very shockingly, included in the plot. In fact, both movies pretty much take for granted that audiences will accept the premise that self-realization and self-fulfillment through sexual pleasure is an important, if not essential, part of adult love at any age.

Moreover that when the promises of earlier love commitments (e.g., in marriage) end in disappointment, there is still time for a new, possibly better, though perhaps briefer, love relationship even in one's 70s. Earlier ideals of permanence, fidelity and the sacred character of sexual relation-ships – aspects of traditional marital love – are completely abandoned in the *Marigold* movies and in many other films with related themes. Moreover, the characters also abandon their homelands and kin for a new life in an adopted country (and former colony) that while reflective of an ancient culture, forms the background for turning back the clock, even at the eleventh hour of a lifetime. Given the age of the actors, a Marigold Three is unlikely.

As for the flower in the title of the movies and the hotel name, more came to light in a conversation I had with an Indian friend I was telling about the film. He explained that marigolds were, indeed, important in Indian culture. "You see them everywhere in the market places, in temples and in homes," he commented. Known as *Genda*, they are widely grown in India and used in garlands that are tied to the frame of the main door of the house and loosely and abundantly heaped onto the steps and altars of shrines to gods such as Vishnu and Lakshmi. What significance did they have, I asked my friend? "Well," he said, "from the way you describe the plot of the movie, I'd say the connection is with passion and creativity. You would see tons of these flowers at weddings." Yes that would fit in with the two movies and it made sense to associate this flower with a hotel. And just when it seemed we had the symbolism all wrapped up, my friend raised a finger in second thought.

"You know, flowers often have multiple meanings. And in the case of the marigold there is at least one more."

I raised my eyebrows.

"Cruelty and jealousy," he replied.

REFERENCES

Barnes, Hazel E. (1997). *The Story I Tell Myself*. Chicago: University of Chicago Press.

Daly, Mary (1990). *Gyn/Ecology: The Metaethics of Radical Feminism*. Boston: Beacon Press.

DeLamater, John and Sara M. Moorman (2007). "Sexual Behavior in Later Life." *Journal of Aging and Health*. 19: 921-945.

Fishel, Deidre and Holtzberg, Diana (2008). *Still Doing It: The Intimate Lives of Women over 65*. New York: Penguin. Documentary film, 2004.

Hegel, G. W. F. (2003). *The Phenomenology of Mind*. Tr. J. B. Baillie. 2nd Revised Edition. Dover Publications.

Kant, Immanuel (1996). The Metaphysics of Morals. Tr. Mary Gregor. Cambridge, UK: Cambridge University Press.

_____ (1963). *Lectures on Ethics*, translated by Louis Infield. New York: Harper & Row.

Kierkegaard, S. (1980). *Concept of Anxiety*. Tr. Reidar Thomte and Albert B. Anderson. Princeton: Princeton University Press.

Sartre, Jean-Paul (1983/1992). *Notebook for an Ethics*. Translated by David Pellauer. Chicago: University of Chicago Press.

Tillich, Hannah (1974). *From Time to Time*. New York: Stein and Day Pub.

Tillich, Paul (1952). *The Courage to Be*. New Haven: Yale University Press.

10. Repetition

Though it's not one of the concepts that the non-specialist would associate with existentialism, "repetition," star number ten, is key to understanding related concepts such as free will, choice, self-determination, authenticity and finitude. How certain patterns repeat in our life and how we willfully or passively experience their reenactment discloses what it means to be an existing human consciousness.

For Kierkegaard, who devoted considerable attention to the term, repetition can mean the experience of either a transforming renewal or a static sameness. Simone de Beauvoir, writing about old age, will warn of the enervating effects of repetitive behaviors that, as habits, have long lost their meaning and efficacy. Repetition can mean continuity of self over time but it can also mean a sameness that hides a hollowing of personhood. Repetition can mean a second or third chance to get something right but it can also entail futile attempts to erase or overcome past failings and disappointments.

Though some habits seem inconsequential, such as sleeping in a certain position, or eating at certain times of day, even the most mundane of routines can, as any skilled novelist will tell you, disclose the most profound aspects of a person's life. Just think of Kafka's hero in *The Metamorphosis* who, when awaking to find he has turned into a cockroach, nevertheless strives to follow his routine – getting to the office on time.

Though far less Kafkaesque, the repetitive patterns of my friend Marc's parents became the topic of a casual conversation.

Tricking Life

We were standing in the parking lot of our neighborhood supermarket where we frequently ran into one another on Friday afternoons on the way home from work. I had casually asked Marc about how his parents were doing. He shook his head. "They eat at the same Mediterranean restaurant at noon every day except Sundays, sit in the same booth, and they order same item on the menu, the humus platter," Marc sighed, shifting his bag of groceries from one arm to the other.

I'd heard about their regular habits and thought it a bit eccentric but not anything to worry about. I just chuckled and shrugged my shoulders. "It's not just a routine," he added. "It's rigidity. Frankly, I'm worried. I think somewhere in the back of their minds they think they can trick life." I must have looked puzzled because he went on to explain. "Look, their bodies are changing, they're having health problems. If they can just do the same exact things, day after day, maybe they can hold back the inevitable."

Repetitive behaviors, habits of everyday life, do seem to multiply as we get older. Look at Marc and me, I mused, with our regularly scheduled supermarket visits. I suspected that were we to look into our shopping bags, we would find that we selected many of the same items week after week, as our diets probably didn't vary much. Were we, too, trying to trick life?

It's not easy to change our habits once they've become second nature. Moreover, habits, when they become routines of everyday life, take on a ritualized quality by lending a reassuring charm to the passage of time. A weekly card game or luncheon with friends, Tuesday's yoga or Pilate's class, and seasonal holiday family gatherings give our lives a sense of constancy and connectivity through activities we share with others. They affirm our identity and imbue the objects around us – coffee mugs, yoga pants, sweet potato pie, with important associative meanings. But when routines and habits become detached from the purposes they were meant to serve, when we do them simply because it feels like we've "always" done them that way, then we may wake up one morning and feel like we've become imprisoned by our lifestyle.

Full or partial retirement can bring major changes to habits and routines. Freed from schedules and obligations related to a career and, perhaps, raising children who are now on their own, we are suddenly granted the opportunity to abandon some existing projects and choose new ones. However, the prospects of a blank to-do list and empty calendar can be daunting. Moreover, we may retain some habits from our working lives that no longer seem necessary. This condition is dramatized in the 2015 movie, *The Intern*.

Robert De Niro plays the retired businessman Ben Whittaker, a 70-year-old widower who finds that despite taking up Tai Chi and other leisure-time activities, he remains lonely, restless and unsatisfied without the challenge and camaraderie of the workplace. He lands an internship at a startup online fashion site run by a young female entrepreneur. In the new high tech office setting, his customary work appendages and apparel – pen and note pad, calculator, jacket, tie and pocket-hand-kerchief become a source of amusement to his millennial generation coworkers decked out in untucked shirts and jeans and wielding smart-phones. However, his career-tested analytical style, willingness to learn, and remarkable empathy toward others – dispositions (may we call them virtuous habits?) acquired from years of experience – soon prove valuable to his young coworkers and, as it turns out, to his frazzled boss who is caught in a family-versus-career squeeze.

HABITS

While she does not address the connection between habits and aging, Claire Carlisle in her compact philosophical survey, *On Habit* (2014), notes that habits are like pathways we make in our daily behavior. The more we journey along a pathway, the more worn and familiar it becomes. Metaphorically, these pathways, says Carlisle, are both "created and maintained by repeated movement." They both facilitate our journey through life and incline us to a particular route from which we find it difficult to diverge, even when conditions necessitate it. Habit, says Carlisle, "is at once a blessing and a curse" (5). In this sense the pathways represent what she calls "the double law of habit" (27-28).

First noted by Anglican Bishop Joseph Butler in a 1736 book of theology, the double law points to the ways in which repeated behavior can dull our senses and lead us into mechanical responses to the world around us but can also, through repeated actions, make them easier and more assured. In short, this double principle reveals how habits can strengthen our receptive capabilities (think of habits of kindness, caring, observation) but also reactive to change (think of habits of intolerance, inflexibility, mechanical routine).

Obviously, the older we get, the more opportunity we have for journey-ing along the worn paths. Simone de Beauvoir discusses the problem of getting into a rut in *The Coming of Age* where she considers two negative conditions of later life – boredom and habit. Both are characterized as con-ditions in which the individual feels trapped in repetitive activities that lack or no longer possess a sense of meaningfulness. She paints a bleak picture of aging when that time of life is increasingly devoid of actions that are geared toward accomplishments that infuse our lives with purpose, curios-ity, and delight. Having either already accomplished what we set out to do or having lost interest in and abandoned some formerly valued projects, we end up confronting "a limited future and a frozen past" (378). Our lives become reduced to "cyclical rhythms of biological necessity."

For the French existentialists, having projects is synonymous with living a life of vital engagement. Projects are willful initiatives that endow our lives with an aura of purpose. They may involve commitments to social justice, artistic endeavors, or any number of ways in which we pursue our self-chosen value agenda toward future fulfillment. Beauvoir emphasizes that projects enable us to transcend the mere maintenance of life insofar as we act productively and in both large and smaller ways contribute to the world. Not to do so leaves us in the mode of passivity, what she calls "immanence."

Once we have chosen them, many of our projects remain ongoing. They are embedded in and supported by routines of daily life. These routines are both necessary and beneficial. For example, for years self-employed authors like Sartre and de Beauvoir pursued the discipline of setting aside certain hours of each day to write and conduct research. Those employed in offices, schools and other job sites are usually not free to set their own schedule. Their routines are prescribed by the demands of the trade or profession.

At home, most of us have an almost invariable sequence of habitual behaviors such as the side of the bed we arise from and how we brush our teeth and comb or brush our hair. Routines save us time and mental energy that we can devote to more challenging and episodic matters that require careful attention. So ingrained are some routines that misplacing a wallet, a pocket book or a cell phone can send us into a tailspin. Indeed, our habits can become so automatic that, preoccupied with a concern (or cell phone conversation), we may drive to work or an appointment with the sudden realization that, having arrived, we cannot recall how we got there.

Over the course of many years, habits and routines that evolved through the compression of efficiency, personal taste and sheer repetition seem to take on a life of their own. This comes out if we're questioned or challenged about some part of our routine. A grown-up son or daughter looks over our shoulder and tells us we need to update our operating system. A granddaughter, a paragon of fitness, tells us we need to change our diet, take up yoga and, patting us on the belly, sign up for membership at a gym.

"But this is the way I do it," we blurt out in exasperation or recite in our minds, "Why do I need to change?" Habits are comforting like favorite old clothes. Still, changing circumstances may cause us to reconsider our wardrobe.

Echoing de Beauvoir's characterization, developmental psychologist and gerontologist Robert Kastenbaum in his research article, "Habituation as a Model of Human Aging," argues that a characteristic of the aging process is what he calls "hyperhabituation." This condition occurs "when novel events and situations are treated as though repetitions of the familiar." In turn, this response leads to the "tendency to overadapt to one's own routines and expectations rather than to adapt flexibly and resourcefully to the world at large."

Kastenbaum notes that habits are good when they equip us to carry out routine activities and to exercise appropriate behavior in familiar situations, thus allowing us to preserve energy and attention for those environmental encounters which are genuinely new, interesting or perhaps threatening. But excessive habituation does the opposite. It restricts our ability to change, adapt and develop in response to new situations and conditions. Inflexibility and maladaptive behaviors impede the development of compensatory strategies as the person says to him- or herself, "Nothing new here, I've seen it all before."

Occupational therapists are familiar with the scenario. The therapist works with a post-surgical or post-stroke patient to show him or her simple and safe ways of conducting activities of daily living (the medical acronym, ADLs) like getting out of bed, dressing, negotiating stairs, sitting and rising or even modifying a golf or tennis swing. Some patients become annoyed. They want to do these things in the manner to which they are accustomed. The hell with the therapist, they mutter. What does he/she know? Perhaps the patient is offered an assistive walking device such as a cane or walker. But the patient, if he or she uses it at all, drags the cane along or leaves the walker parked at the bedside.

Old habits are hard to change. In fact, they qualify as "old habits" when they become instances of hyperhabituation. Kastenbaum's research raises an interesting question. Can we overcome the tendency to become set in our ways and increasingly inflexible in the face of our own detriment? Clearly, this is an existential question.

SILVER LINING

Philosopher and women's studies professor Helen Fielding finds a silver lining in the dismal cloud de Beauvoir pictures hovering over the habituated elderly. She notes de Beauvoir's optimistic concession in *The Coming of Age* that a habit that is "thoroughly integrated" into someone's life "makes it richer, for the habit has a kind of poetry" (*Fielding, 70*). Beauvoir mentions the English custom of taking afternoon tea as an example of a habit imbued with a measured rhythm. Late afternoon teatime enfolds its participants into a ceremonial reenactment of an English custom dating back in popularity to the early nineteenth century. Even recent immigrants to the UK emulate the tradition that is also a practical one since the English supper is usually not put out until around eight o'clock. One feels very English in joining the generational tradition of taking afternoon tea.

However, neither de Beauvoir nor Fielding are particularly interested in Earl Grey or cucumber sandwiches. De Beauvoir is simply suggesting that there might be some repetitive activities like culturally endowed habits that could have some merit in that they bring comfort to the participants and serve as a context for ongoing meaning making.

While de Beauvoir plays the role of the great liberator of the elderly, she still holds a rather dire and narrow view of the aging process. In her moral condemnation of the inner or spiritual life as an example of escapist false consciousness, she leaves few alternatives to living a vital and meaningful old age besides having authentically self-selected projects and deflecting the dehumanizing stereotypes that younger people may project onto members of the older generation. Her solution has been characterized among gerontologists as pushing the values and activities of middle age right to the cemetery gates – a path very few people can manage to steer.

To contrast this viewpoint, Harry Moody, in his gerontology textbook, *Aging: Concepts and Controversies* (2012), includes a selection from *The Coming of Age* alongside a piece by Carl Jung. The founder of Analytic Psychology advocates that older people should let go of the socially conforming, humdrum endeavors of outward worldly activities to explore the "afternoon of human life" and the promise it holds of deeper meanings that are reachable through reflection and spiritual pursuits.

In a similar vein, American philosopher David Norton argues in *Personal Destinies: A Philosophy of Ethical Individualism* that some habits of the elderly bespeak a sense of serenity and "a taste of eternity." He describes his grandfather's daily attention to three cherished possessions, "his pipe, his pen, and his pocketknife." Weekly trolley trips to a familiar store and dedicated gardening time gave his grandfather's life a "cyclical movement" that lent it "sanctification" by "expressing the eternal within it" (208). Norton, contrary to de Beauvoir, says older people no longer need to orient themselves to a novel future. He believes it is possible to lead a self-actualized, "post-mortem" life of contentment in old age that is free of the now outlived ambitions of midlife. Norton's account offers us a stark contrast to the existentialist, de Beauvoir.

Fielding, too, seeks an alternative to an exclusive focus on future-oriented projects. She explores the "poetry of habit" to suggest that without venturing into the realm of spiritual practices, older people might find a "disclosure of meaning" (80) in ceremonial acts like teatime if they use the opportunity for fresh experiences and genuine intimacy rather than the dreary tedium of going through the motions of brewing, pouring, sipping and engaging in idle chitchat. Fielding suggests that not every meaningful activity needs to be powered by a high degree of willfulness. Here she verges on the familiar distinction between Being and Doing where the apparent passivity of just being – for instance, lingering in the interval of teatime, is actually a way of opening oneself to the world of others and to the potential of receiving fresh insights and thoughts. Surely de Beauvoir would not find fault with such ways of engagement with life.

The poetry of habits could embrace other such ritualized activities as meditation, prayer, washing dishes, cooking, bird watching, dancing, playing chess and so on. These types of activities, says Fielding, hold the "poetical possibility" of allowing a person to be open to the unexpected and to creative encounters with the unknown. But this only works, qualifies Fielding, tipping her hat to de Beauvoir's concern for the working class, "if the person in question is not beset by anxiety over daily survival."

When habits are imposed rather than freely chosen, such as in the regulated routines of nursing homes or the limited taste choices of a Meals on Wheels delivery service, some aspects of life lose their meaning as the individual feels powerless. Even for the more hale and affluent older person living independently, what might appear to be meaningful routines can be quite the opposite. De Beauvoir gives the example of a member of a card players' group that gathers on weekday afternoons at a certain cafe. She observes that the man has on more than one occasion flown into a rage because other customers have inadvertently occupied "their table." Of this person, says de Beauvoir, "It means a lifeless requirement has come into existence, one that prevents him from adapting himself to the situation."

We should not be surprised by de Beauvoir's critique of dulling habits and routines since they reverse the momentum of being-for-oneself, which is the possibility of freedom through spontaneous behavior and self-chosen projects. Once spontaneity is curtailed, life becomes mechanical and enervating. However, to follow in the path of commentator Helen Fielding, we too seek an alternative. How, we ask, despite or in light of the accumulation of habits and routines, can we find our way to innovatively and creatively adaptive ways for conducting our lives? Part of the answer comes from lessons learned from antiquated buildings. I will explain.

Pillow Talk

Some years ago I stumbled on a technique that proved usable as the opening gambit of a lecture on "Keys to A Creative Retirement." A premise of my talk is that, as we age, some of our habits and routines hinder, rather than help us enjoy life and keep things fresh. I always try to find some way to add an element of surprise and audience involvement to my talks to offset the passivity of using PowerPoint slides. An idea occurred to me one day while helping my wife change our linens. She noticed the clumsy way I was inserting a pillow into a pillowcase and offered to show me the "right method."

After she demonstrated her technique and awaited my approval, I said: "I'm sure there are many ways of doing this." We bantered a bit further and I decided to prove my point by searching the Internet on how to enclose a pillow in a pillowcase. Instantly, I found website texts and video demonstrations of at least six techniques for putting a pillow in or, as it turns out, pulling a pillowcase over a pillow. Suddenly, I realized that one's preferred pillow-stuffing technique was related to habit formation.

I was invited to give the keynote address on "Creativity and Aging" at a fall semester kickoff event at a Minnesota university's lifelong learning program. After being introduced to the audience, and with a snazzy, professional looking title slide on the screen behind me, I greeted my audience and commented that in order to talk about ways to stay creative as we age, I would begin by displaying a model of the human brain. I reached down and lifted up a black athletic bag, unzipped it as if I were going to pull out one of those plaster models of the cranium that unhinge to show the cauliflower-like brain inside. I looked down into the bag, looked up with an abashed countenance on my face, and declared: "I'm so sorry. I must have taken the wrong bag." Then I pulled the fluffy pillow out of the bag and, holding it up, sheepishly declared: "For my afternoon nap." Then I reached back into the bag and extracted the pillowcase, sighing: "And look, someone forgot to put on the pillowcase."

At that moment, members of the audience began shifting in their seats and eyeing one another. A few audible chuckles or sighs rose up and a couple of chairs made the sounds of people preparing to escape. I had to quickly launch into my spiel telling the audience: "My mother advised me that you should always make do with what you have." And then, holding up the pillow and the pillowcase, I asked: "Can anyone tell me how to place this pillow inside the pillowcase?"

After a couple of seconds of uncertainty, a woman said: "Why don't you turn the pillowcase inside out and then pull it over the pillow." I clumsily started to do as she described but then in mock exasperation asked: "Is there any other way to do this?" Another woman said: "Hold the pillow under your chin and then lower it gently into the open end of the pillow-case." Then another voice told me to fold the pillow in half, grip the two corners and "jamb the thing into the pillowcase." By this time, most of the audience members had caught on. Disagreements were voiced. More techniques were offered. Some people began to laugh. A man proclaimed that he always deferred to his wife in the matter of pillows. This brought several boos and his face reddened. The times had changed.

I then advanced my slide to a chart showing numerous ways to stuff a pillow, each with their own special name – chin drop, inside out/pull over, and so on. The point I then made is that while there are many ways of doing something apparently as simple and mundane as stuffing a pillow, we become habituated to following an approach either that someone taught us long ago or one we presume is the best if not the only way. And aren't we a little disturbed when someone tries to convince us that there might be an alternative?

I then invited the audience to give examples of other routine activities that become habituated. Tying a bowtie or necktie was offered. Ways of folding laundry, packing a suitcase, and making hardboiled eggs were debated. Then a scientific type kicked the discussion up a notch with his recommendations on the right way of building an outdoor fire. There followed techniques for organizing files, hanging shirts, and, called out a pundit, tricking an audience to get involved in a lecturer's topic.

By now there was general agreement that, as we age, it's easy to get stuck in habits and routines to the point that we no longer remember how or why we chose them in the first place. How did we become so inflexible and what can we do about it? At this point I transitioned into our main topic: how can we retain or renew our creativity in later life? That's when I presented the analogy to what architects call "adaptive reuse."

I flashed on the screen a slide of a boarded up, red brick warehouse that showed rhythmically arched window openings and elaborate cornices. The structure became (next slide) transformed into a bustling public marketplace. Or consider a fire station erected when horses pulled the engines. This had become (next slide) a popular neighborhood restaurant. By analogy, I proposed, our accumulation of structured habits and routines, based as they are on time-tested experiences and knowledge, can be reconsidered to explore options for innovation and modification. The solution to updating is not to tear something down but to remodel and, hence, reinterpret it. Creativity, in this context, means putting the old to new uses. If we can just tweak some of our habits to find subtly different ways to accomplish the task of everyday life, we may experience a ripple effect opening up new possibilities.

I then asked audience members for some personal examples of habits and routines that they had for one reason or another chosen to change. Several were quickly forthcoming. "Following hip replacement surgery," said one woman, "I had to learn a new way of throwing a bowling ball." Another disclosed that she had come to the realization that she had to give up telling her daughter-in-law how to get her grandson to try new foods. "My husband," quipped another, "has finally recognized the superior wisdom of our GPS." Acknowledging these examples, I invited the audience members to share their stories in several breakout sessions, each led by a different facilitator chosen by the group.

Adages

In our smaller meeting room holding about 30 people, we got to talking about how we acquire habits. The conversation quickly veered in a direction I hadn't anticipated.

"You know," commented a man in a black turtleneck sweater, "a lot of our habits come from how we're raised." He paused as if what might follow was self-evident.

"How so?" I asked.

He looked around as if he was not expecting to be put in the limelight. Realizing we were all waiting, he continued. "What I mean is, when I was growing up there was a lot of what I was taught to do by my parents that didn't seem to require any explanation. 'When you meet someone,' said my dad, 'always put out your right hand and when you shake be sure to look the other person in the eye.' My dad didn't say do this because it's the polite thing to do or it's the way you show respect or the way you express your dignity and recognize the dignity of the other person. Understanding all that came way later."

"Ah," I exclaimed. "Aristotle."

"The Greek shipping magnate who married Jackie?" quipped a woman in an embroidered, quilted vests.

"Ah no, the other Aristotle," I said. "The ancient Greek philosopher."

People laughed. Of course, they all knew whom I meant.

"Aristotle says that virtues like courage, generosity and friendliness toward strangers are inculcated in us when we're young. We're taught good habits and proper dispositions before we're really able to understand the principles they're based upon. Over time, says Aristotle, we learn how to exercise good judgment in when and how these habits should be applied in particular situations. Like knowing when to charge and when to retreat in battle and to practice moderation in drinking and eating.

"Right," said the man in the black turtleneck. "That's what I mean. I can't tell you how much that simple lesson about shaking hands paid off for me in both my business and personal life. But now," he paused and looked around at the other participants, "our esteemed guest speaker is telling us we should ditch these old habits of ours because they stifle our creativity. Is that the deal here?"

Now I was put on the spot. And before I could defend myself, the woman in the quilted vest jumped in. "Here's how my kids shake hands," she said, flapping her hands and shouting, "Hey man. What's happening, dude?"

There followed another round of laughter at my expense. "Well," she said, sitting down. "Am I being creative?"

The group was certainly having fun with me. I suppose this was an instance of Midwestern humor. Teasing authority figures. Then something more from Aristotle occurred to me.

"*Gnomi*," I shouted out.

"Okay, we'll stop," said the man next to me who smiled and patted me on the shoulder.

"Ah, no, no, this is great," I replied. "What we're doing is identifying what Aristotle called good sense. His term was the Greek word *gnomi*. I guess it means something like wise adages or truths that are communicated through folklore. We learn them growing up. They're all around us. They help shape our habits."

"Oh," said the man who had tried to come to my aid. "Like 'early to bed and early to rise make a man healthy, wealthy and wise.' You mean stuff like that?"

"Yes," I nodded. "What else? What adages did you grow up with?"

A woman in a green jacket waved her hand. "Give a man a fish and he will eat for today. Teach him how to fish and you'll feed him for a lifetime."

"Yes," I said. "That's another one."

The participants in the breakout session reminded me that many of the habits we acquire come from what we might call cultural conditioning. In our teens, we may begin to question and even rebel against accepted forms of politeness or good manners. Certainly traditional adages, many gleaned from Proverbs or books like Aesop's fables, have been replaced by the wisdom expressed in rock and roll lyrics ("Love is all you need.") and Sci-Fi movies ("May the force be with you.")

What is special about habits and routines is that they are made up of repeated patterns that must be acted anew while they contain a self-defining sameness. When the patterns are enacted impulsively, independent of practical utility, we call it repetition compulsion or obsessive-compulsive disorder. But when the repetition is appropriate and beneficial to carrying out a given task, like stuffing a pillow in a pillowcase, we consider it normal.

Clearly, some repetitive habits verge on the pathological. For example, a long life can mean a vast accumulation of stored items ranging from children's art works to the now obsolete DVD collection of a departed spouse. Unable to decide to let go of these "treasures," we may find ourselves surrounded by dangerous piles of clutter. The diagnosis, Diogenes Syndrome or "senile squalor syndrome," is a mental health classification for older adult hoarders. According to the American Geriatrics Society, the affliction is related to "self-neglect, social withdrawal, apathy, compulsive hoarding of rubbish and lack of shame." It is this last characteristic, lack of shame, which connects the addictive behavior to the ancient Greek philosopher, Diogenes of Sinope, also known as Diogenes the Cynic, a man who flaunted his personal hygiene in public places and, a street person of his time, who slept in a large broken urn in the market place. Those were the habits that turned his name into a mental health diagnostic classification. Fortunately, most of our habits are not pathological. They do, however, reflect our identity to others.

Habits and Identity

Anyone who has attended a school reunion, especially after a long interval of twenty, thirty or more years will have experienced that uncanny feeling that I had at my elementary school conclave. As we stood around identifying the sixth graders in the photo from over fifty years ago, we put names to faces as we remembered them back then, not as we might have associated those faces with our presently gathered alumni.

If a stranger, say, one of the current teachers, were handed the picture and asked to identify the individual children with our group of old class-mates, she would likely have a difficult time of it. For even those of us who had not been in direct touch with our old classmates on some reoccurring basis would have a hard time matching the faces in the photo with the onlookers in the school hallway. Most of us had changed so dramatically in appearance as to be unrecognizable.

There were – there always are – exceptions, people who even as older adults still resemble their former childhood guise. Is it that they had somehow managed to age well or that the distinctive contours of some people's faces had only been etched more deeply by time? And as we stood around chatting and catching up on the monumental life-changing events of fifty years, certain features of personality also began to surface. Here, once again, was the class clown, the cynic, the flirt, the brain, the playboy and the fidgety one. They emerged from behind the mask of a graying beard and mustache, from under the long blonde bangs or the taut skin of a worked-on face.

These observations are, of course, conjectures from one person's point of view. It is through my own memories and associations that these resemblances are derived. Nevertheless, I think it's fair to say that what makes a school reunion both poignant and perplexing is that though a great deal about us has changed enough has stayed the same to make these comparisons possible.

All of us have been repeating ourselves day after day for decades. And with each repetition of how we approach the world, give utterance to our thoughts and feelings or conceal them, choose what to eat and how we eat it, even how we carry our bodies and enact our gestures and facial expressions, we have also continued to make ever so slight adjustments and modifica-tions. The paradox of repetition is that we can maintain the apparent unity of identity only by infinitesimally introducing something new. And these tiny modifications, of which from day to day we remain largely unaware, accumulate like the grains of sand that compose shifting dunes.

One might say, yes, personality traits are remarkably persistent whether the path of our lives has been rough or smooth. Having traits seems like a term of passivity, as if we don't possess traits, but they possess us. Some are perhaps genetically coded, some come from involuntarily imitating our parents' voices, mannerisms, and cheerful or bleak outlook on life. Nevertheless, we reenact these traits and sometimes find ways to modify them through the invited intervention of a psychotherapist, teacher, friend, coach or spiritual advisor. For a great many people world-wide, Kierkegaard was one such person. The Socrates of Copenhagen wrote a book on repetition.

Kierkegaard's Repetition

Kierkegaard played teasingly with the Danish word for repetition, *gentagelse*, which literally means to take something back. He explored the paradox of identity, that in the context of development, we change yet experience ourselves as a unity, even when this totality of self is formed by elements in strong oppositional tension. Sometimes we call these "inner conflicts" or "ambivalences."

Kierkegaard drew attention to the opposing ancient Greek schools of thought, the Eleatics, represented by Parmenides, and that of Heraclitus. The first held that all change is illusory and that the world always has been and could not have come into being. The latter, that all is flux and that "we cannot step into the same river twice, for the waters flow on." Similarly, he contrasted repetition with recollection. The latter was at the heart of Plato's theory of knowledge.

Presented in a quasi-mythological way, Plato argued that each person has an immortal soul that possesses timeless and immutable truths such as might be found in the rules of geometry or rationally deduced universals. Subject to reincarnation, when the soul returns from an incorporeal to a corporeal state, it undergoes forgetting due to the distractions of the physical senses. But through a process of question-inspired investigation, the soul or mind moves from fragments of knowledge to larger amalgamations. He calls the process "recollection." So for Plato learning is a matter of drawing out of the soul what it latently possesses. In this way, recollection is a gateway to the timeless, to eternity, and ultimately to contemplation of the unchanging.

Kierkegaard sought to refute Plato by insisting that no process that required time and that was undertaken by mortals could lead to an apprehension of eternity. Insisting that the path back through time to eternity must, ironically, be an endless one, Kierkegaard, echoing Zeno's paradox, argued it was impossible to complete this temporal journey.

For Kierkegaard, opening a backdoor into eternity through delving into memory was impossible for mortals. Only the forward movement of repetition was possible. For Kierkegaard the ultimate paradigm of repetition was the rebirth of the self through the miraculous and paradoxical intervention of the divine spirit into the temporal order of humanity – that is, the paradigm of Christianity. Kierkegaard also drew a parallel for repetition to the story of the Biblical Job, from whom everything was taken but to whom, through faith, everything was "given back." Kierkegaard's religious repetition is really a kind of liberation; the former self relinquished in order to be born again. Indeed, for Kierkegaard the Eucharist (taking of communion) was one of those repetitive behaviors that renewed the individual's spirituality through the experience of the God-in-time.

Kierkegaard's idea of freedom is quite opposite to Sartre's and Simone de Beauvoir's since it calls for the will to surrender exclusive reliance on oneself. The individual makes him- or herself free for redemption by forgoing the futile search for meanings that one believes are waiting for release within one's own psyche. The yearning for transcendence can only be achieved through faith and receptivity to the divine.

REINVENTING ONESELF

In more contemporary and secular terms, a transforming repetition of identity, when enacted in mid- or later life, has been captured in the dubious phrase "reinventing yourself." Popular magazines laud middle-aged housewives who turn into skydivers, retired accountants who tap into a hidden talent and become standup comedians, wizened rural dwellers who through storytelling interviews become wisdom keepers. Clearly, some have made reaching into the past their future-oriented project, while others pursue the image of a fresh or freshened identity as a way to repackage their former self.

The sharp distinction between recollection and repetition that Kierkegaard poses is largely polemical. He is advocating a Christian theology of the chasm between the human and the divine, between immanence (we have the power to save ourselves) and transcendence (redemption can only come as a gift from God). Reinventing oneself could be seen as either one. And as for the Sartrean notion that only the present can drive the future and reclaim the past, what of guilt and remorse as motivators? The following story, one I sometimes share in my "Pillow Talk," reflects this dichotomy.

DAVE'S REDEMPTION

Over the years I spent time with Dave as a participant in our lifelong learning program, he engaged in several projects to make amends for neglecting his children while devoting himself to becoming a success in business, for neglecting his first wife who suffered from mental illness, and for turning away from the career he had hoped to pursue after returning from the battlefields of World War II. To an extent, Dave was quite aware that he was trying to rectify the past.

A warm brown face and a perpetual twinkle in his eye, Dave once asked me: "You want to know how I planned for retirement?" The answer had to be something ironic, so I waited.

"Death," he announced with a grin. "Death was my plan." Yet there he was, retired and very much alive. "I got sick. Thought I was a goner. I was in bed for weeks. Just my little dog keeping me company and Dorothy bringing me her special health food potions. 'David,' she told me, 'you gotta quit the business. It's killing you.' And you know what? She was right. So I went to my boss, Mr. Klein, and told him I was retiring. 'Dave,' he said, 'you're a young man. So soon?'" Dave grinned and leaned forward as if to whisper, "You see, Mr. Klein was 92."

After the couple moved to Asheville, Dave traded the suits and ties of decades of competition and ambition in the women's fashion industry for his standard around-town outfit: blue jeans, a sweatshirt and a NY Yankees baseball cap. He once told me, "In my closet I keep two suits and a few nice ties. They're for weddings and funerals."

"I was all set to sign up for journalism at Columbia University. But there was a long line of people waiting to register." Dave shook his head. "In the service I'd waited in too many lines. I saw another, a shorter line for the business school. So that's where I went."

His father and uncles wanted Dave to come into their business, but he said no, he wanted to be his own man. Yet, impulsively, he denied himself the career he loved, one that he even practiced while in the army where he helped edit a battalion newspaper.

In retirement, Dave became a Big Brother to an eight-year-old boy who lived with his grandparents. He took the boy, Jesse, to baseball games, tutored him in reading, spelling and math and with Dorothy provided him with a second family that was able to open doors for him and give him the support necessary to make something of himself.

"I knew I was trying to make up for the things I didn't do for my own kids. Leaving them alone so much with their mother, that was a big mistake. We all paid for it," he said.

Dave decided to write a screenplay about his relationship with Jesse. He found a teacher who could help him learn the tricks of the trade and succeeded in producing a completed script, which he set out to place in the hands of a literary agent. Dave had connections through a cousin. The script was sent.

However, Dave did not get to see this part of his deferred dream come to fruition. Diagnosed with pancreatic cancer, Dave succumbed after six months of futile treatment. Asked by Dorothy to give his eulogy at the Veterans Cemetery, I read a portion of one of Dave's essays that he turned in for an intergenerational class I conducted. It was about the day he returned from overseas.

Dave had written to his parents that he didn't want any hoopla. But when he got out of the taxi in front of the family brownstone in The Bronx, he was met by a crowd of relatives waving flags and throwing streamers. At the party, the well-intentioned aunts and uncles prodded him to tell about the girls of France and his heroic adventures in combat. Dave explained in the essay how he had gone away a teenager and come home a man. His mother's eyebrows went up when, during the party, he asked for a beer. Later, as the party wound down, Dave wrote, he retreated into his boyhood bedroom, lay down and sobbed into his pillow.

Once in my office, where Dave liked to drop in unannounced, he told me another story about how he had altered a lifelong pattern of behavior. Dave volunteered to help with a newly forming annual conclave of Native American tribes from the southeastern part of the U.S., especially the Cherokee whose large reservation was about two hours from Asheville. Called Kituah, the event was being planned by tribal members and local citizens. Dave, who was culturally Jewish, said he tended to identify with "the underdog." So he volunteered to help out on the planning committee.

What happened is that in meetings he had many ideas to offer but he was largely ignored.

"They wouldn't call on me. That upset me," said Dave. "I was used to being Number One. I always had to be, you know, out there in front." Dave said he talked about this with Dorothy who told him to stop being such a big shot, that he wasn't working in the Garment District anymore. "And you know what," said Dave with his favorite refrain, "she was right."

So he altered his strategy. He kept quiet in meetings. Just listened to what everybody else had to say. "And you know what?" I waited for the shoe to fall. "They called on me. 'Dave, what do you think about this idea? Dave, do you have any suggestions for how we should accomplish this goal?'" Dave quoted the tribal leaders.

While Dave's self-reinvention could be one of those AARP magazine kinds of stories, the truth is that the mistakes of the past could never be fully erased. Visiting him in the hospital, I could hear Dave's labored breath as he slept or was in a coma, betokening that the end was near. Leaning over his father, cell phone in hand, Dave's son was pleading with his sister that she should come as soon as possible. His sister's reluctance or resistance registered on Dave's son's anguished face, which made it all too clear that while Dave may have found a way to redeem himself, his daughter still suffered the effects of her growing up years.

SUPERMARKET

Several years after the conversation about his parents I met Marc coming out of the same supermarket, though it was a Sunday. I was surprised to see him at the new time of the week. "Oh," he said, "we decided to go on this new vegetarian diet and so I find I have to come to the market more often." Marc's father, Ben, had passed away. I had attended the funeral. His mother was afflicted with Parkinson's disease and Marc and his wife, Deborah, had chosen to become her caretakers and bring her into their home.

"You know," said Marc, "I've learned a lot more about my mother's life since she's come to live with us. I knew that she and her sister and parents had fled Belgium as the Nazis closed in and that they eventually made their way to southern France, then Spain, then Portugal and finally to New York. She was studying to become a pharmacist."

"That must have been a traumatic experience. Hadn't she told you any of this when you were growing up?"

"Well, yes. But only in very general terms. Mom was reluctant to talk much about her youth and all that happened to her and her family. She'd always say, 'life is for living in the here and now. The past is past.' But really, I think it was just too painful for her to talk much about that time in her life. Now that she's living with us, Deborah got the idea to interview her as part of a series on Jews of Asheville who had survived the Holocaust. It was only when Deborah explained how important it was to preserve these stories for future generations that Mom relented."

"Are all these stories accessible? Could I read about her life?" I asked.

"Yes," said Marc. "In fact, you can go to the website through the university library archives."

"I'd like to do that."

"There's something else that I began to realize about my parents' routines."

"Oh, yes, their routines. I heard they got mad at the guy who owns the Mediterranean place and switched over to that sandwich shop on Second Avenue."

Marc smiled. "Yeah, they did that a year before my father died. New loyalty, the same fixed time, place and, well, they had to switch from humus to the veggie burgers. He rolled his eyes. Then Marc turned and pointed at the window of the supermarket. "Speaking of routines." He raised up his the tote bags he held in each hand and smiled. "I think part of their way of keeping their lives very regular, even to the point of obsession, was this earlier time of life. I mean, the chaotic, life-threatening and uprooting experiences that Mom faced. I don't think she ever got over it."

I said I supposed that made sense but what about his father?

"You know, my father was a soldier in World War II. His battalion liberated one of the concentration camps. I think that what he saw and felt, which he had to suppress and just do his duty, well, I think that took a toll on him too. It's no accident that my father would fall in love with a Jewish refugee from Belgium.

REFERENCES

Carlisle, Claire (2014). *On Habit*. New York: Routledge.

Fielding, Helen A. ((2014). "The Poetry of Habit." *Simone de Beauvoir's Philosophy of Age: Gender, Ethics and Time*. Edited by Silvia Stoller. Berlin/Boston: De Gruyter. 69-81.

Kastenbaum, Robert. (1981) "Habituation as a Model of Human Aging." *International Journal of Aging and Human Development*, 12 (3), 151-170.

_____ (1984) "When Aging Begins: A Lifespan Developmental Approach." *Research on Aging*, (1), 105-117.

Kierkegaard, Søren (1843/1964). *Repetition: an essay in experimental psychology*. Translated by Walter Lowrie. New York: Harper & Row.

Moody, Harry R. and Sasser, Jennifer. (2012). *Aging: Concepts and Controversies*, Seventh Edition. Los Angeles: Sage.

Norton, David (1976), *Personal Destinies: A Philosophy of Ethical Individualism*. Princeton: Princeton University Press.

11. Death

Confrontation with death, our 11th star, is one of the existentialist writers' and thinkers' most profound themes – one that evokes both the head and the heart. Often handling it with realistic detail in their novels and short stories, writers linked to the tradition, from Tolstoy in *The Death of Ivan Ilyich* (1886) to Simone de Beauvoir in her heart-rending account of her mother's final days in the ironically titled, *A Very Easy Death* (1964), do not cringe from seeking to make sense of life amidst the throes of pain, suffering and loss.

We remember that it is in the face of his certain death by guillotine that Camus' Meursault (*The Stranger*) finally emerges from the shell of his indifference. Only in the travails of a seemingly terminal disease does Gide's Michel (*The Immoralist*) discover the hidden passion of homoerotic love that, once kindled, restores him to vitality with a new lease on life.

Contributing philosophically to this theme, Camus declares in the opening lines of his *Myth of Sisyphus:* "There is but one truly serious philosophical problem and that is suicide. Judging whether life is or is not worth living amounts to answering the fundamental question of philosophy" (3).

And why is this question fundamental? Because, when we are mature enough to reflect on our mortality we at times realize that our lives are like that of Sisyphus who is condemned by the gods to push a rock up a hill only to have it come rolling down. In other words, given its ultimate futility, life can seem an absurd enterprise. And is there no escape from this plight? No, insists Camus, none that are not a matter of self-deception. And he cites as examples belief in a beneficent immortality or a rational trust that human reason can render the universe intelligible so as to reflectively affirm the significance of human life. Rejecting both as false hopes, Camus transforms Sisyphus from a tragically victimized to a nobly heroic character, the quintessential "rebel" who persists despite his inescapable fate.

For his take on death, the more inwardly oriented Heidegger asserts: "If I take death into my life, acknowledge it, and face it squarely, I will free myself from the anxiety of death and the pettiness of life – and only then will I be free to become myself." Only by embracing our own eventual demise can we live in the light of our finitude and experience our uniqueness as the being that lives in dread such that he or she experiences *ekstasis*, "standing out" into existence. Yes, but can we truly know what another person's death is like?

Heidegger says no. In *Being and Time*, he argues that while we may have had intense close-up experiences with other peoples' deaths, we nevertheless can never know "the loss of Being that the dead person has suffered" (282). However, the death of others does heighten our awareness of the inevitability of our own death. He gives his phenomenological analysis of this awareness a paradoxical twist.

While we cannot anticipatorily experience the actuality of our dying, our death enters into our consciousness as "the possibility of the impossibility of any existence at all" (307). While we may speculate on it, the finality of our own death remains impossible to imagine or, more precisely, we can only imagine the impossibility of our no longer being. But it is precisely when we come up against this conceptual impossibility that our actual condition is disclosed to us. My death is mine in a radical sense: it is the moment at which all my relations to others will disappear. This condition of no longer being in relationship to others Heidegger dubs our "ownmost possibility" (294). And it is precisely by acknowledging the limited condition of my very own not-Being that my own being-able-to-be is intensified and brought into sharper focus.

Heidegger's description of the prospect of non-relationality is captured in the 1971 film documentary and 1973 book title, *How Could I Not Be Among You?* The book of poems comes from the hand of poet Ted Rosenthal who, at age thirty, learns that he has leukemia and only a short time to live. In the last line of the book's title poem, Rosenthal addresses the reader: "O people, I am so sorry,/Nothing can be hid./ No circle in the round." And he concludes, "Keep moving people. How could I not be among you?"

For Heidegger, this "disclosure" of my own-most possibility of not-being cannot be "outstripped" (294) unless, falling into a state of inauthenticity, we delude ourselves with fantasies of an unending existence or pursue ways to distract ourselves through immersion in busy work or frantic socializing – in other words, finding ways to deny the truth of our mortality. For Heidegger, the authentic mode of living with awareness of my possible impossibility is what he calls "being-towards-death."

It seems that to qualify as an existentialist, one must become a student of death. This may strike some as a doleful preoccupation but death and dying hold the potential to teach us important lessons about what it means to exist, to be alive. A study of death requires not only reading and contemplation but also practical fieldwork.

A Student of Death

My closest presence to the actual moment of a person's death was when I held my mother's hand as she lay dying in a nursing home. After two days of labored breathing and anxious restlessness, her face went slack and her heart stopped beating. One moment, despite fleeting conscious-ness, she was there and in the next this woman, my mother, was gone, leaving her loved ones to internalize her outward presence into the store-house of our memories.

The period of my mother's active dying drew me to her bedside along with my sister, brother-in-law and my mother's sister, my aunt Edith. Mother had been in a skilled care facility for over four years. For about a decade, she had suffered periodic TIAs or mini-strokes that, while they caused her disorientation – going down to breakfast or knocking on a neighbor's door at 3:00 a.m. when she dwelt in an independent living facility apartment – their impact seemed short term. A few days later, she would have regained awareness of her surroundings and reentered her normal daily routine.

Additionally, a serious ankle fracture years earlier had failed to heal properly and while she wore a prosthetic boot for many years, eventually she could no longer ambulate even with the aid of a walker. Mom suffered periodic hallucinations, telling me that a band of gypsy-like people had invaded her apartment by coming in through the window blinds, and later, in her nursing home room, reporting that they came through a crack in the wall and refused to leave until an aide came and scared them off.

Though she could be disoriented at times, my mother had the bitter-sweet plight of the rare nursing home patient who, while needing 24-hour care, is among the handful of alert patients who know what is going on around them. During my infrequent visits, flying in for a weekend or driving up with my family for a longer stay, I would find certain aides hovering about her as she gave advice on whether this one should complete his GED, that one stay with an abusive spouse, and how another one could get her kids to stay in school. My mother, the mentor to these disadvantaged, mainly people of color, was a throwback to her youth and the rough-and-tumble multicultural neighborhood where she grew up. I had not seen this side of her until her nursing home days. I should have recognized it was a sign of her fierce determination to adapt to an otherwise unacceptable situation, one from which my sister and I had hoped to protect her.

My mother's dying was not what gerontologists would call a "good death," meaning a gentle exiting from life, surrounded by loved ones, retaining some semblance of personal dignity, not heavily sedated or multiple-intubated and, ideally, prepared for death, having reached a stage of acceptance and completeness. The staff at the nursing home called her condition a "failure to thrive," which is medical terminology for exhibiting clear signs of rapid decline in wakefulness, appetite and respiration, though the exact cause remains unclear.

Our mother was in a semi-conscious state for two days and she struggled to try to get out of bed as she mumbled the sounds of a troubled soul. From the perspective of an observer, it seemed like she was fighting to stay alive as if there was one more wedding, birthday party or bat mitzvah she hoped to attend. Our hospice nurse encouraged us to tell her that it was all right to let go and that we loved her. Her sister held her hand and whispered stories about their childhood and good times they'd had together. She received some morphine both to help calm her and to control any pain. I felt distress at the idea of trying to assist my mother to step into the void of non-being. I suppose if I held a belief that some part of her would survive in the great beyond, I might have been more comforted and, perhaps, more comforting to her. My mother was a few weeks from turning 95 (she was a 01-01-1911 baby) when she died on December 8, 2006.

Generally speaking, we cannot choose how we are going to die. Even a suicidal attempt may go awry. For some, death comes unexpected and swift – an automobile accident, a massive stroke. For others, dying entails a long period of decline, disability and perhaps accompanying despair. People die the way they have lived, say some experts such as gerontological nursing professor, Sarah Kagan in her 2009 book *Cancer in the Lives of Older Americans: Blessings and Battles*, but I cannot personally verify that observation, even after serving for several years as a hospice home visitor.

It is often poignantly ironic that those whom Alzheimer's disease befalls would seem to be its unlikeliest victims – a Margaret Thatcher, Iris Murdoch, Aaron Copland, or a Rosa Parks. And so it is with the insults of mortal illnesses, for apart from genetic predispositions and poor self-care behaviors, when and how we will become afflicted remains unpredictable. Moreover, we have few means to practice for our own death, though various sects of Buddhism do have scriptures that offer guidance to passage through stages of the dying process and the guidelines of the medieval text *Ars moriendi*, "The Art of Dying," were widely followed as part of a Christian consolatory death practice well into the 19th century.

I did not want to die the way my mother had if, in fact, I was correct that she fought anxiously to stay alive despite her limited mobility, severely curtailed possibilities for enjoying life, and the fact that she had already lived decades beyond her life expectancy at birth. That is why I decided to become a hospice volunteer.

HOSPICE

Spending time with the dying or, as we were instructed to remember, the "the very much still living," was my way of trying to gain more comfort with my own eventual passing away. I sought to be matched with patients who were able and welcomed the opportunity to share stories, talk about events of the day, and to explore the meaning of our own mortality. For the most part, these would be people still living at home.

As part of our hospice training program, we were instructed not to impose our values, beliefs or personal agenda on our patients. Rather we were to let them lead in determining how they would like to spend time with us. This could sometimes mean just sitting together silently for long periods of time or chatting about politics, sports or grandchildren for an hour at a time. We learned that some patients would want to talk about their anticipation of passing from this world and about what may lie on the other side, while others would never bring up the subject, at least not with us. Others, we were advised, could be quite talkative on the subject. As it turned out, I had many conversations with one patient about how she wanted to be attired for her cremation even though we both recognized the comic aspects of this topic since she did not even want a viewing of her body to occur before incineration.

My duties as a hospice home visitor were to provide company for the dying person in the months remaining ("socialization" is the term used) and to give the caregiver a break to leave the home to shop, visit a doctor, or go out to lunch with a friend (called "respite"). By accompanying another person to the proverbial "death's door," I thought I would gain greater insight into my own fears of death. I hoped that at least I would become less anxious.

Among the hospice patients I visited was D. who suffered from advanced kidney disease. Having weighed her options, she had decided against dialysis, preferring to let the disease take its course while allowing her independence from a time-consuming medical process (hemodialysis) which, as she told me, probably would not have added much to the quality or length of her life. Her lab reports indicated that she qualified for home hospice care, meaning that it was expected she had less than six months to live. When she filled out a request form, D. indicated she welcomed having a home visitor with whom she could talk about literature, writing and maybe politics if the person was of a liberal orientation. I seemed to match these requirements.

D. resided in one of eight stucco and metal-roofed, attached ground level rental units located on what was until recently a country road. Now a scattering of new houses and apartment complexes were popping up among apple orchards and disused tobacco plots. She had an L-shaped living room and kitchen, a bathroom and two bedrooms, one of which she used as a TV room and for storage. The living room held a few favorite objects: a vase from Guatemala, an embroidered pillow from Ecuador, an antique double-sided desk, the kind long ago used in accounting offices, some landscape painting of a New England scene and a hand-hooked rug from somewhere in Africa.

Additionally, there was the cat, Roosevelt, about whom I was warned to be wary as he had an unpredictable temperament. I would usually find D. seated in the saddle of her walker pulled up to her desk where she might be reading, writing a note or responding to emails on her laptop computer. Her standard attire was a loose gray sweatshirt and baggy sweatpants. She wore her hair in two long braids that framed an almost wrinkle-free face, though her yellowing skin showed the bony structure of her cheeks and jaw.

I visited D. weekly, about one and a half hours each time, depending on her mood and energy level. Mood was the main determinant, though I could not always tell whether it was her most recent lab report, physical discomfort (she was losing the use of one of her legs) or sadness over the shortness of her days ahead that influenced her spirits. She was an intelligent, articulate and unsentimental person and she often criticized her various hospice visitors – the nurse, social worker, physical therapist, for what she perceived as their shortcomings. Ironically, it was the young music therapist whom she adored and with whom she wrote songs about episodes in her life.

I, too, came under her critical eye and more than once was dismissed. "I don't think I need you to visit anymore, Ron," she would say. "You're very nice. A caring person. But my needs have changed." There was nothing I could say, as I was there at her discretion, not mine. What had happened to bring about this rupture in our relationship, I would not know. But a few months later I would receive a message that D. might like me to resume my visits, "on a trial basis."

One day D. handed me a small paperback book entitled *Sum: Forty Tales from the Afterlife*, written by neuroscientist David Eagleman and published in 2009. D. was not religious and she had made it quite clear to me that she held no beliefs in life after death. So why she gave me this book was something of a puzzle. But I had learned from past experiences to simply accept this gift and do with it what I would.

In the book Eagleman imagines 40 different ways of experiencing the afterlife. For example, the one with the existential title "Angst" begins: "As humans we spend our time seeking big, meaningful experiences. So the afterlife may surprise you when your body wears out." In a version vaguely reminiscent of Plotinus's notion of the human soul forgoing its individual uniqueness when returning to the cosmic flame of Being, Eagleman's imagines us returning to "our true bodies," which are communities of celestial size energy fields whose task it is to maintain and uphold the cosmos to prevent it from "re-collapsing."

Here Eagleman is likely drawing on the prevailing Big Bang theory of the origins of the universe, its expansion and hypothesized inevitable "re-collapsing" into the state of a Black Hole. After "three decades," says the narrator, Eagleman, we get a reprieve from our task and can choose a "vacation" option. Most of the energy phantoms choose their former earthly existences, which the author presents as a resort-like retreat from the arduousness of preventing cosmic disaster.

Earth dwellers once again, they do the things Eagleman says humans do such as watch comedies on TV, consume alcohol and engage in conflictive relationships. There's something about being in a human body, a kind of sensation-distracted forgetfulness that renders the re-embodied humans indifferent to the perils of universal collapse. Over time, once again, our bodies wear out and our respite from tending the cosmic collapse comes to an end. Eagleman's narrator offers a concluding observation. "It is not uncommon," he says, "to see us lying prostrate in the breeze of the solar winds, tools in hand, looking out into the cosmos, wet-eyed, searching for meaninglessness."

This teasingly ambiguous ending raises a number of questions about the parable. Does it mean our this-worldly search for meaning is a way we hold back the chaos into which our lives would otherwise descend, or do we hope for meaninglessness to relieve us from the stressful task of preserving or finding meaning? Or is the whole idea of seeking meaning in a universe that is unimaginably vast, billions of years old and cycling endlessly through modes of expansion and contraction simply laughable? I wondered what D. thought.

What I said to D. after I had read the book was that Eagleman made the brilliant observation that the ways in which we humans conceive of the afterlife seem to reflect the issues and concerns of this mortal side of existence. D. smiled benevolently with a gleam of mischievousness in her eye and remarked, "Yes, death mocks us." She reached across her desk and picked up a hand mirror with a wooden handle. "Look," she said, beckoning me to move beside her. With our heads side by side she showed me our two mortal faces, at which point we both burst out laughing.

Driving home, I suddenly remembered an image of a mirror. This time it was a full-length one that served as a portal into the nether world of death. The mirror was in a now-classic film whose director was Simone de Beauvoir's good friend, the playwright and filmmaker Jean Cocteau.

ORPHÉE

The opening scene of Jean Cocteau's 1949 movie *Orphée* presents the confident, handsome, yet at that moment disgruntled, young poet, Orpheus, who is drifting among the tables at his favorite Parisian haunt, the Café des Poètes. Cocteau quickly creates the atmosphere of the post-war Left Bank milieu as cafe patrons debate the merits of existentialism and the meaning of the absurd while they sip wine and inhale the pungent smoke of Gauloises.

There's tension among the habitués – artistic and political rivalries. Jazz, the gift of the American liberators, plays in the background. As in the ancient Greek myth, the story is going to be about love, death and immortality. In this version of the tale, Orpheus becomes enamored with the angel of death, in the movie played by a hauntingly beautiful figure, the Princess who arrives in a black chauffeur-driven limousine and who, against the rules of the underworld, falls in love with Orpheus and aims to take and keep him.

Meanwhile, Orpheus' wife, Eurydice, is also abducted into the under-world by the jealous Princess and he, the poet, is bound to rescue her by donning a pair of surgical gloves given to him by the Princess's driver. The gloves enable Orpheus to walk through his reflection in a full-length bedroom mirror and to descend into the gloom (Cocteau uses film nega-tive to create these eerie scenes) of the world of the dead. There are many highly symbolic and evocatively surreal moments in the movie such as the way the henchmen of death arrive in the guise of two black leather-clad and helmeted motorcyclists who run down their victims and whose bodies the Princess whisks away to her mist-enshrouded castle before they are taken into the netherworld. Parisian filmgoers could not have missed this reference to the recently departed Nazi occupiers.

When the Princess steps from her limo and stands before the body of Orpheus's poet friend, Cegeste, who has been injured at a fight at the cafe and then run down in the street by the motorcyclists, she address the prone body, "Do you know me?" Prompted, Cegeste arises from the pavement to answer in a voice devoid of emotion: *"Ma morte."* My death. An amazing line that in its brevity and simplicity asserts Heidegger's "unstrippable" truth that there is death, meaning the death of others, but there is only one's "ownmost possibility" of death. *"Ma morte."* And yet Cocteau presents a counter to this oh-so-existential revelation. Late in the film, after he has once again passed into the underworld through the mirror of his own image, Orpheus asks the Princess to strangle him so that they can stay together forever. Though it's against the rules of the officials of the netherworld, she complies.

This death within death's domain, the negation of not-being, serves Cocteau as an allegory of the artist's ascension into the Pantheon of fame and immortality. For what is the doubling of death if not a transfiguration? Consider how many poets, painters, or writers (straight away we think of Emily Dickinson, Franz Kafka, and Vincent Van Gogh), for whom it was only after their deaths that they attained their literary or artistic immortality. Nevertheless, in the film Orpheus must eventually return to his wife, who awakens in their bedroom, reporting that she has had the strangest of dreams.

Unlike the ancient classic tale, Cocteau's version of the Orpheus-Eurydice myth ends with the lovers reunited, apparently death overcome. Eurydice believes it was all a dream but Orpheus, who has met the angel of death face to face, knows otherwise. Simone de Beauvoir would likely see the story as an illustration of the human plight: tragic ambiguity.

SCENES FROM AN AFTERLIFE

I wondered about my mother's apparent frightful struggle to stay alive in her last days. At certain moments she even tried to rise from her bed. Was there anything that could have been done to help her prepare for what we might like to think of as a "transition" from this, our "mortal coil," to whatever lies beyond? Various people aimed to provide companionship and to comfort her during the last year of her life. Might they have been of help?

A qualified clinical psychologist or psychiatrist is required by nursing home protocol to make weekly visit to patients receiving medication for depression, anxiety, hallucinations and other psychological problems. For a time Dr. G. visited my mother. A burly, bearded, gray-haired man with wire-rimmed glasses, he once mentioned that he had studied in Mexico City with famed psychoanalyst Erich Fromm. Dr. G. told me how much he enjoyed visiting with my mother, though what they talked about remained a mystery as he adhered to the principle of confidentiality. I asked my mother about Dr. G. "Oh, that man?" she nodded. "I don't know why he comes to see me. He strolls in, sits down, and asks me how I'm feeling. I say, fine, how about you? And then he tells me his troubles. I don't mind his visiting if it helps him."

My mother was as seemingly indifferent to a second frequent visitor. I'm not sure how the Rabbi L. came to be a weekly visitor. My brother-in-law had been advising the local (ultra-orthodox) Chabad group on building a new synagogue so perhaps they were aware that his mother-in-law was in a nursing home and assigned someone who did pastoral care to visit her. I also asked my mother, who for many years remained a non-practicing Jew and who expressed grave doubts about rabbis, what she thought of this man. "It's nice that he visits. Sometimes he just sits there not saying anything and after a while he'll get up, mumble a prayer, and leave. Maybe he has nothing else to do with his time. But it's fine with me if he wants to come sit here," she said, pointing to the chair where I was seated. However, as it turned out, my sister told me that our mother wanted her funeral conducted by Rabbi L., as he was the only clergy of her faith who knew her, the others having died off years ago.

From the time of death, someone had to sit with my mother's body. Once members of the Chevra Kadisha, the burial society, had washed and dressed her body in a shroud and laid her in a casket made without screws or nails, volunteers took shifts sitting with the body. The ceremony, conducted in the funeral home's sanctuary, was mostly in Hebrew. A couple of eulogies were allowed. Besides the one Rabbi L. prepared after meeting with the family in advance of the service, I spoke on behalf of our family and made a point to praise my sister Arleen's undaunted performance as my mother's advocate in the nursing home and her persistent efforts to keep my mother's spirits buoyed up by arranging transport in a handicap van to the various family affairs.

.er the cemetery interment when I watched my mother's casket being lowered into a waterlogged grave, I thanked Rabbi L. for his services. It was then that I asked him about whether he and my mother had ever discussed beliefs about death and the afterlife. He hesitated. Shifted from foot to foot. "No," he said. "She never brought up the subject."

This amazed me, as it seemed to me that it would have been helpful to my mother to express her fears and perhaps to be consoled by the kindly Rabbi. Even if his assurances did not convince her, at least she would have been able to share her fears with a receptive person. But then I also thought, maybe Rabbi L. was withholding information in accordance with clergy-patient confidentiality. But he could have told me that. It seemed to me that Rabbi L. might have found subtle ways of encouraging my mother to speak her mind. And if she had, in fact, done so, what might she have told him?

Rabbi L. brushed some beard dandruff off his lapel and nodded thoughtfully. "And you, Yirachmeel," he said, using my Hebrew name. "Did you speak with your mother about such matters?"

"I tried to draw her out a couple of times but she didn't seem to under-stand what I was getting at," I responded.

"Ah," he said. "It can be difficult. Not everyone wants to face the unknown."

He was right about this. How ill equipped I felt trying to engage my mother in conversation about what death meant to her. While rationally I was a complete disbeliever in life after death, I entertained the fantasy I had fabricated from reading Plotinus that at death the soul departs the body and returns to an undifferentiated union with the One. I was drawn to the idea that the biographical person jettisoned his or her history-laden identity like the boosters of a rocket that fall away once they have provided the thrust necessary to send the projectile into space. My own ambivalence and muddled formulation would have done little to ease my mother's fears. And then it hit me; it was my own anxiety that stifled my efforts to walk beside her into Rabbi L.'s "unknown."

The traditional eight days of mourning were observed with nightly services conducted at my sister's home. Because I knew a little about the beliefs held by this ultra-orthodox sect, I invited one of Rabbi L.'s colleagues, who was also a friend of my brother-in-law, Sam, and my sister, to say a little about their views of life after death. At first a bit reluctant, he acceded to my persistent request.

"Let me tell you about the *Olam Ha-Ba*," began Rabbi Z., who looked at the blank expression on the faces of the gathering of aunts, uncles, cousins and assorted friends seated in folding chairs in my sister's living room. "Ahem," he cleared his throat. "The world to come, that is." One of my cousins gave me a sideways glance and winked. One of my uncles, a Reform Jew, closed his eyes and shook his head.

Rabbi Z. proceeded to explain that according to true Jewish belief, the soul of the person already exists even before birth and possesses knowledge of God as the soul is at one with the divine. But when this soul enters its bodily state the baby receives a kind of slap on the mouth that causes it to forget all that it knows of what is eternal. And so begins the process of relearning, which is to say reawakening, what the soul has forgotten. Since according to the theory of thermodynamics nothing of the material cosmos ever completely disappears but only recycles between matter and energy, so it is with the stuff of souls.

Many souls return to earthly existence in a process like reincarnation because these souls have more work to do in helping to bring about *tikkun olam*, the perfection of the world and the healing of man's inhumanity to man, which can only be brought about by observing the 613 commandments written in the Hebrew Bible. Other souls return because they have been wrenched from life before they could fulfill their destiny. Rabbi Z. held back from mentioning this but I had read that his group believed that the souls of millions of those who died in the Shoah, the Holocaust, had returned to continue the process of completing their earthly destinies.

The family members on my father's side were already several generations into Reform Judaism or had gone completely secular. My mother's parents were old-country (Russia and Lithuania) first-generation American Jews and so what they were familiar with of Judaism was the orthodox tradition. From the stories my mother and aunt had told, it would be a stretch to say they had observed even a tenth of these commandments. For one, my grandfather had abandoned a wife and child in Russia and, for another, my grandparents engaged in bootlegging during Prohibition and had been raided more than once. My maternal grandmother did keep a kosher kitchen and she lit candles on Shabbat eve.

Consequently, for this group, mostly insulated from orthodoxy, the Rabbi's words brought many a raised eyebrow and a furrowed brow. One of my daughters nudged me and asked, "Do we really believe this? You never told us." I whispered I would explain later.

THE DEATH OF OTHERS

Simone de Beauvoir looked death and dying directly in the faces of the two most important people in her life. Writing with candor and compassion, de Beauvoir gave philosophical consideration to serious illness and the dying process in two books from the later part of her career – one about the last days of her mother's life, as mentioned, ironically titled *A Very Easy Death* (1964), and the other about Sartre's decline over a ten-year period and his final days, *Adieux: A Farewell to Sartre* (1981).

Francoise de Beauvoir was seventy-seven and had been in fragile health while also suffering the pains of arthritis for many years. After a fall in her apartment, doctors discovered that not only had she broken her femur bone but also after a series of investigations, that she had a sarcoma involving the small intestine. A laparotomy was performed, pus was drained, and the tumor resected. Complications ensued and she died four weeks after the operation. Her daughter points out that at no stage was either her diagnosis or prognosis discussed with Madame de Beauvoir.

Like my mother, de Beauvoir's fought against death, insisting to the two daughters beside her hospital bed, "I do not want to die." Both Simone and sister Poupette had ambivalent feelings about their mother but more so her famous daughter with whom she clashed over many years about such matters as Simone's defection from Catholicism, her Bohemian life-style and her leftwing politics. Simone maintained a dutiful but distant relationship, letting her younger sister pick up the slack.

As is so often the case in conflictive parent-child relationships, a parent's illness, decline and increasing dependency bring about a defenselessness and vulnerability that arouse feelings of pity and remorse in adult children. In the accompanying walk up to death's door surprising changes may take place that bring about reconciliation, revelations and an intimacy long ago lost in childhood or young adulthood. This was the case for Simone and is the subject matter of her witnessing her mother's last months and days.

Ever the existential observer, Simone also pays close attention to her mother's surrounding – the hospital with its rules and regulations, the doctors, often arrogant, immured to patients' sufferings, preoccupied with their skills and medical procedures, differences in how the privileged classes are treated in medical settings compared to the poor, and even the role of visiting clergy. The Paris hospital setting of 1963 that is described in her book stands decades before the "death with dignity" movement and the patient's self-determination legislation that would be enacted in many post-industrial countries. So what de Beauvoir observes about unnecessary and painful procedures inflicted upon her mother to keep her alive should come as no surprise to contemporary readers. But for the daughters, Simone and Poupette, these medical interventions were highly disturbing. Indeed, de Beauvoir's book entered the annals of the newly emerging bioethics movement concerning end of life decision-making already in the 1970s. She bore witness, as she had done in *The Second Sex*, to the attitude of superiority of the male-dominated ranks of the men in white who considered any question of their authority as an insult to their status as incontrovertible experts.

Simone was also struggling with the finality of separation from her mother, an emotional severing that had occurred years earlier but now resurfaced with fresh and intense emotion as the realization of the absoluteness of death brought the moment to a crisis. "This time my despair escaped from my control," writes de Beauvoir of her usual stoic attitude towards her mother's criticisms. "Someone other than my self was weeping in me," she explains to Sartre. And she feels that upon her own face, her mother's mouth with its expression of hope, distress and loneliness, has become her own mouth (*A Very Easy Death*, 28).

After decades of regarding her mother as the kind of person she chose adamantly not to become, she suddenly is overtaken by her mother's suffering and her plight as a dying person, overtaken as the adult child of a mother who cannot be so distanced so as to make Simone a mere accidental offspring. Simone, who is often distressed by feelings of growing old and unattractive, sees her own destiny as one day lying in such a hospital bed surrounded by indifferent medical attendants and well-wishers who cannot save her from perishing. And as she is wont to do when overwhelmed by critical life experiences, she decides to take pen to paper and find a way to give narrative reality to what she has observed.

In the case of her beloved Sartre, the situation was quite different. Sartre chose to arch towards death like a flaming meteor burning out as it streaks across the sky. Despite his doctor's recommendations, Sartre continued to consume alcohol, smoke, take large quantities of uppers (Corydane) and fill himself with rich and fatty foods. He suffered several strokes, lost most of his vision, became incontinent, lost considerable mobility and strength while he drove himself to finish his multi-volume study of the French novelist Flaubert and write articles for magazines and newspapers.

He continued to make the rounds of his several former lovers whom he helped to support financially and entered into a new relationship with a young Greek admirer who had knocked on his apartment door one morning. Eventually, he became incapable of going out on his own. His adopted daughter, Arlette Elkaim, and Simone took turns staying overnight in a guest bedroom in his apartment in case something were to befall him and he could not get help. The way of life that he had long lived was the only life he knew or wanted to know and if persisting in this manner would accelerate the end of his life, so be it, insisted Sartre.

"To be dead is to be prey for the living" (593), Sartre wrote in *Being and Nothingness*, and there is little to show in his subsequent work that he held another position. We may leave a legacy, a reputation, images stored in the memories of those whom we loved and hated, inspired and offended. But in Sartre's world to come there is only oblivion. What remains of us is an objectification that will be turned this way and that by our interpreters, biographers and critics.

Death is a repetition of the problem of the Other whose view of us we cannot control. Though we may seek ways to insure how we will be remembered, we are almost defenseless against the words that others use to reinvent us in their own minds as they attempt to re-inscribe us in the minds of others. For the few that are chosen to dwell in the Parthenon of the history of their chosen field (though subject to periodic dismissal and reinstatement), their reputation persists in a struggle between their legacy and the judgments of those who claim the authority to speak for, against and about them.

The immortal ones are not, however, completely defenseless, even in death. They have equipped the fortress of their work with labyrinths of puzzling paradoxes and hidden ironies to beguile the naïve who tread into waters over their heads. Some have planted conceptual landmines to wound the unsuspecting, and they have enlisted a host of self-perpetuating living acolytes who serve as guardsmen capable of shooting paralyzing arrows of counter-criticism into their detractors. Until the rise of secular societies and constitutional protections of free speech, the profession of philosophy was one fraught with the risks of social ostracism, banishment, imprisonment and being burned at the stake. From Socrates to Walter Benjamin and Simone Weil, the list of notable philosophers who have died at the hands of executioners, taken their own lives or died a political prisoner is lengthy. But even in death many of these epoch-making philosophers remain dangerous. Hence, their books are burned, they are erased from history school texts, or pundits declare their ideas as irrelevant and obsolete.

The scenes of Simone de Beauvoir hovering over her dying mother and trying to advocate for her in that Parisian hospital and later doting on the intractable Sartre to try to keep him alive and functioning serve as testimony to the primal bonds of love in the face of impending loss. Impending loss may intensify the love we have for others and for the memory of those already lost, as I was repeatedly to discover.

LOVE AND DEATH

One of my hospice assignments was to visit with a man living in the assisted living portion of a church-sponsored nursing home. "Jack" had moved there several years earlier because his wife suffered from middle-stage dementia and needed around the clock care and supervision. He moved her into the dementia wing and, so he could visit with her daily, moved himself into the adjoining assisted living section. This, I took it, was a testimony to love.

Jack suffered from COPD (a lung disease) and some type of cancer. Usually in good spirits and eager to talk about the past and current affairs, he was now starting to complain about how tired and breathless he was becoming. Even getting out of his La-Z-Boy and taking the few steps to his bathroom was exhausting. He could not go without oxygen. I tried to console him: "This must be tough." He nodded. Smiled sadly.

"I'm ready," he said during one of my visits after he had offered me chocolates from a box someone had left. I gave him a quizzical look.

"I don't have much longer to go," he commented, matter-of-factly. "And Jenny doesn't recognize me anymore. I don't think she'll know I'm gone. She can't last much longer either." He paused to catch his breath. "I'm comforted that I could arrange it so." He paused again. "So she's going to be cared for right to the end."

"Is there anything I can do?" I asked.

"Well," he said, giving a little laugh and then coughing. "If you have any pull with St. Peter, you could put in a good word for me."

I wasn't sure how to respond. I had not mentioned until that moment that I was not of the same faith tradition as was Jack. Moreover, given my skeptical views about the hereafter, I felt uncertain whether venturing down this conversational path was a good idea. Still, I wanted to say something.

"I don't know much about St. Peter, I'm afraid. I'm Jewish."

He looked at me in silence for several seconds. "Jewish? Yes." He nodded as if some missing piece of a puzzle had just dropped into place.

I had no idea what might come next. After all, we were in a Protestant denominational care center. There was a clergyman who came to visit Jack but Jack indicated that he didn't like the man because he didn't think he was a truly compassionate person. "He makes the rounds," Jack had told me with a shrug.

"I once dated a beautiful Jewish woman," Jack began, adjusting the tubes that went into his nostrils. "After my first wife died." He paused to either catch his breath or quiet his emotions or maybe both. "We'd been happily married and even worked in the business together for many years. That was a loss. Mmm."

Just then a knock on the door interrupted Jack and an aide came in to take his vital signs. Jack and I watched one another and he winked, as the aide prattled on about how beautiful was the weather. Noticing the box of chocolates she remarked, "Oh, those look good." Jack lifted the box. "Yours, darlin'," he drawled. The aide pocketed a couple of the chocolates. Thanked him. Nodded to me and went out. Would Jack remember where he left off?

"It was a few years later and naturally I was lonely. I met this woman through a mutual friend. For some reason, she had never been married. Dorothy. That was her name. Dorothy S." Jack smiled.

I immediately recognized the woman's last name. Could she have been a sister of my former optometrist, Dr. S.? I also knew him from a synagogue I used to attend where he served as what in the Baptist church would be called a Deacon.

"Jack," I said. "Did she have a brother, an optometrist, Dr. S.?"

"Yup," he replied. "That's her brother. You know him?"

"Yes. Not very well. I went to him for glasses and I knew him from a synagogue I attended."

"Did you know Dorothy?"

"No, I only knew Dr. S. and his wife. And not very well."

"Oh," he said, smiling. "The sister-in-law. She was a force of nature."

That I suspected was true from what I had seen of her. A take-charge woman who bustled around giving advice both to the receptive and the indifferent.

Jack then told me the story of how he and Dorothy hit it off right away and how they went dancing and took several trips together. He was considering proposing. But this was not to be.

"Dorothy had a condo somewhere in Hawaii. Must have been from some inheritance money, or so I heard. She'd go there for months at a time. And even though we were becoming a, you know, a known entity, off she went as she was wont to do." He paused and took a couple of deep breaths. "I felt kind of deserted even though she insisted she'd be back before I'd even begin to miss her. But I missed her right away. As fate would have it, a few weeks later someone introduced me to Jenny. She reminded me so much of my first wife, you know."

"And that did it," I said.

"Uh-huh. That did it."

I stayed with Jack for a few more minutes but when I saw that he was growing weary and his speech more halting, I said my goodbyes and reminded him when I was coming the next time. He nodded and waved his hand. The following week I received word from the hospice coordinator that Jack had died.

I don't think Jack would have believed Heidegger that our own death is always a possible impossibility. Maybe when we're younger but when you've reached the point in your life when every breath is an uncertainty and you see people around you disappearing from their usual breakfast or lunch seat, you are pretty certain the death is no longer impossible to consider impossible. Still, on the brink of speculating on the afterlife, our conversation veered to the romance of Jack and Dorothy. That was the Jewish connection, one that I could not in the least have suspected might be the outcome of my confession: "I'm Jewish."

What Jack taught me is that, even on the brink of death, a love affair, a romance, a fleeting memory of an embrace may hold us back from falling into despair as we face our demise even if we believe, however vaguely, that something of us will persist onto the other side of the mirror.

MISSING

During the time of my visits with D. I attended the high school 50th anniversary class reunion described elsewhere. There was an additional follow up to that event that I visit from time to time – a website.

The website for my high school graduating class includes a listing entitled "In Memory." Ours was a large graduating class of about 800. I counted up those who were known to have died, currently close to 200 names or about 18 percent.

About that many names are listed under a category of Whereabouts Unknown. An asterisk on the heading asks us if we can supply information about these "lost" individuals. Therefore we may surmise that many additional deaths have gone unreported to the organizers of the class reunion's website. A conservative estimate would put the percentage closer to 25 or 30. Life expectancy for those born around 1943 is 71.7 for males and 77.5 for females (the combined average would be 74). So 55+ years after graduation, it's surprising that the actual mortality rate is not higher for our cohort. This is in part testimony to the lengthening of the life course after age 65 due, in part, to improvements in medical care and the use of antibiotics, environmental and food safety, and life extending technologies such as pacemakers and dialysis machines. Also race, educational attainment and other social class factors favor the white middle classes, which we mainly were.

As I run my eye down the list of names, I hear a drum roll. Not only did I know many of these individuals during four years of high school, I knew many of them from my elementary school days forward. One day my name will be on this list. One day there will be no one interested enough to click on the list and one day the list and website will become permanently unvisited. Such is the plight of every generation. In the meantime, each name of the departed conjures up a picture: a giddy redheaded girl who told jokes as I stood waiting impatiently beside her under her parent's front porch light; a boy who encouraged me to run for president of a youth organization when I had little sense of myself as a leader; and a 50s rock and roll idol-looking blond boy whose mere glance, I enviously noticed, caused the girls in our circle of friends to blush. The blond boy died in his 40s of stomach cancer, the encourager died close to age 50 of complications of Crohn's Disease, but of the redheaded girl's death indicated by the list as in her early 60s, I know nothing since I had not seen her in over 50 years.

And though I know it's irrational and runs counter to Heidegger, I cannot help asking myself: How could they not be among us?

REFERENCES

Beauvoir, Simone de (1965). *A Very Easy Death*. Translated from the French by Andre Deutch. New York: Pantheon.

_____ (1984). *Adieux: A Farewell to Sartre*. Translated from the French by Patrick O'Brian. New York: Pantheon.

Camus, Albert (1955). *The Myth of Sisyphus and other Essays*. Translated from the French by Justin O'Brien. New York: Knopf.

Eagleman, David (2009). *Sum: Forty Tales from the Afterlives*. New York: Pantheon.

Heidegger, Martin (1962). *Being and Time*. Tr. J. Macquarrie and E. Robinson. Oxford: Basil Blackwell.

Kagan, Sarah (2009). Cancer in the Lives of Older Americans: Blessings and Battles. University of Pennsylvania Press.

12. CONSCIOUSNESS

One of a small number of individuals to be draped with a doctoral hood from the History of Consciousness program, ironically I have to admit that I have been anything but historically self-aware. My life has been marked by a series of cultural shocks that show me to have been slow and often reactive to the changes going on around me. So this raises some interesting questions about the concept of consciousness, the twelfth star in the existential night sky.

Consciousness may refer to complex states of individual or collective contextual self-awareness (e.g. Kierkegaard writing about cultural attitudes of mid-nineteenth century Europe in his 1846 book, *The Present Age*) or to the minimal conditions of pre-conceptual sensations and perceptions (Merleau-Ponty writing about "the lived body," in his 1945 published study, *The Phenomenology of Perception*). In the existential tradition, consciousness is considered a dynamic process, not a fixed state, one that is best understood by tracking both its subtle, individual (subjective) and culturally epochal (objective) transformations. These individual and widespread cultural changes, and our awareness of them, often seem to arise as a bolt out of the blue. We gain special insight into the workings of consciousness when waves of social change break over us. Several immediately come to mind.

THE WAVES

One day in the mid-1960s the girlfriend of my friend "Harold," whom I had known since high school and on into college, explained to me that she and Harold had come to the conclusion that he was more attracted to men than to women but that for years he had struggled against admitting these feelings. I realized that I hadn't known Harold as well as I had assumed.

Not only was his identity changing in my mind but my assumptions about sexual orientation were shaken. I didn't like admitting it to myself, but I realized I was, at least initially, uncomfortable with regarding Harold as a man who was sexually attracted to other men... and perhaps to me.

As mentioned, during my last year in undergraduate college I became active in the Civil Rights movement. Since I had a car and she did not, I volunteered to drive "Claudette," one of the black leaders of the local Student Non-violent Coordinating Committee (SNCC), to meetings. On this particular day we were heading to an AME church for a meeting with black ministers. Claudette turned to me and said that she had received a call from the national headquarters informing her that all the white members of SNCC were being asked to withdraw from the organization. I took Claudette to the meeting and then back to campus. Driving home, suddenly her message sank in, we white people were no longer welcomed. Anger, confusion and then guilt surged up as if I had done something against Claudette and other African Americans. But what was it? The whole history of white racism came flooding into my mind.

As a graduate student I held a teaching assistant position that helped pay most of my living expenses. One semester I was assigned to assist a visual artist conduct a class for general liberal arts students on sculpture making. The students' materials consisted of assorted wood scraps that came from tool and die shops and furniture factories. The students made assemblages with just the use of white glue. My role was to lead the reading and discussion sessions to acquaint students with aesthetic theories. Norm, the artist I was assisting, insisted that I take part in the studio portion of the course so I would understand what the students were experiencing.

One evening, after dinner in the campus cafeteria, I drifted over to the studio to do a little work on an abstract piece I had recently started. After a while, I looked at my watch and discovered it was one o'clock in the morning. I had been gluing wood shapes together for five hours. On the table in front of me stood a wooden configuration that I suddenly realized looked like a motorcycle. Its wheels seemed to be throwing off geometric shapes that reminded me of the signs of the zodiac. In my hand I held a pie-shaped piece of wood that was curved at the large end and flat at the other. Without thinking, I put glue on the flat end and pressed it onto a disc shape in the middle of the handlebars. Voilà, it became a headlight beam.

How is it that certain deep-seated and in some cases culturally ingrained attitudes can be challenged and overturned, leading to a state of disorientation accompanied by emotional perplexity? The first example, Harold's coming out, is one that I'm sure has occurred among millions of people. A friend or family member going public challenges our assumptions about gender, acceptable forms of sexuality, love between men and between women, and the certainty (or uncertainty) of one's own sexual identity. This dawning of a new type of consciousness also calls forth a new vocabulary – words like partner, queen, Gay and so on.

The second example concerns the shock of being told that despite your seeming best intentions, inadvertently you're a participant in institutionalized racism. Case in point, along with your white counterparts, you tend to usurp the power of the black people you believe you've been assisting. Consequently, we are forced to see ourselves in an unfamiliar and, perhaps, unattractive context of history.

The third example is an alteration in consciousness that has been called "flow." Customary awareness of the passing of time is transformed into an experience of expansive duration in which preconscious and seemingly autonomous physical gestures – in this instance handling wooden shapes and a squeeze bottle of white glue – produce a recognizable form but only as the trance-like state comes to an end and awareness recalibrates to clock time. One might say this third example of altered consciousness is the discovery of inner creativity, a discovery that entails an entirely new way of looking at materials and compositions as well as the enigmatic powers of imagination.

Some changes in how we engage with and encounter other people, objects, institutions, environments and ideas only require minor retooling – small adjustment to accommodate the unexpected, the anomalous, the exceptional. But other challenges are of a magnitude great enough to require a major overhaul or "paradigm shift." The mental machinery running our fundamental operating procedures has broken down to the extent that fixing it by replacing a few parts has now become impossible. The whole machine, we realize, is obsolete. These and many other instances should make us wonder: how is a change of consciousness possible? Clearly, from these few examples, we see that changes in individual consciousness are in many ways inseparable from large-scale social upheavals.

THEORIES OF CONSCIOUSNESS

Changes in awareness raise some interesting questions. For example, if there is a sense of discontinuity when a set of my assumptions is overturned, what provides the bridge to a new outlook such that I can even report the states of before and after? If changes in awareness feel as though they happen to or overtake me, to what extent am I a "willing" participant – that is, do I choose to change or is it somehow forced upon me? And if many dramatic alterations in conscious awareness turn out also to be shared by millions of other people, is it the case that, knowingly or not, I am simply being carried along "with the times?"

The terms awareness and consciousness are not identical. Much of my day is spent in conscious activities like navigating around furniture, hearing the doorbell, putting the right amount of cream and sugar in my coffee to suit my taste, and perceiving that the one-half visible side of my coffee mug is, in fact, an actual three-dimensional shape. In these examples, I am conscious but not actively aware. I'm apparently not conscious when I'm in a deep sleep and usually cannot recall anything that happened between, say, midnight and six-thirty a.m.

My dog is conscious, too. She barks at me when she needs to go out and she immediately comes to stand beside the container of treats when we return from our outing. She's trained me. However, she does not seem particularly aware of herself or given to moments of reflection.

When I choose to pay attention to what I'm doing because the activity requires care or caution – like setting the timer when hard-boiling eggs or putting on my left turn signal when blending into traffic from the on ramp lane of the freeway, I tend to be much less on automatic pilot. When I attend a live performance at a theater, I'm swept up in the plot and engaged with the characters, if the play is successful, and I am simultaneously alert to understanding what's going on and making sense of what the play means to its audience, and especially to me. Afterwards, my wife and I discuss how we liked the play and I become more self-conscious that we each have taken away something different, occasionally oppositional, from what we both just observed. Noting that difference increases my self-consciousness.

When philosophers talk about consciousness they may be focusing on different types of phenomena, depending on what they're trying to get at.

Merleau-Ponty, following the late work of Edmund Husserl, wanted to prove that a lot of the things humans do in their interactions with their environment are actions of the "lived body" rather than some conscious process. Seeing the world as three-dimensional even when we only see objects one side at a time is not a reflective process. It isn't that we learn to see in three-dimensions or that it takes an act of will, we are just "wired" to do so. Consciously but not self-consciously, potters and surgeons learn to think with their hands in what chemist-philosopher Michael Polanyi called "tacit knowledge."

Clearly, there are a great many things that we do successfully without deliberation. But then how about the unreflective experience of falling in love? The very idiomatic nature of the phrase, which is qualified by "falling," suggests an involuntary activity. We meet a certain someone and wham, the electric sparks fly. We want to touch the person and we want them to touch us. We adore and want to be adored. It's so irrational. Maybe they're not even the "right type" for us. Later, we may discover, they weren't or we weren't the right type for them. But how can that be when our initial emotional response seemed to announce itself with such absolute certainty? Is it timing, our biochemistry or the alignment of the stars? We're conscious of falling in love. We tell our best friends about it. Conscious, yes, but we initially lack critical awareness until the bubble bursts or lifts us heavenwards.

Theories of consciousness are important because they raise serious questions about identity, the self, free will, responsibility and even the actions of collectivities we call social movements. A good deal of the debate among philosophers in recent times has been about matters such as how consciousness is related to the acquisition of knowledge, to the human capacity for certainty, the status of what constitutes "reality," the mind-brain and the mind-brain-body connections.

For some philosophers, ones especially influenced by research from the neurosciences, mind-body dualisms of the Cartesian sort must be rejected, as it's clear that no mind is disconnected from its home in the body as long as one is alive. They show how parts of the brain function to "map" the body as a set of reference points. These are crucial to the various states of consciousness such as feelings, emotions, the senses of spatial and temporal perception, as well as higher order acts such as the inner narrative of our autobiographical self.

In differentiating human consciousness from that of other animals, the "nature" of consciousness that is human is distinguished by the capacity for self-modification, not just in behavior but also in the formation of concepts and categories that help us make the world and ourselves intelligible. It would seem there are lower and higher states of consciousness with humans exhibiting the perhaps unique capacity of "consciousness of consciousness." From the time of Descartes, many European philosophers have made consciousness, as exhibited in the individual subject, the starting point of their theoretical constructions.

However, this approach has not gone unchallenged. More so in recent times as evidence has poured in from the natural sciences about genetics, the workings of the brain and the psychology of economic behavior, e.g. Daniel Kahneman's study of innate cognitive bias in his work on two systems of brain activity, "thinking fast and thinking slow." These theories mock the pretenses of conscious awareness.

In recent decades research into states of consciousness have benefitted from the tools of brain imaging that allow scientists to watch computer screens as regions of the brain "light up" while patients or study subjects respond to various stimuli. Other types of research on choice making have shown precognitive inclinations and impulsive behaviors (e.g. compulsive gambling, buying, hoarding and other forms of addiction) that seem to go against a person's more rational self-interest. The thrust of emerging theories of consciousness is that there is a great deal in how we behave that is unconscious or that reveals levels of what could be called pre-reflective consciousness. Such studies tell us that we seem to have little or no control over how we live our lives. In other words, how we are "wired" determines a great deal about our actions and beliefs.

These revelations would make dubious the existentialist argument that we are the sum total of our (conscious) actions and choices. Yet, in support of the conscious choices premise, there is little doubt that in post-industrial, religiously tolerant societies the range of available life-style choices has never been greater. For example, a 2015 Pew Research Center study found that "42 percent of Americans no longer consider themselves part of the religion in which they were raised." While many no longer belong to any organized religious body, others have migrated to a new religious group that, they believe, better meets their spiritual needs.

Indeed, today's choice making, in large parts of the world, is historically unprecedented. Some women choose to serve in the military, even in combat brigades, or they join the ranks of firefighters, and some men choose to stay at home to raise their children or enter fields traditionally occupied by women such as nursing. Increasingly, LGBTQ people choose to publically live out their gender orientation rather than hiding their deeper identities. In these and countless other ways, people make significant conscious, and often difficult, life-defining choices.

While philosophers whom we associate with existentialism and phenomenology certainly made a study of subjectivity their point of departure, other historically concurrent schools of thought such as empiricism, analytical philosophy, and, particularly in post-war France, structuralism, poststructuralism and deconstructionism, largely rejected the existentialists' emphasis on consciousness.

Broadly speaking, each of these philosophical orientations rejected the notion that our ideas about the world depend on an adequate theory of consciousness. Rather, they tend to argue that most of the ways that humans behave and perceive are consequences of unconscious influences or that individual consciousness is simply too small a unit of study since individuals only know the world through perceptual filters such as culturally ingrained values, species adaptation to changing environments, linguistic behavior, or to the neurophysiology of the brain.

Starting with the Subject

A theory of consciousness is perhaps the most central and also most vulnerable ontological construct of Sartrean-Beauvoirian existentialism. For this brand of existentialism, consciousness, rather than rationality, opens the gateway to knowledge. Consciousness precedes rationality and encompasses the pre-rational, irrational and pre-reflective. As a light bulb in a dark room is switched on to reveal both the interior space and the bulb itself as the source of light, so does consciousness illumine itself when engaged in turning upon itself. Unlike reason, which comes imbued with an affinity to detect causality, consciousness is neutral, it is a function empty of values, vacant of hidden structures and eternal ideas, and for Sartre it is not even the focal point of a master networking organization, a transcendental ego. The ego, the switchman, the self, these all are constructs generated by consciousness through its interaction with its world and its other consciousnesses.

Sartre's formulation was an attempt to refute his teacher Husserl's notion of a transcendental ego, the home and hearth, so to speak, of subjectivity. For Sartre, that theoretical ego was nothing but an unfortunate tendency in Husserl's late work, his falling back into a type of philosophical idealism from which students like Sartre and others associated with existentialism had sought to escape in order to stay focused on the concreteness of human existence.

Sartre's formulation that the subject, the individual, emerges out of consciousness and that the reflective activity that we call the self is, as a construct or invention of self-consciousness, a fiction or perhaps, in light of Sartre account of his own self-formation in his autobiography, *The Words,* the deliberate choice of one or more biographical narratives. Sartre's claim, "I was born to fulfill the great need I had of myself" (69), is testimony to this radical philosophical position. This notion of the self as neither singular, immanent nor innate, but dispersed, multiple, and a malleable process, would certainly qualify it as a harbinger of postmodern theories of identity.

Returning to Sartre's formulation, the most amazing feature of consciousness is that it can disrupt itself from its state of Being and like a creation *ex nihilo,* produce its opposite, not unconsciousness but, regarding itself as Other or object, a self-consciousness which Sartre calls the "being-for-itself." Premised upon this capability of self-disruption, this negation of consciousness in its acts of intending an object, this act of regarding itself as other than itself, is the primal openness to freedom to make choices or, perhaps even more primitively put, to become the creature that brings choices into existence.

While de Beauvoir was less inclined to engage in ontological speculation, she drew on Sartre's abstract formulations to investigate social issues such as the suppression of the native peoples of colonized countries, the plight of the working classes and the poor, the subjugation of women and, later in her career, the often deplorable conditions of the elderly. Sartre moved on to increasingly embrace Marxism and to retract his theory of the radical freedom imputed to self-consciousness in its ability to transcend itself, instead placing greater emphasis on what he had earlier termed "facticity," the limiting conditions in which a self-conscious being might find itself.

In his 1960 work, *Critique of Dialectical Reason*, Sartre sought to preserve some semblance of his earlier notion of the freedom of subjectivity while locating this subject in the midst of historical, social and economic reality. The individual could no longer transcend what Sartre called the "situations" in which it found itself without joining forces with other individuals caught in a similar plight. Even the privileged of society must recognize their attachment with and dependency upon those whose labors make their lives comfortable and secure. As the masters enslave others, so do those they exploit and depend on also enslave them. It seemed to Sartre that only through acts of social protest and even violence could the downtrodden awaken the bourgeoisie from the hypnotic trance in which they were captured. The privileged classes were lulled by the false rhetoric of capitalist ideology that proclaimed everyone benefitted from a competitive market system and that the formation of social classes was an inevitable condition of life.

In mid-career Sartre still believed that the novelist, playwright, poet and visual artist could penetrate the fog of self-deception that surrounded the consciousnesses of the privileged classes to wake them to the conditions of inequality and exploitation that supported their way of life. But he grew doubtful that even the most committed and provocative of artistic creators could affect a broad transformation of social consciousness. Instead, awards, royalties, and fame would ensnare the most talented of such provocateurs, as the capitalist engine turned their work into an array of fashionable and consumable products. Sartre was himself awarded the Nobel Prize for literature in 1964 but he refused it for just this reason.

Late in his life and career (he continued publishing articles and books, sometimes with collaborators, into his last years) Sartre adopted the term *le vécu*, lived experience, to describe the opacity of human consciousness rather than, as earlier, its transparency to itself. By the time of his massive multi-volume psychoanalytic-Marxist study of the life and works of the novelist Gustav Flaubert (1971), Sartre no longer thought of the subject as a "nihilating consciousness" but rather as a function of the society in which that subject lived. The individual was influenced by the modes of industrial production, technical knowledge available at the time, the structure of the family, "the historic future which reveals itself" as one's "destiny," along with the individual's inherited predispositions and biological characteristics. All of these factors shape one's consciousness and make it impossible to ever completely comprehend oneself since comprehension is itself a function of the ways in which consciousness is shaped.

How different from that of his friend, Simone de Beauvoir, had become Sartre's increasing emphasis on the opacity of consciousness and the difficulty of both self and societal change. For her part, de Beauvoir's more practical focus on altering the consciousness of millions of people about the inequalities concerning gender, age, race and social class, could be likened to a famous allegory concerning appearance and reality.

The idea that higher states of consciousness are achieved by differentiating between appearance and reality goes back to the world of the ancient Greek philosophers. In Plato's allegory of the cave, the enchained prisoner, who has been staring at shadow shapes on the rear wall of the enclosure all his life, is provoked to turn around to discover puppeteer-like people causing these shadows to appear as real. In shock and dismay, he frees himself and strides upward past the shadow-projecting puppeteers with their silhouettes and light sources (some kind of fire) toward the entrance to the cave and out into the initially blinding sunlight of, allegorically speaking, true reality.

In her own version of emergence from a cave of falsehood, Simone de Beauvoir freed herself from stereotypes of women and their socially approved roles. Liberated from these shadows, she could see in almost every domain she studied – history, anthropology, biology, sociology, economics, psychology and theology – how the shadow play that favored men and cast women into secondary roles had been carried out over the centuries. Like Plato's freed prisoner, she chose to go back into the cave and liberate the others rather than bask in the sunlight of liberated self-awareness.

Systematically identifying how others were ensnared, de Beauvoir drew the ire of those that denied they served as puppeteers. Sometimes it was those she described as the prisoners who would refuse the idea that they were the hapless victims of a shadow play. She courageously deflected her detractors' vitriol, perhaps realizing she had helped to usher in this tremendous change in consciousness. She did not, as did the allegorizing

Plato, claim there was some absolutely true or essential idea – the Good, for Plato, an idealized authentic Woman, for de Beauvoir – that could now be grasped and toward which everyone should henceforth stride. There was no essence of Woman; rather being a woman was a matter of how to become a woman once the individual had turned away from the culturally projected, shadow illusions that had imprisoned her.

By implication, consciousness was that human activity through which, in this case, a woman was capable of casting off a shadow play and becoming the innovator of her own character development. Initially de Beauvoir did not think a worldwide social movement was called for. Just as she had been able to accomplish her own liberation, so other women would find their way. But eventually she came to the realization that, as Sartre had advocated about the downtrodden and the colonized, mass solidarity was necessary if advances were to be made. Becoming part of the women's movement, she advocated for legalizing abortion and for changing French laws to promote economic equity in cases of divorce. What women could now demand were certain legal rights, equal employment opportunities, changes in how men treated women in the workplace, and ways the society could accommodate a revolution in gender identities.

The underlying lesson de Beauvoir sought to convey to readers who followed her methodology was to challenge every claim that a "scientific" study of nature gave evidence to how human choices are predetermined. Were these theories hiding an ideological investment in the status quo while supporting and sustaining the power and authority of entrenched experts? The kind of choices de Beauvoir had in mind were not trivial ones, such as a preference for a certain type of éclair or *petite four*, as Sartre pointed out in the question-and-answer period following his famous 1945 lecture at the Club Maintenant. Rather the choices were those that concerned the values by which one chooses to conduct his or her life, the qualities that defined one's aspirations, the ways one would engage in the social, political and economic spheres of life with others both near and far, and so on.

When we encounter the vast new territory of the scientific studies of consciousness, many of which aim to show that consciousness is a metaphysical fiction or that much of our behavior is in fact not a function of consciousness but of the body's built in capacity of dealing in immediacy, we should be on alert for what comes next in the guise of a seemingly empirically based conclusion. Let us take, for example, the approach of an influential French anthropologist, one of whose works still in manuscript form (*The Elementary Forms of Kinship*) Simone de Beauvoir studied as a background resource while writing *The Second Sex* and whose subsequent writing helped to push existentialism to the sidelines of intellectual life in France and beyond.

STRUCTURALISM

By the early 1960s, existentialism in France had been eclipsed by other intellectual movements that tended to dismiss any notion that understanding the human condition must begin with a focus on the individual subject, the dynamics of consciousness, and the free will side of the age-old dichotomy of free will versus determinism.

Foremost among these movements was what became known as "structuralism." In 1962, Claude Levi-Strauss published a work in the field of anthropology entitled *La Pensée Sauvage*, translated into English in 1966 as *The Savage Mind*. The "savage mind" did not refer to the mentality of primitive peoples. Instead the theory aimed to describe the mind's natural state through which humans process experience by classifying, distinguishing and ordering the world.

For Levi-Strauss, who indulged himself in puns and plays on words, the French *sauvage* connoted something wild or untamed, hardly captured in the English "savage." Based on his study of certain tribal peoples (such as Indians in the Brazilian rainforest) but also by looking at modern forms of social organization, Levi-Strauss argued that across time and geography, binary oppositions such as the sacred and profane, raw and cooked foods, and designations of pure and impure, formed the basis of how people utilized systems of classification. "The savage mind totalizes," said Levi-Strauss, it "builds mental structures which facilitate an understanding of the world in as much as they resemble it" (263).

Levi-Strauss's exciting new theories were regarded as "scientific" and not speculative. And though they dealt with large aggregates such as tribes and nations, they focused on highly diverse peoples living in vastly different conditions in vastly different parts of the world. This was consistent with structuralism's premise that the human mind functions in the same ways everywhere – and perhaps even always.

The major thesis of *The Savage Mind* is that, at the deepest level, no fundamental differences exist in the ways that modern humans and so-called "primitive" peoples think and perceive reality. All mature humans with normally functioning brains are capable of complex thought, including critical analysis and inference about cause-and-effect relationships, Lévi-Strauss declared. Therefore, it is fallacious to assume, as had most anthropologist and philosophers, there existed a "dichotomy between logical and pre-logical mentality." Rather, argued Levi-Strauss, the "the savage mind is logical in the same sense and the same fashion as ours" (that is, "non-primitive" peoples). All cultures, moreover, contain common components, including myths and systems of classification, and the differences in the content of myths and classifications are primarily a result of variations in environment, knowledge and technology.

Levi-Strauss regarded culture after the manner of groundbreaking linguist, Ferdinand de Saussure who treated language as a system of structures made up of discrete elements or units that could be combined, recombined, and re-ordered in many different ways, but always according to consistent patterns that ultimately rest on binary oppositions such as general/particular, up/down, God/human, etc. Analyses of their formations reveal ways in which languages shape cultures by establishing "deep structures" operating beneath surface phenomena. Once these deep structures are disclosed, they can unlock organizing principles such as tribal kinship systems, ritual practices, the uses of magic, as well as purportedly rational attitudes about class differences in industrialized societies.

Levi-Strauss's structural anthropology demolished theories of social Darwinism ("survival of the fittest") and contravened the long-held views of evolutionary psychologists who believed human progress was a matter of passing through stages of belief in magic, then religion and ultimately in philosophical and scientific methodology. Levi-Strauss sought to refute this presumption of the superiority of the rational mind. Rather he tried to show on the one hand the "scientific" in the ways that tribal people interacted with their environment and, on the other, elements of magical thinking in the accounts of modern science. He aimed to dismantle the then well-established distinction between "concrete" (i.e. "primitive") and "abstract" ("scientific") thinking by pointing to the large number of abstract terms in the languages of tribal people, and the achievements of so-called primitive pre-literate peoples, including skills of pottery-making, weaving, metallurgy, agriculture and the domestication of plants and animals.

Levi-Strauss revealed in his 1995 anthropological memoir, *Tristes Tropiques*, the extent to which missionaries from "advanced" cultures had contributed to the horrifying demise of tribal peoples and their cultures by bringing to them disease, alcohol and alien religions. As for existentialism, Levi-Strauss argued, albeit indirectly, that its ontology of consciousness as the ground of self-creation via negativity (doubt, distancing, making objective, in short, transcending), was sheer nonsense, since every person was born into a language group and culture with its own inherent way of structuring how the world would be perceived and understood.

In "History and Dialectic," the last chapter of *The Savage Mind*, Levi-Strauss, who had already made numerous references to Sartre, threw down the proverbial gauntlet by aiming to ridicule Sartre's notion that "dialectical reason" is distinct from and superior to "analytical reason." For Sartre, dialectical reason involves the give and take of both self-interrogation and the conflictive nature of social and historical development.

Dialectical reason is the engine described by both Hegel and Marx as the driving force of self-overcoming or transcendence. It's what allows individuals and collectivities to, in a sense, think outside the box of the given (e.g. mathematical formulas, political theories, enculturated values) and, through the power of the negative (doubt, contradiction, rebellion, the discovery of anomalies) to generate new options. Analytic reason's tools such as logic, language analysis, model-building, measurement, quantification, and empirical observations of the external world tended only to reinforce or sustain knowledge that stays within the box of cultural attitudes and the dominant political ideology of a society.

Levi-Strauss argued that Sartre was completely wrong and that he lacked an understanding of not only anthropology but also modern science. Sartre, he argued, he had fallen into the trap of Eurocentric presumptions that improvements to the human condition only occurred after the rise of literacy and development of abstract thinking.

While a considerable amount of debate raged between Sartre and Levi-Strauss, it seemed clear, at least in the early 1960s, that Levi-Strauss and the school of structuralism had won the day. But this was, in part, because Sartre had by then tried to wed existentialism's focus on the individuals with Marxism's focus on the collective with the result being a very dysfunctional marriage. The attempted union wound up alienating both Marxists and old-school existentialists.

To many of the French intelligentsia, Sartre had knuckled under to the French Communist Party's "with us or against us" line of thinking. For his part, Sartre believed that despite the flaws and failures of the Soviet regime, the communists held the only hope for bringing about widespread social justice in overcoming colonialism, worker poverty, the tyrannical regimes of European countries such as Spain and Portugal and many countries of South America such as Chile and Argentina that were supported by the democracies of capitalism. The Cold War atmosphere, fear of aggression from the Soviet Union (the Hungarian Uprising had occurred in 1956), fascination with American movies, cars and rising affluence, and astonishing advances in technology, helped make the concepts of structuralism seem more modern and enlightened than the tired terms of existentialism's "human condition."

Structuralism's dominance did not last. The student uprising of 1968 and structuralism's difficulty in explaining the upsurge of personal agency and the ferment of social change in France and elsewhere revealed serious deficiencies in the theory. Indeed, in 1969, as a sign that structuralism was losing its intellectual dominance, Levi-Strauss bemoaned the fact (as quoted in the *New York Times*) that "the position of the youth now corresponds to that of Sartre."

The post-structuralism movement followed suit with (among the various theorists associated with the orientation) a critique of the notion of linguistically influenced binary opposites and the more undermining critical standpoint that every universalizing intellectual project could be shown to reveal the distorting influences of cultural (primarily Western) hegemony. In other words, there were no objective truths and every observation of a "foreign" or "primitive" culture inevitably led to a mirror of its own making or the distorting effects of its own conceptual tools.

NARRATIVES OF CONSCIOUSNESS

Clearly, every philosophical movement has its heyday and its advocates, many of whom are academics who earn a living by writing and teaching about their school of thought. And, clearly, subsequent movements arise that build upon a philosophical position or aim to find fault with and point to the need for revision if not the complete replacement of their predecessors' constructs. Sometimes the most powerful critics are teachers' former students. One-upmanship is well known to those who work in an academic setting and while the particular philosophical issues can seem arcane to outsiders, there is almost always something important at stake – that is, besides fame, fortune and power – in these intellectual skirmishes.

Those within the walls of academia, the intellectual elites, are able to grasp the subtleties of theoretical conflicts that spill over into who gets promoted and what type of people get hired who promote a certain theoretical disposition. Members of these elites are in possession of the complex terminology and historical background out of which the battles have emerged. But the conflicts do "trickle down," so to speak, to the non-specialists (who may also be academics from other fields), a vastly larger number of people who are able to glean from the din of battle and the waving of banners just what the contestants stand for and against. Simply put, they (and we) respond to the epic themes conveyed at a certain level of narrative availability. Fans of Public Television may have enjoyed David Eagleman's amusing and informative 2015 documentary on the unconscious brain during the *Closer to the Truth* series on "Consciousness." The battle of free will versus determinism continues unabated.

In the arena of theories of consciousness, as I have pointed out, the Sartrean epic narrative from the era of *Being and Nothingness* was that consciousness is the gift that human beings give to themselves when they accept the burden of freedom presented through the power of negation. While couched in the context of a highly idiosyncratic vocabulary derived in part from the three great Hs of modern European philosophy, Hegel, Heidegger and Husserl, Sartre, through his "phenomenological ontology," but also Camus, through his hero of the absurd, Sisyphus, sent a powerful message across the world that people could forge their own destinies and overcome seemingly insurmountable obstacles through the sheer force of being true to themselves and making authentic choices.

In Sartre's subsequent writing he veered in a sharply different direction by aiming to demonstrate that it wasn't enough to go it alone, because the oppressive forces of class structure and the means and control of capitalist production imposed enormous restrictions that individuals, acting alone or in isolation, could not overcome. Not only was commitment required of the writer and philosopher but solidarity with the masses. Moreover, it was not only the subjugated classes who suffered. It was also the oppressors, the bourgeoisie and other privileged elites, who were caught in the web of entanglements and self-deceptions. Camus, as we have pointed out elsewhere, was sympathetic to Sartre's liberationist cause but he feared the influence of ideologies, those of both the left wing and the right, because too often, he observed, they justified further intolerance and acts of inhumanity.

For her part, Simone de Beauvoir shifted from an earlier preoccupation in her novels on interpersonal consciousness (conflicts of relationships such as the lovers' triangle) to the larger social context of the plight of Woman as Other and, later, the Elder as Other.

As mentioned, in her 1955 novel, *The Mandarins*, she created a multi-level story of individuals caught up in conflictive love relationships simultaneously buffeted by events of post-war European society and political ideology. She captured the ways individual lives can be overwhelmed by the winds of war and political upheaval. Wars and revolutions often force people to choose sides under extreme circumstances that, in their own eyes and those of others, make some people heroes and others villains or cowards.

Like Sartre, de Beauvoir's message also proclaims the right to freedom of choice and the individual's assertion of personal worth against the oppressive forces of prejudice, stereotyping and exploitation. Later social activists, feminists and opponents of ageism (e.g. the Gray Panthers in the U.S.), extracted from de Beauvoir's dense and scholarly studies the information they needed to launch consciousness-raising movements among women and, later, the elderly.

Though it is perhaps a bit simplistic to put it this way, the credibility of conflicting theories of consciousness comes down to the persuasiveness of the narratives that aim to describe the theories. While only a small number of people across the world could make their way through the highly technical vocabulary of Sartre, de Beauvoir and, to a lesser extent, Camus' major philosophical works, the sheer force of their convictions came through their more accessible and widely translated short stories, plays and novels, and through interviews published in magazines, newspapers and on newsreels, and by way of commentators and editors of anthologies who distilled their messages for countless millions of people.

Unlike most academic philosophers who are relatively unknown to the general educated citizenry, Sartre, de Beauvoir and Camus were world famous, their works translated into multiple languages. They embodied their principles and ideas and paraded them before the public after decades of widespread poverty, devastating wars and massive political upheavals. Eventually, however, their stories lost their freshness and headline-grabbing power.

Also the times changed. Suddenly structuralism was in because it combined increasing interest in theories of language and grammar, fascination with new methods in anthropology that honored rather than degraded so-called "primitive" people, and because post-1960s life in most Europe countries became more comfortable and secure after decades of war and political strife. Acquiring freedom seemed less critical than understanding the construction of meaning in the latest Godard or Truffaut French New Wave film, in the initiation rituals of a Brazilian tribe or whether the Book of Job revealed a literary form similar to that of a Greek tragedy.

Given this trend of regarding consciousness as structurally enculturated, it is not surprising that in 1979, my alma mater, UC Santa Cruz chose as its new director of the History of Consciousness program Hayden White, author of the provocative 1973 book entitled *Metahistory*, which challenged the assumptions of historians' ways of writing history. White proposed the idea that historical accounts (he focused mainly on nineteenth-century historians) were essentially literary art forms that directly or indirectly gave a shape and meaning to the collections of facts, dates and actors that make up a historical chronology. One of the key influences on White's view that history, whether public or personal, is always a matter of interpretation came from his reading of Sartre's Being and Nothingness. In the section entitled "My Past," Sartre argues that it is always in light of one's present projects that one infuses the past with meaning and renders it intelligible. (I, too, have found this an inescapable truth. Hence, this book.)

Narratives of history are, in White's view, influenced by one of several master narratives or "tropes" that impose a particular order, sense of causality, and temporality upon the complex maze of reported and documented events that go into historical research. His theory would seem to undermine a trend in the work of historians to operate in a meticulous objective, scientific way. In fact, according to White, they hardly differ from the writers of fiction. In this sense, the same set of historical events could be described in multiple, perhaps equally valid, ways. White was not arguing for relativism in historical narratives, rather that every written account of a particular history always bears the stylistic stamp, the signature, of the author/historian. Implying, by inference, that theirs is never the final word and that the meaning of events is always open to another interpretation and another narrative account.

White's approach seems to harbor a built-in paradox. He believes that a central purpose of historical writing is to "liberate" knowledgeable readers from "the burden of the past," by showing them that history is full of disruptions and discontinuities, and that it is not the smooth flow of the inevitable. Yet every historical account is overtly or covertly committed to a paradigm of what a historical account means, a paradigm revealed in the structure of the narrative itself. So, for example, in satirical narratives of history, folly and chance are shown to govern human affairs, while in tragic narrative accounts human conflicts invariably end in death and despair. A third narrative mode, the comedic, depicts shared values prevailing against the forces of disruption, and so on. But this imputed typology suggests that narrative structures of history are somehow linguistically or, perhaps better, rhetorically determined; that is, the authors may not be aware they are embracing a certain narrative paradigm. The "liberated" reader of history is unburdened from the weight of the past by understanding how these multiple modes of narrative structure function to convey meanings. But because each narrative account seems to offer its own veracity and internal consistency, the resulting narratives leave history readers, as it were, untethered.

White's approach provides an additional meaning to what might be called the macro level of historical consciousness. Unsurprisingly, White's approach retains the tension between a liberationist and a determinist view of historical consciousness. How then did the History of Consciousness program fare under the master of historical tropes?

In response to the changes in historical consciousness in the 1970s and 80s, White and his colleagues sought to make the graduate program more receptive to minority, feminist and LGBTQ students and far less focused on the European tradition of dead white males, particularly those of an existentialist and phenomenologist persuasion that prevailed from the time of the program's inception in 1966. Ironically, White (in an oral history interview from 2012) expressed disappointment that his university colleagues in anthropology and feminist studies remained unfazed by the attention he called to the problems of historical narratives. Should he have been surprised? The kind of critical self-consciousness that White's approach calls for can have the effect of undermining the certainty one might possess in developing a narrative account. Few people passionate about their research findings and dedicated to political liberation want to question the very way they tell their story. Hayden White retired in 1995 and was made a UCSC professor emeritus. The program continues to thrive.

Since the era of structuralism many new philosophical approaches have come into vogue in intellectual circles, bringing with them new vocabularies and descriptive and demonstrative narratives. Many of these narratives (e.g. deconstructionist, post-structuralist) have been influenced by the writings of Husserl, Heidegger, Nietzsche, Kierkegaard, Merleau-Ponty, de Beauvoir and Sartre and others closely or loosely associated with existentialism. And some of these philosophical positions have engaged with those whose narratives stem from brain imaging and neurolinguistics.

Can human consciousness be usefully compared to how spiders spin their webs or beavers build their dams? Philosopher and cognitive scientist Daniel Dennett's account of human consciousness makes it a wired-in, language-based facet of human adaptability. Dennett, author of *Consciousness Explained*, argues that autobiographical narratives only manage to create illusions of selfhood. Neuroscientist Antonio Damasio, in his 2010 book, *Self Comes to Mind: Constructing the Conscious Brain*, equates human consciousness with self-consciousness, in spite of all the recent examples of autonomous (i.e. non-conscious) brain activities, and still sees value in the notion of an "autobiographical self." This ongoing debate illustrates that there will always be a gap between first-person (subjective) and third-person (scientific) accounts of consciousness. Given Hayden White's claims, even the latter would remain a function of literary tropes.

PERENNIAL PHILOSOPHY

Several decades after my initial discovery of my friend Harold's sexual orientation, I sat with him and his long-time partner Mitch at a Manhattan restaurant. They were sharing stories of traveling throughout Southeast Asia where they visited their many gay friends and even walked in the Kolkata Rainbow Pride Festival. Listening, I marveled at the huge changes in social tolerance and acceptance of the diverse ways in which people choose to lead their lives. But I also heard from them of their many other friends who dare not reveal their sexual orientation for fear of reprisal and even imprisonment. Choosing oneself always includes an element of risk, especially if you find yourself, from a societal point of view, an "outsider." Because the struggle to free oneself from prejudices of one sort or another and to find the courage to be the person one needs to become is a perennial challenge, existentialism will never become outdated but, rather, will be rediscovered and reinterpreted for whatever is "the present age.

The existentialists did not invent the quest for self-determination, being true to oneself, taking responsibility for one's choices, demonstrating solidarity with oppressed populations or confronting one's finitude. But they supplied a fresh (albeit sometimes clumsy) vocabulary, a rich, manifold and often compelling narrative and a conceptual framework for the middle decades of the 20th century that continues to resonate into the 21st.

EXISTENTIAL AWAKENING

It's not easy to pinpoint those moments when the life and reality that one had not only taken for granted but had done so unknowingly suddenly come into question. Such moments that feel like a kind of awakening (but who knew they were asleep?) can arrive in powerfully overt or faintly subtle ways. Wars, political upheavals, and economic reversals were contexts for the existentialists from Kierkegaard (the revolutions of 1848 and the coming of the constitutional monarchy in Denmark) to de Beauvoir (the rise of Fascism, the lead-up to World War II and the Occupation).

These events helped to shatter the calm of ordinary, taken-for-granted life. But less overtly dramatic events may also play a role. A child observing family disputes over religion (de Beauvoir's mother was an observant Catholic, her father indifferent to religion), or a father sharing the burden of his melancholy and religious inner life with a favored child

(Kierkegaard) can produce an early awakening to the fact that there are multiple ways of understanding the mind of others as well as one's own mind. Sometimes it's difficult to identify any particular event or situation that would break open the shell of the taken for granted.

The experiences with which I began this chapter came from my adult life. But what I regard as my earliest awakening came in childhood. When I was around seven I experienced one such moment walking home from elementary school, a journey of perhaps 15 minutes. It was a windy fall afternoon – Indian summer. Leaves swirled around on the lawns beside the sidewalk. Suddenly, I felt strange; felt that as the boy walking along the sidewalk I had vanished, had stepped out of my body. Someone was continuing to move forward but someone else had drifted off. It was as if another reality, though one without distinct content, opened to me. A pang of anxiety surged up. Was this dying, was I sick, would my mind switch back to normal?

The disruption was not so much one of entering a different reality as in suddenly becoming aware that, all along, I had inhabited one. The word "suddenly" is misleading in this context because there was no clear line of temporal demarcation. Phrases now occur to me like: "I walked out of time," or "Time seemed to stand still." I realize these are paradoxical statement based on the confusion between spatial and temporal sequences. While I could not then formulate this question, my physical self was asking: Is there more than one reality? I wouldn't have had the vocabulary that included a word like "reality." I just kept on walking and, in a few minutes, everything seemed as it had been. I said nothing about this experience to anyone but I tucked it away in a tiny recess of my mind.

A few months later when, at a routine check-up with our pediatrician, I decided to describe the experience. I thought maybe as a doctor he'd heard other similar accounts and he would be able to attach a name to it. "Hmm. Interesting," he said, smiling and giving me a reassuring shrug that, I assumed meant, 'You will be fine. This happens to a lot of kids.' And since he dismissed the experience as of no consequence, I dismissed it, too. Only it wouldn't go away. Years later, I decided that what psychologists might call a "dissociative experience" was the kind of invitation to wonder about one's life and the world in which that life is enfolded that probably everyone receives some time or other. I just happened to be one of those people who couldn't let it pass unexamined. On rare occasions, like right now, writing these words, I am revisiting that moment – existentially.

Vanishing or hovering above the scene of a fall day with the leaves kicking around along the sidewalk, I could say that this was the announcement of the possibility of my not being. My existence was not necessary. I might not ever have been. Like Sartre, I had to invent my own necessity to be. And like Heidegger, I saw that I was an existent flung into being, a spirit of imagination, a dreamer, a mind that could find its way into unexpected realms, make discoveries, experience the thrill of suddenly understanding what Kierkegaard meant by the collision of the finite and the infinite as the paradox of our humanity. Was this an instance of de Beauvoir's "tragic ambiguity?"

Revisiting the perplexity of a moment on a perfectly ordinary fall afternoon on the way home from school, repeatedly over a lifetime, episodically when it seems to recall itself, that's enough of an exercise in ambiguity, but not one that I would describe as tragic. A wound, perhaps, a slight tear in the tissue of inviolability that would never perfectly heal. To recollect this moment is to touch a scar.

REFERENCES

Damasio, Antonio (2010). *Self Comes to Mind: Constructing the Human Brain.* New York: Pantheon.

Dennett, Daniel (1992). *Consciousness Explained.* New York: Back Bay Books.

Levi-Strauss, Claude (1966). *The Savage Mind.* Translated from the French by George Weidenfield and Nicholson Ltd. Chicago: The University of Chicago Press.

_____ (1973) *Tristes Tropiques.* English translation, Jonathan Cape Ltd. Retranslated with complete text by Doreen and John Weightman in 1992 as a Penguin Book.

Polanyi, Michael (1958). *Personal Knowledge: Towards a Post-Critical Philosophy.* Chicago: University of Chicago Press.

Sartre, Jean-Paul (1976). *Critique of Dialectical Reason.* Translated from the 1960 French edition by Alan Sheridan-Smith.

White, Hayden (2012). *Frontiers of Consciousness at UCSC.* Interviewed and edited by Cameron Vanderscoff. UC Santa Cruz Digital Collections. Accessible at: http://digitalcollections.ucsc.edu/cdm/ref/collection/p265101coll13/id/3849